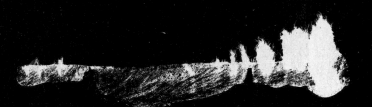

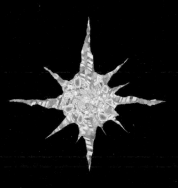

PLANETARY

Warren Ellis & John Cassaday
Writer/Co-Creators/Artist

Laura Martin
Colorist

Bill O'Neil issues 13-15
Richard Starkings issues 16-18
Letters

Jim Lee, Editorial Director   John Nee, VP–Business Development   Scott Dunbier, Executive Editor
Paul Levitz, President & Publisher   Georg Brewer, VP–Design & Retail Product Development
Richard Bruning, Senior VP–Creative Director   Patrick Caldon, Senior VP–Finance & Operations
Chris Caramalis, VP–Finance   Terri Cunningham, VP–Managing Editor
Dan DiDio, VP–Editorial   Alison Gill, VP–Manufacturing   Rich Johnson, VP–Book Trade Sales
Hank Kanalz, VP–General Manager, WildStorm   Lillian Laserson, Senior VP & General Counsel
David McKillips, VP–Advertising & Custom Publishing   Gregory Noveck, Senior VP–Creative Affairs
Cheryl Rubin, VP–Brand Management   Bob Wayne, VP–Sales & Marketing

LEAVING THE 20TH CENTURY

John Layman & Scott Dunbier
Original Series Editors

John Cassaday
Cover Art

Larry Berry
Collected Edition Design

PLANETARY: LEAVING THE 20th CENTURY, published by WildStorm Productions. 888 Prospect St. #240, La Jolla, CA 92037. Cover and compilation Copyright © 2004 WildStorm Productions, an imprint of DC Comics. All Rights Reserved. WildStorm and logo, PLANETARY, all characters, the distinctive likenesses thereof and all related elements are trademarks of DC Comics. The stories, characters, and incidents mentioned in this magazine are entirely fictional. Originally published in single magazine form as PLANETARY #13-18, © 2001, 2003, 2004. Printed on recyclable paper. WildStorm does not read or accept unsolicited submissions of ideas, stories or artwork. Printed in Canada. This book is manufactured at a facility holding chain-of-custody certification. This paper is made with sustainably managed North American fiber. Third Printing.

DC Comics, a Warner Bros. Entertainment Company.

ISBN: 978-1-4012-0294-1

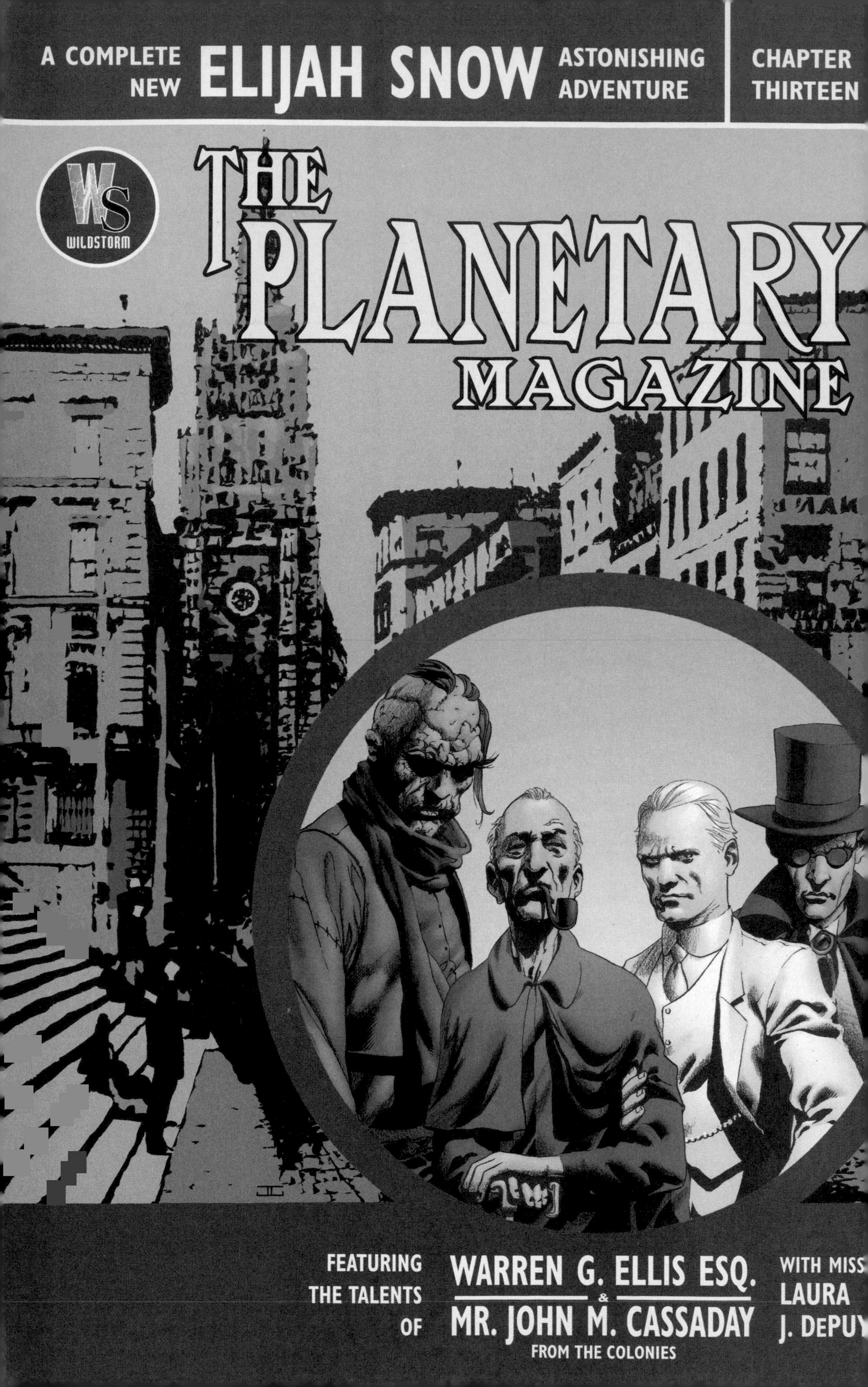
A COMPLETE NEW
ELIJAH SNOW
ASTONISHING ADVENTURE
CHAPTER THIRTEEN
WILDSTORM
THE PLANETARY MAGAZINE
FEATURING THE TALENTS OF
WARREN G. ELLIS ESQ.
&
MR. JOHN M. CASSADAY
FROM THE COLONIES
WITH MISS LAURA J. DePUY

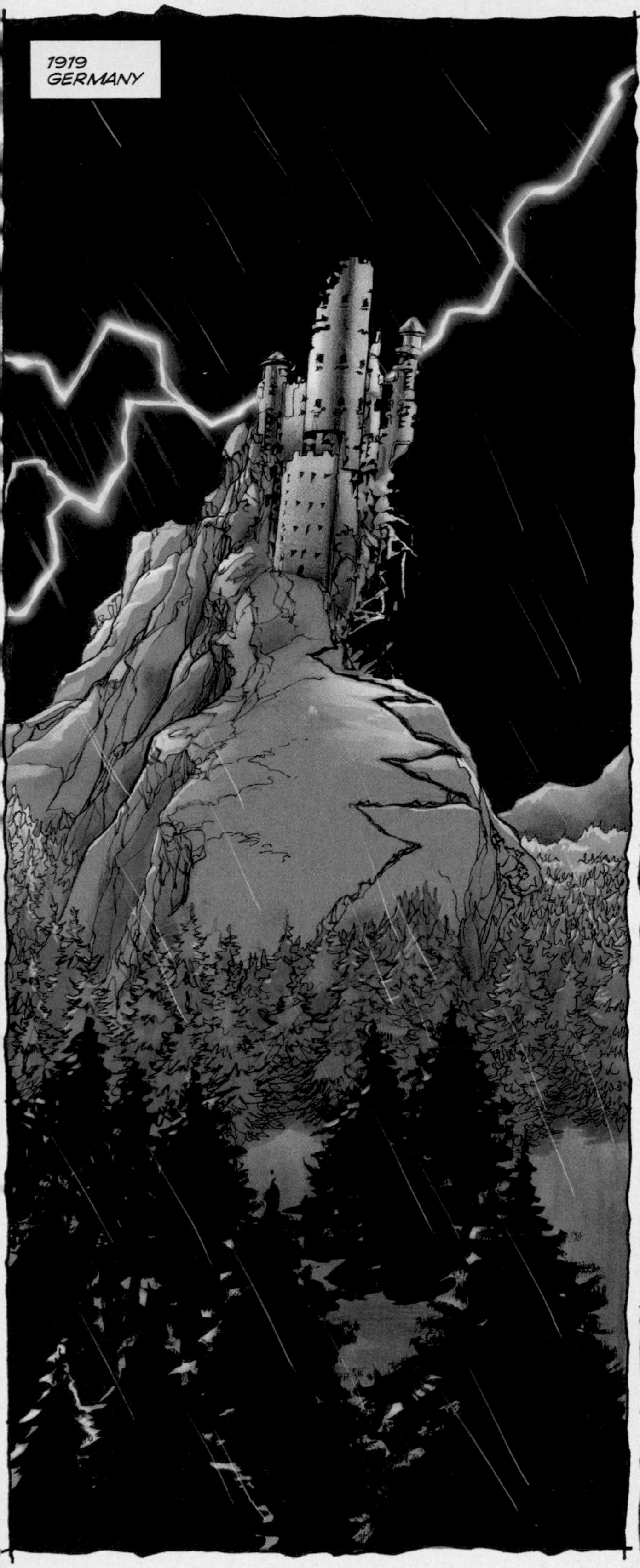
1919
GERMANY

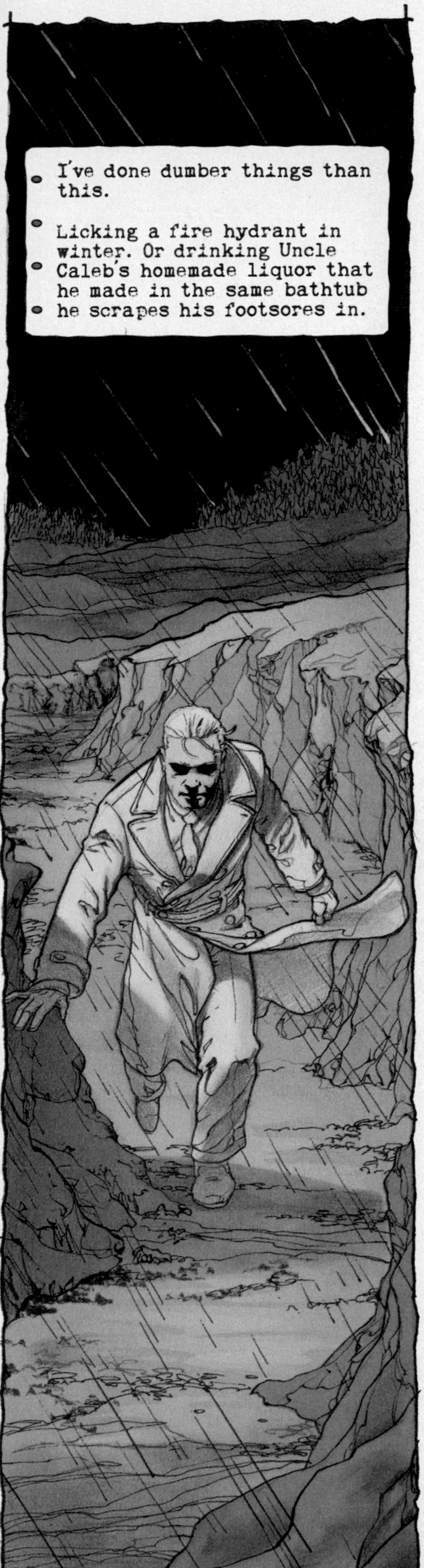
I've done dumber things than this.
Licking a fire hydrant in winter. Or drinking Uncle Caleb's homemade liquor that he made in the same bathtub he scrapes his footsores in.

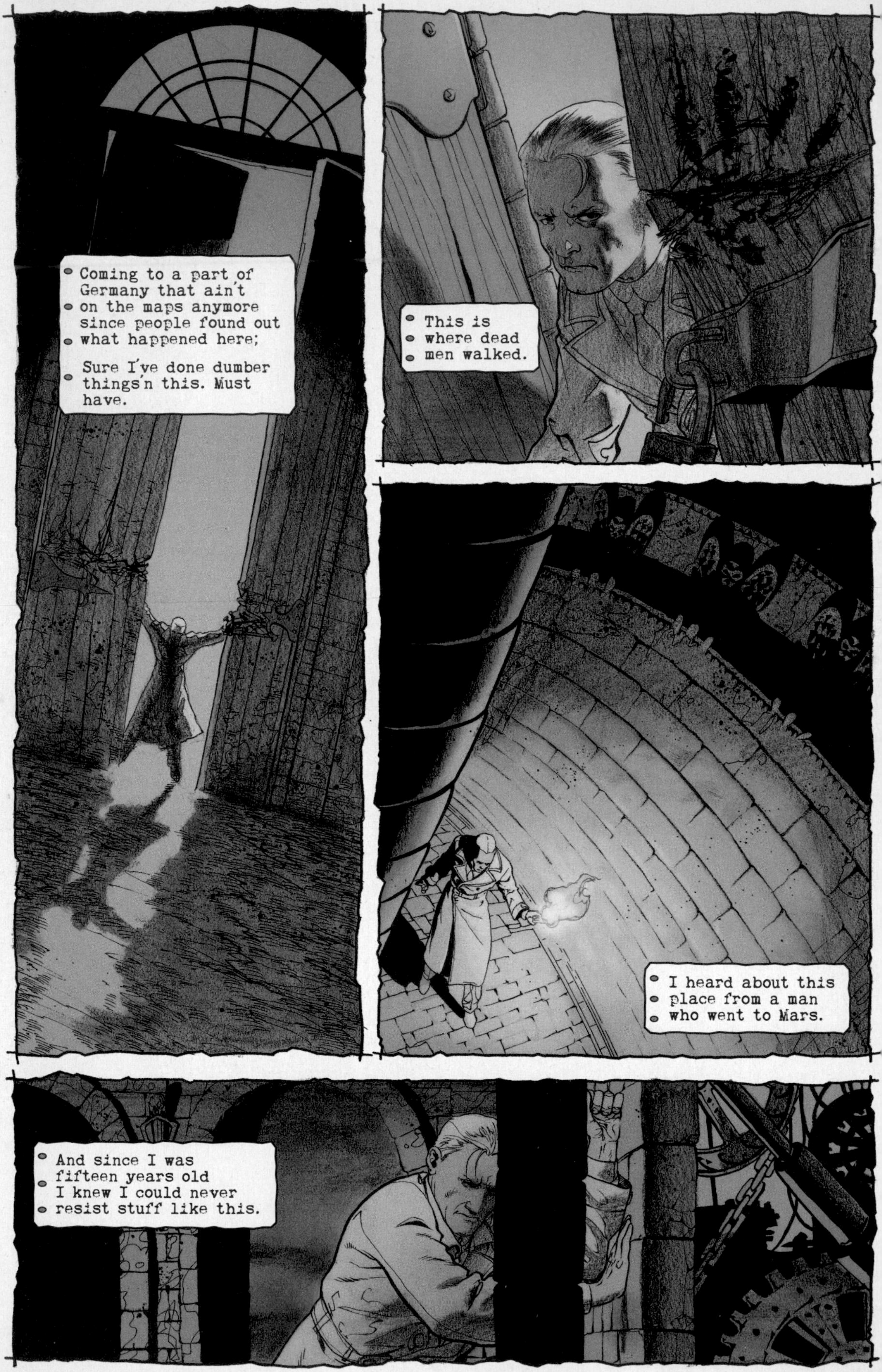
Coming to a part of Germany that ain't on the maps anymore since people found out what happened here;
Sure I've done dumber things'n this. Must have.
This is where dead men walked.
I heard about this place from a man who went to Mars.
And since I was fifteen years old I knew I could never resist stuff like this.

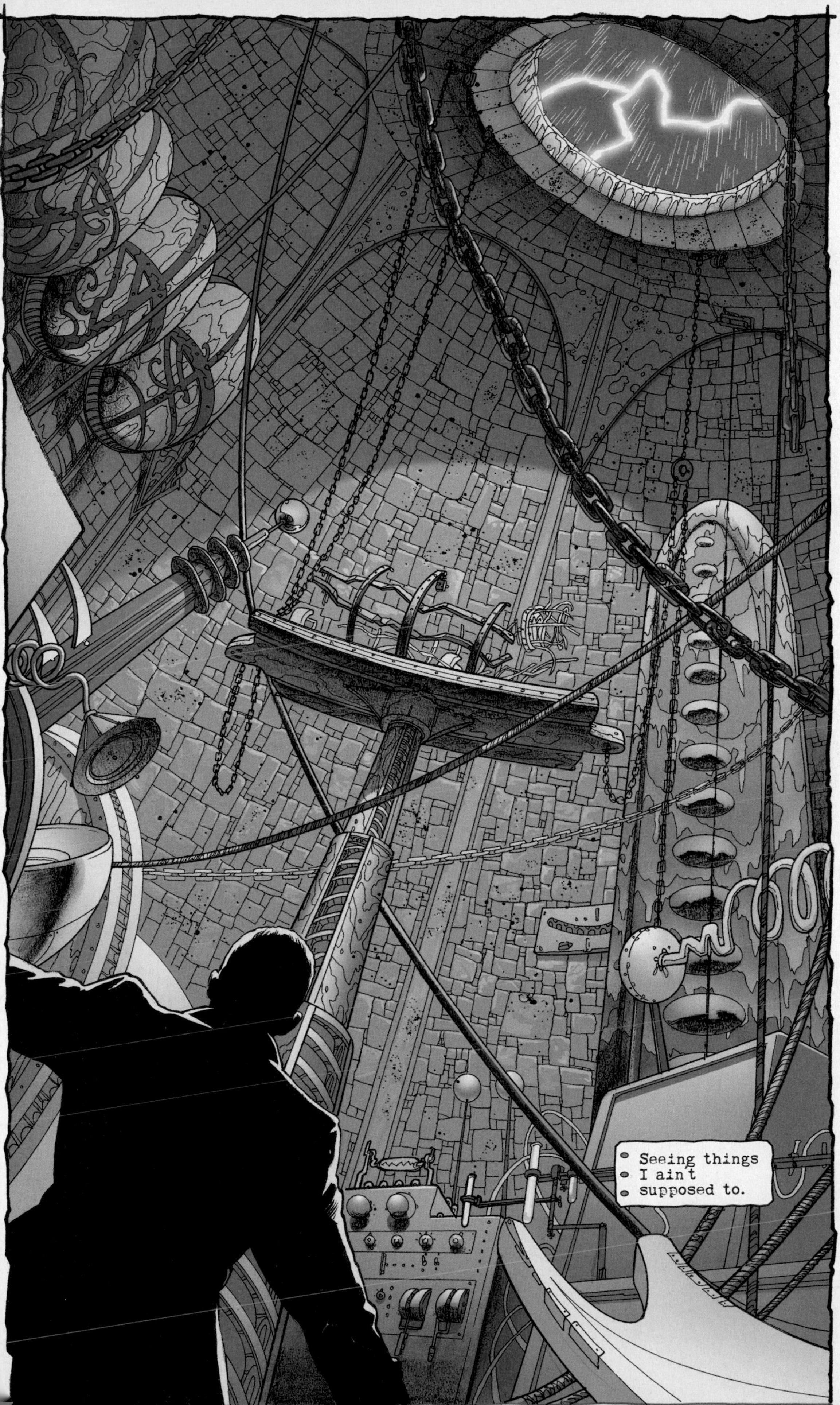
Seeing things
I aint
supposed to.

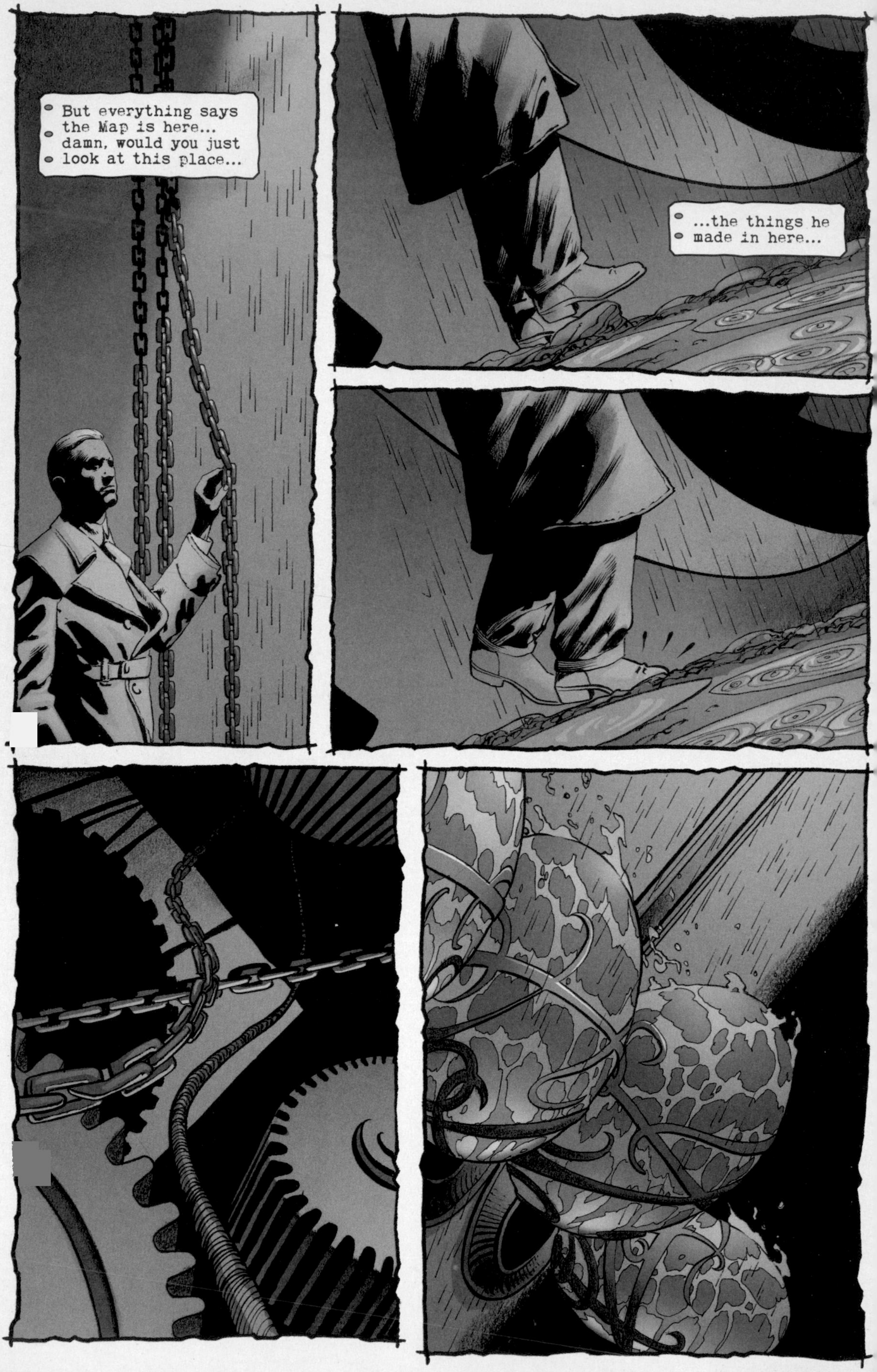
But everything says the Map is here... damn, would you just look at this place...
...the things he made in here...

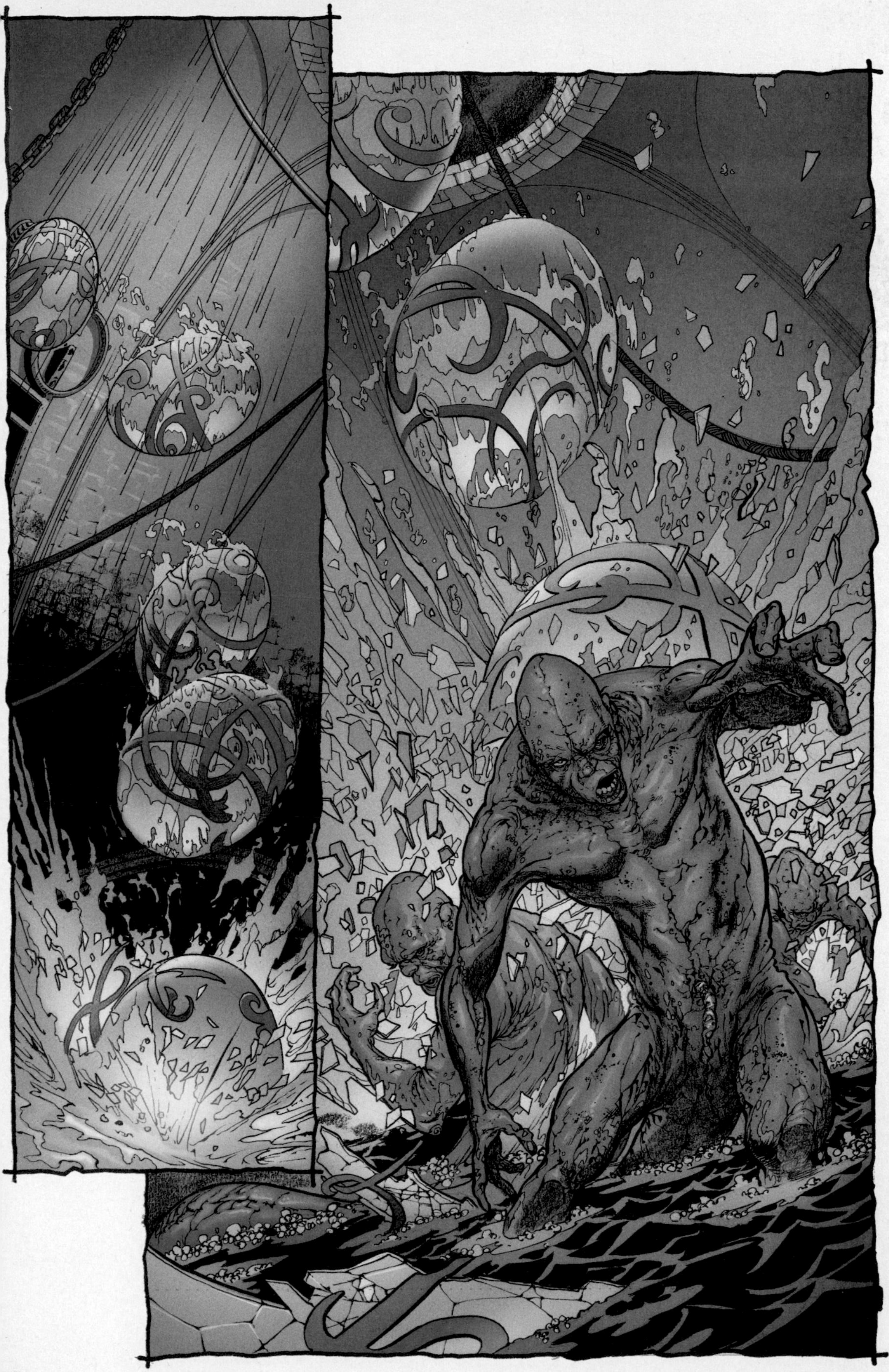

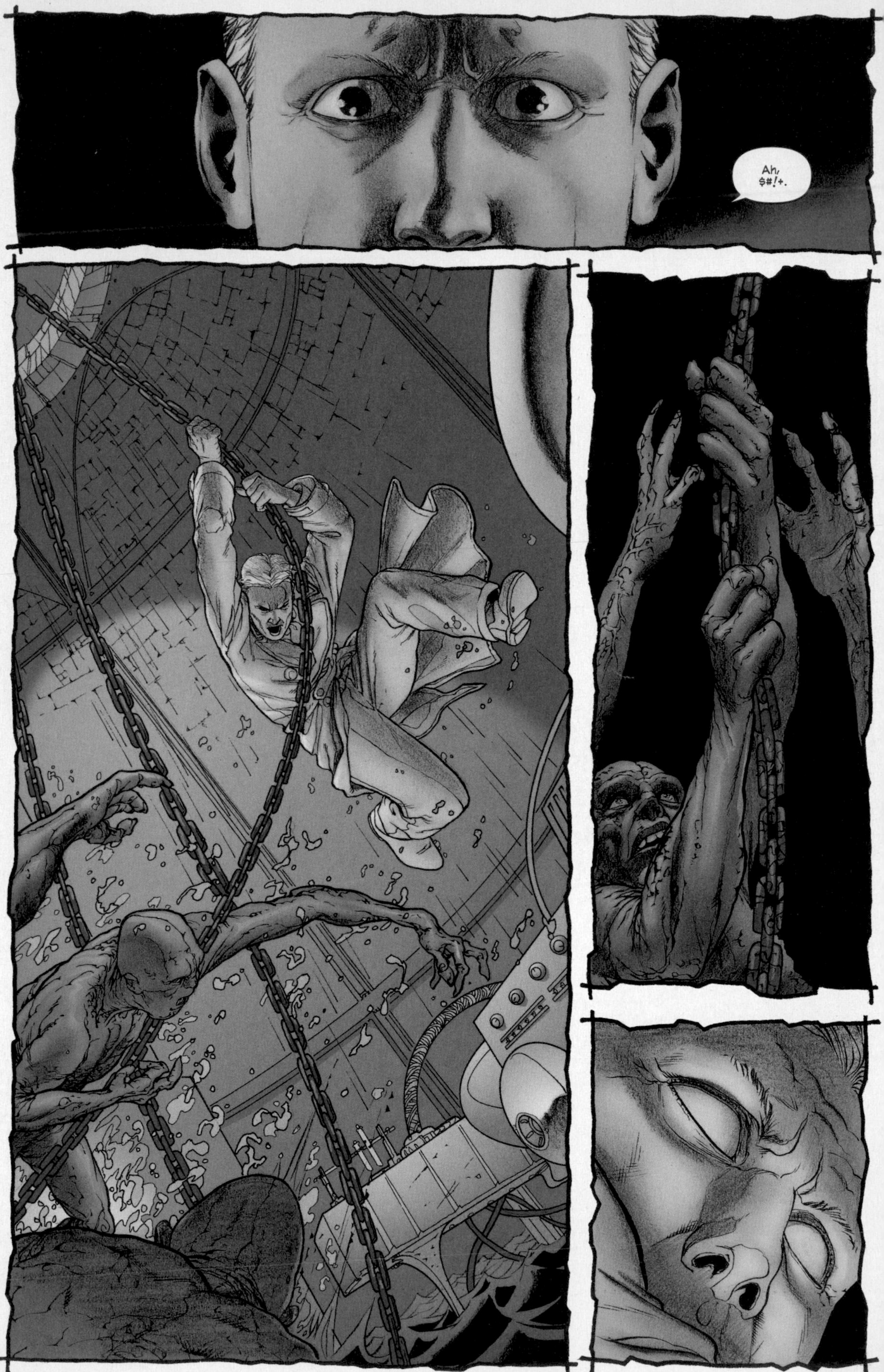
Ah, $#!+.

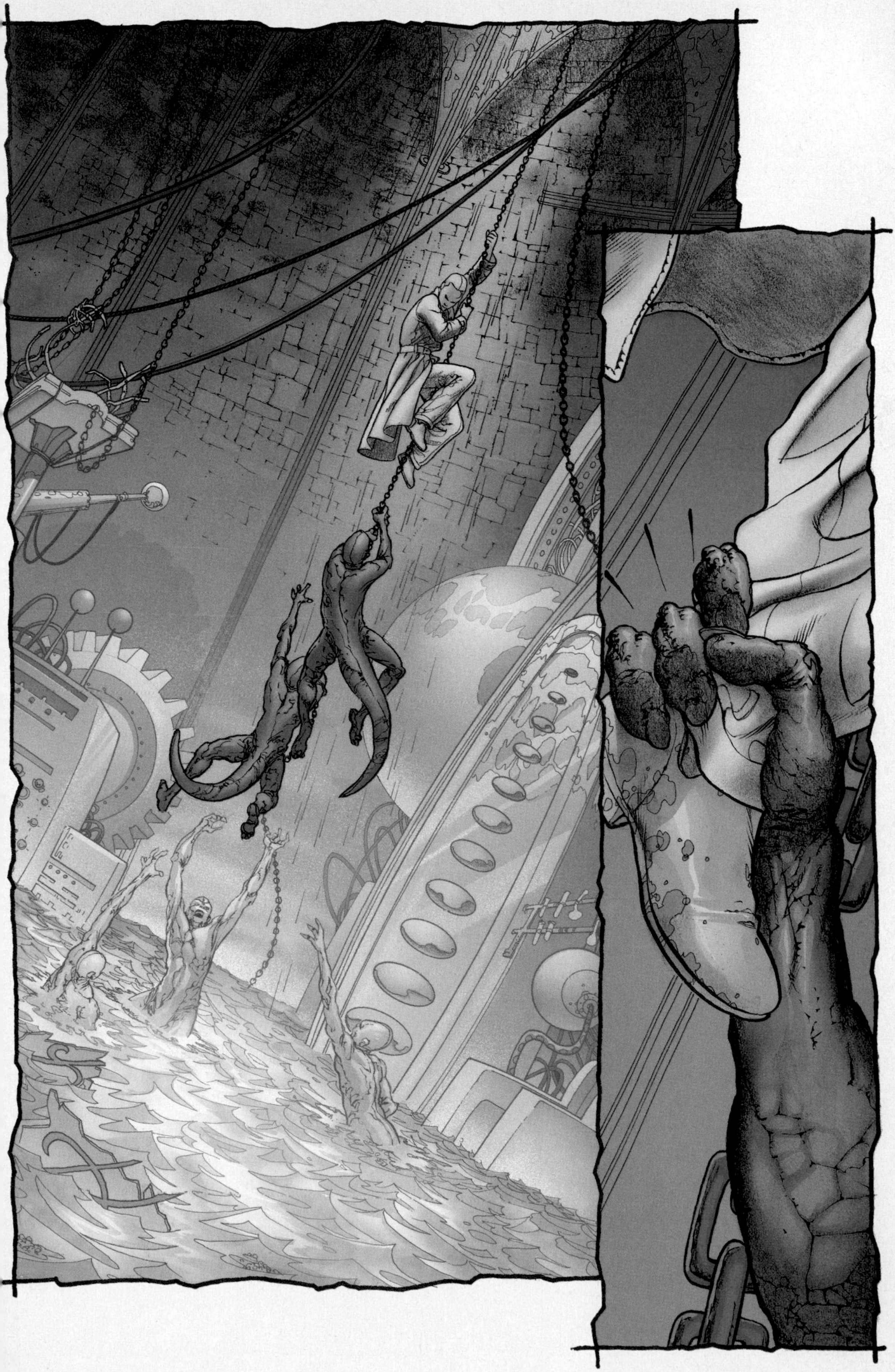

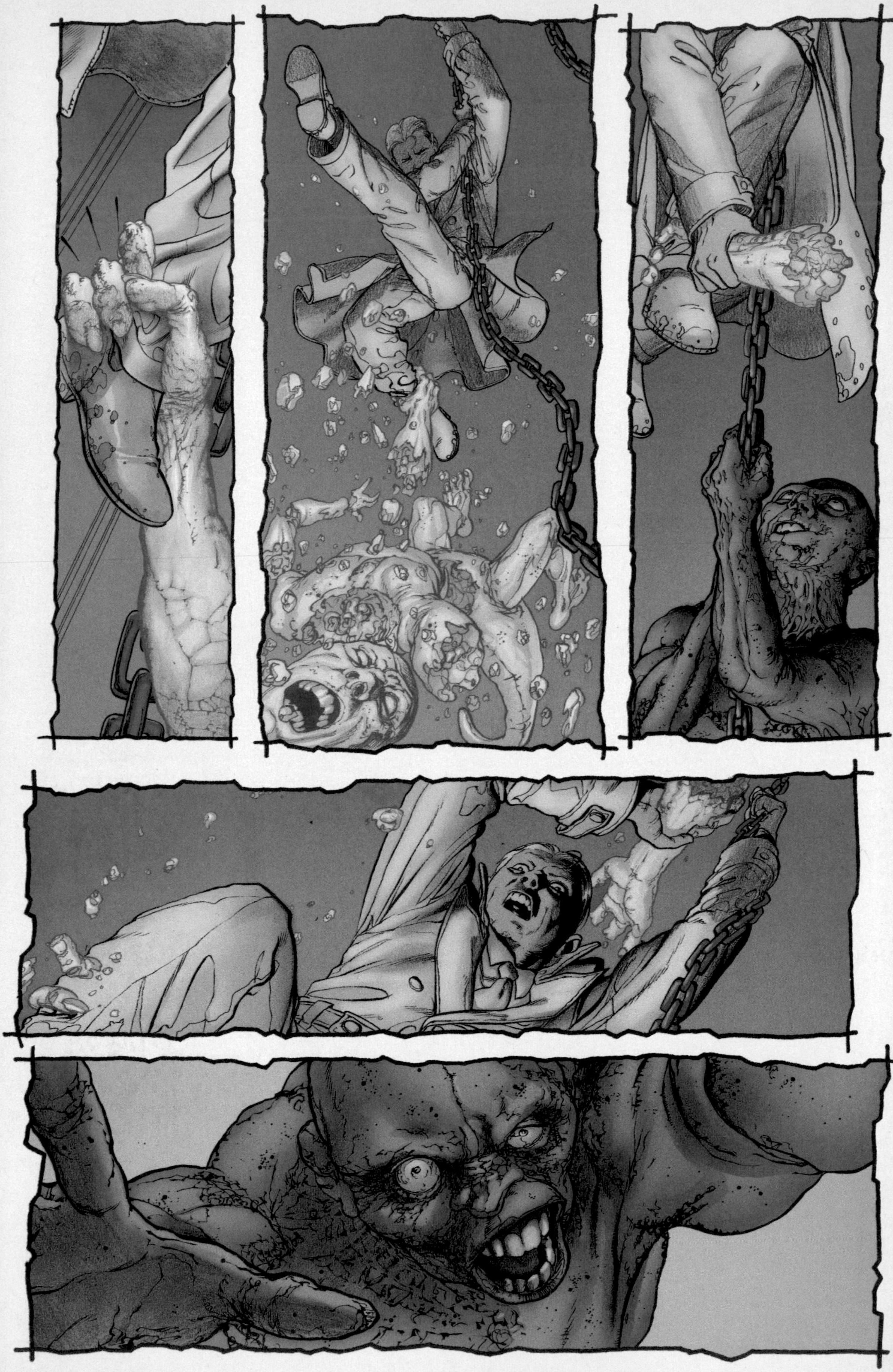

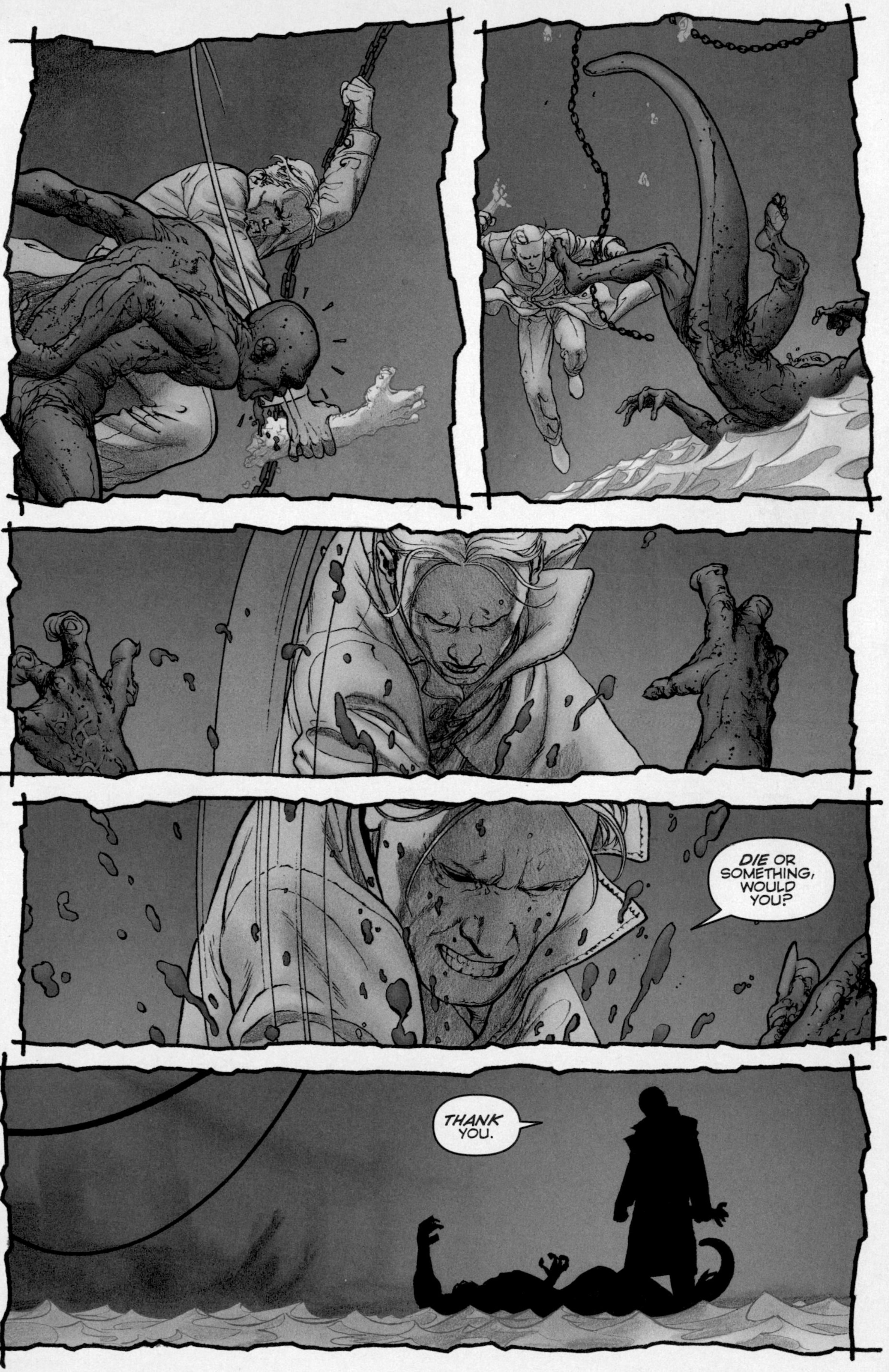
DIE OR SOMETHING, WOULD YOU?
THANK YOU.

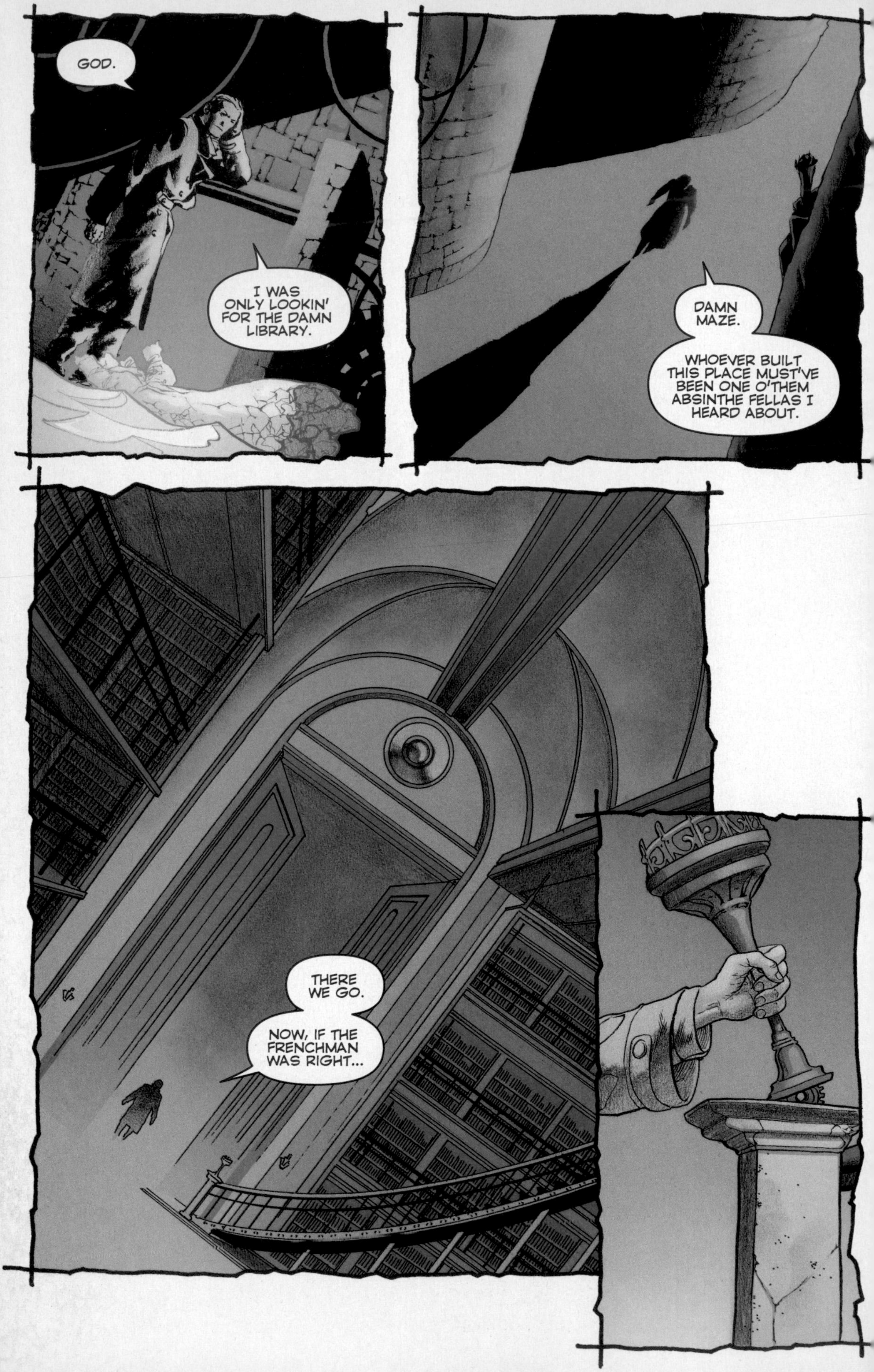
GOD.
I WAS ONLY LOOKIN' FOR THE DAMN LIBRARY.
DAMN MAZE.
WHOEVER BUILT THIS PLACE MUST'VE BEEN ONE O'THEM ABSINTHE FELLAS I HEARD ABOUT.
THERE WE GO.
NOW, IF THE FRENCHMAN WAS RIGHT...

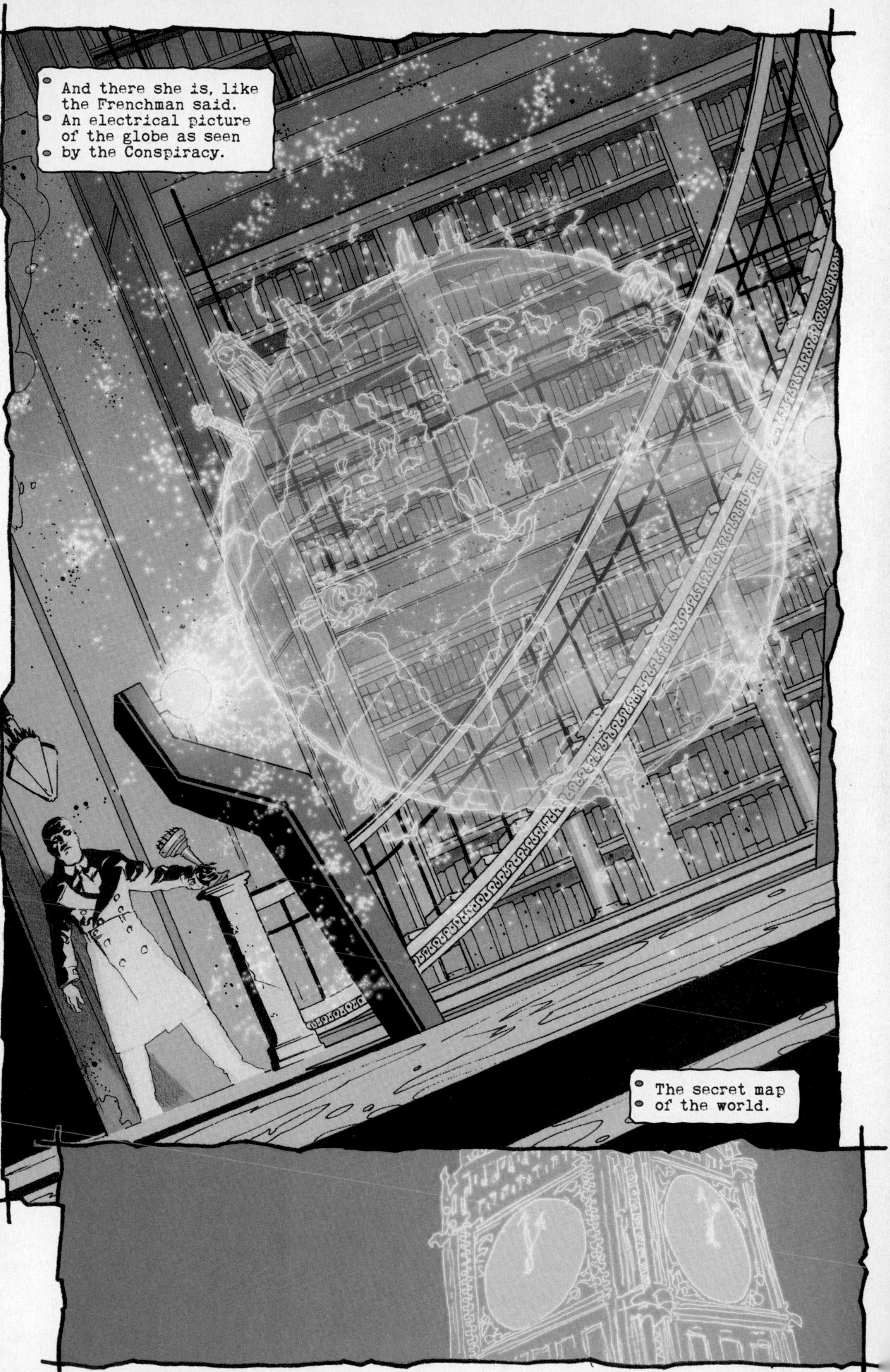
And there she is, like the Frenchman said. An electrical picture of the globe as seen by the Conspiracy.
The secret map of the world.

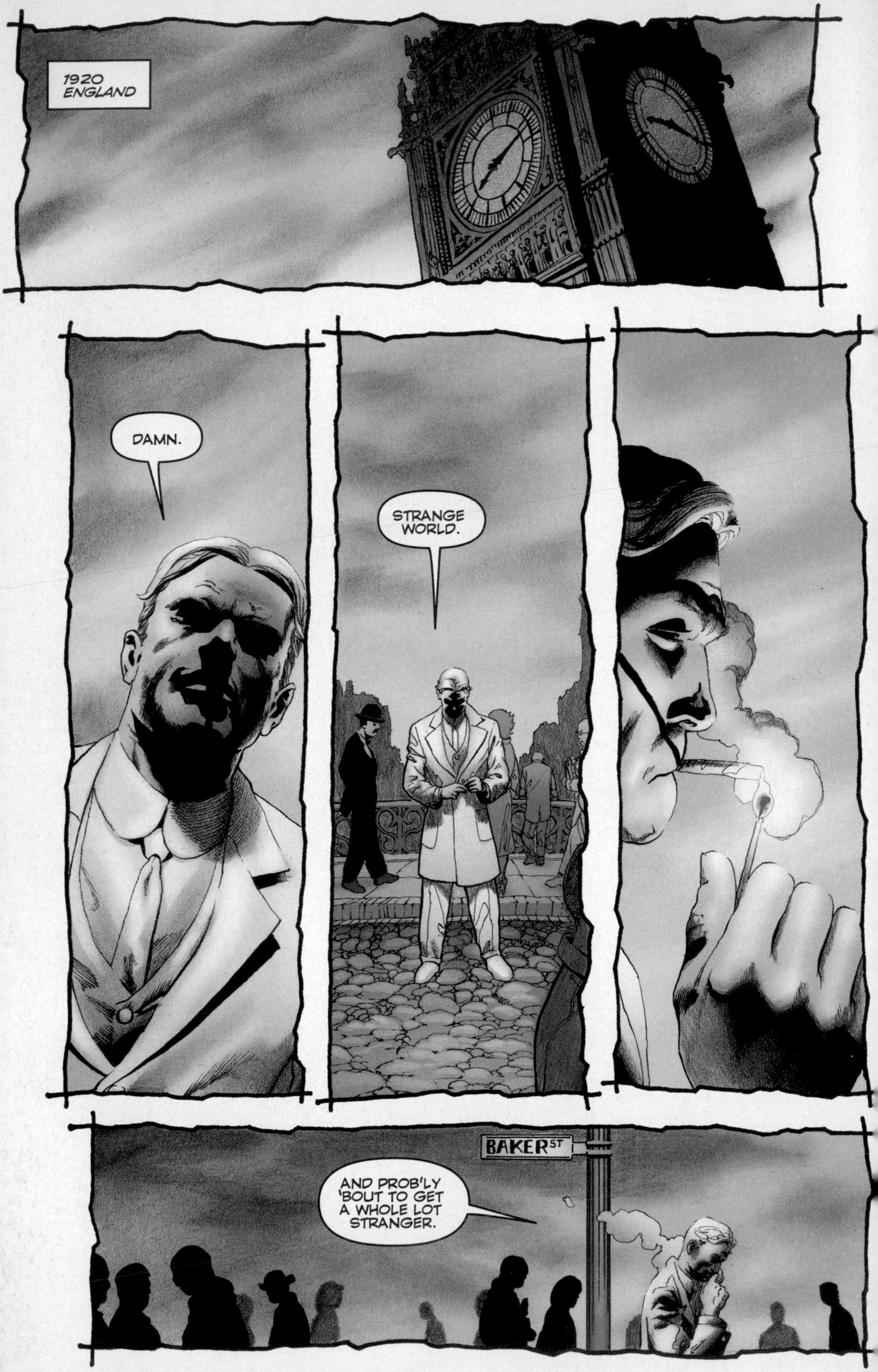
1920
ENGLAND
DAMN.
STRANGE WORLD.
BAKER ST
AND PROB'LY 'BOUT TO GET A WHOLE LOT STRANGER.

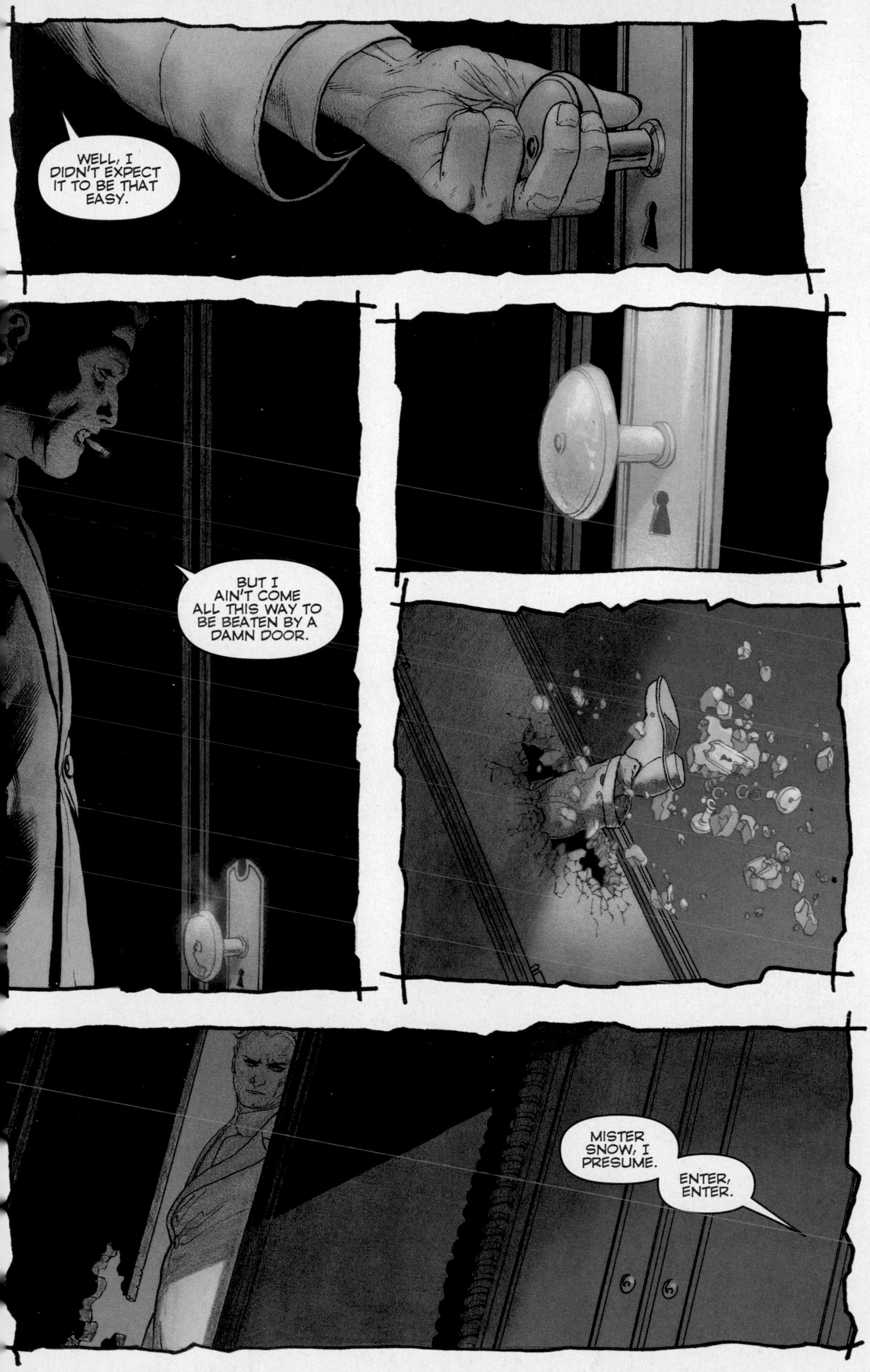
WELL, I DIDN'T EXPECT IT TO BE THAT EASY.
BUT I AIN'T COME ALL THIS WAY TO BE BEATEN BY A DAMN DOOR.
MISTER SNOW, I PRESUME.
ENTER, ENTER.

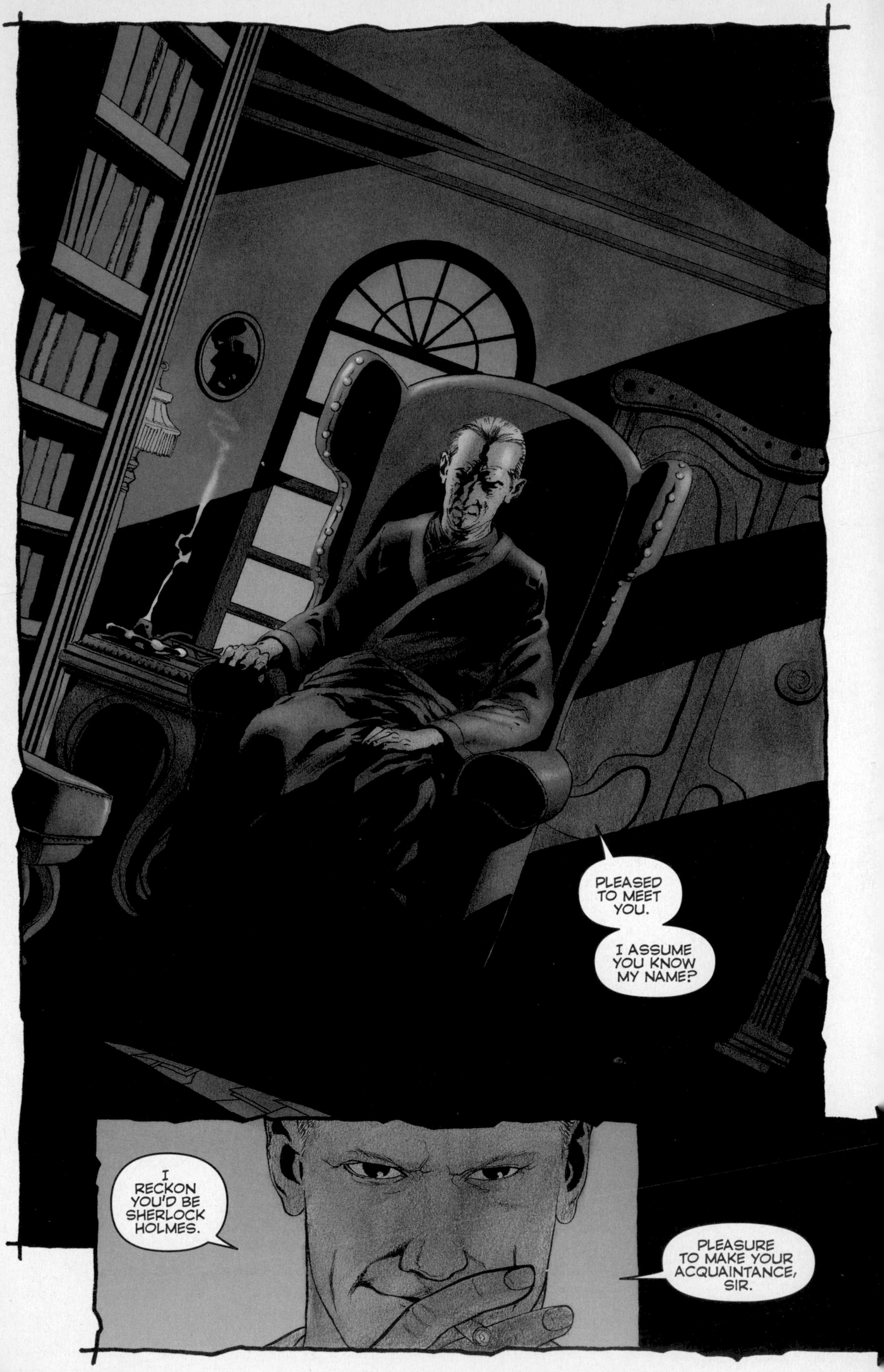

PLEASED TO MEET YOU.
I ASSUME YOU KNOW MY NAME?
I RECKON YOU'D BE SHERLOCK HOLMES.
PLEASURE TO MAKE YOUR ACQUAINTANCE, SIR.

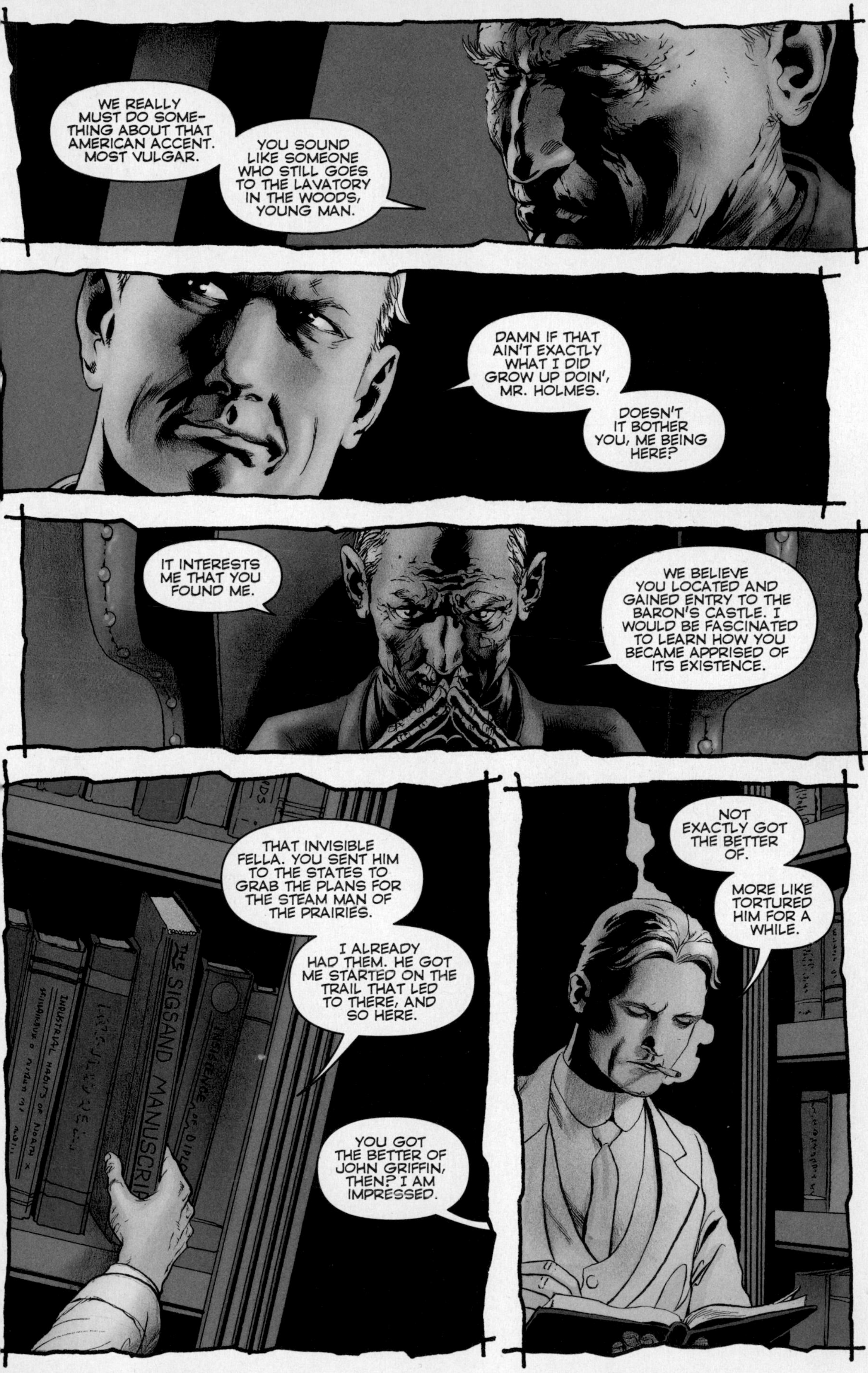
WE REALLY MUST DO SOMETHING ABOUT THAT AMERICAN ACCENT. MOST VULGAR.
YOU SOUND LIKE SOMEONE WHO STILL GOES TO THE LAVATORY IN THE WOODS, YOUNG MAN.
DAMN IF THAT AIN'T EXACTLY WHAT I DID GROW UP DOIN', MR. HOLMES.
DOESN'T IT BOTHER YOU, ME BEING HERE?
IT INTERESTS ME THAT YOU FOUND ME.
WE BELIEVE YOU LOCATED AND GAINED ENTRY TO THE BARON'S CASTLE. I WOULD BE FASCINATED TO LEARN HOW YOU BECAME APPRISED OF ITS EXISTENCE.
THAT INVISIBLE FELLA. YOU SENT HIM TO THE STATES TO GRAB THE PLANS FOR THE STEAM MAN OF THE PRAIRIES.
I ALREADY HAD THEM. HE GOT ME STARTED ON THE TRAIL THAT LED TO THERE, AND SO HERE.
YOU GOT THE BETTER OF JOHN GRIFFIN, THEN? I AM IMPRESSED.
NOT EXACTLY GOT THE BETTER OF.
MORE LIKE TORTURED HIM FOR A WHILE.

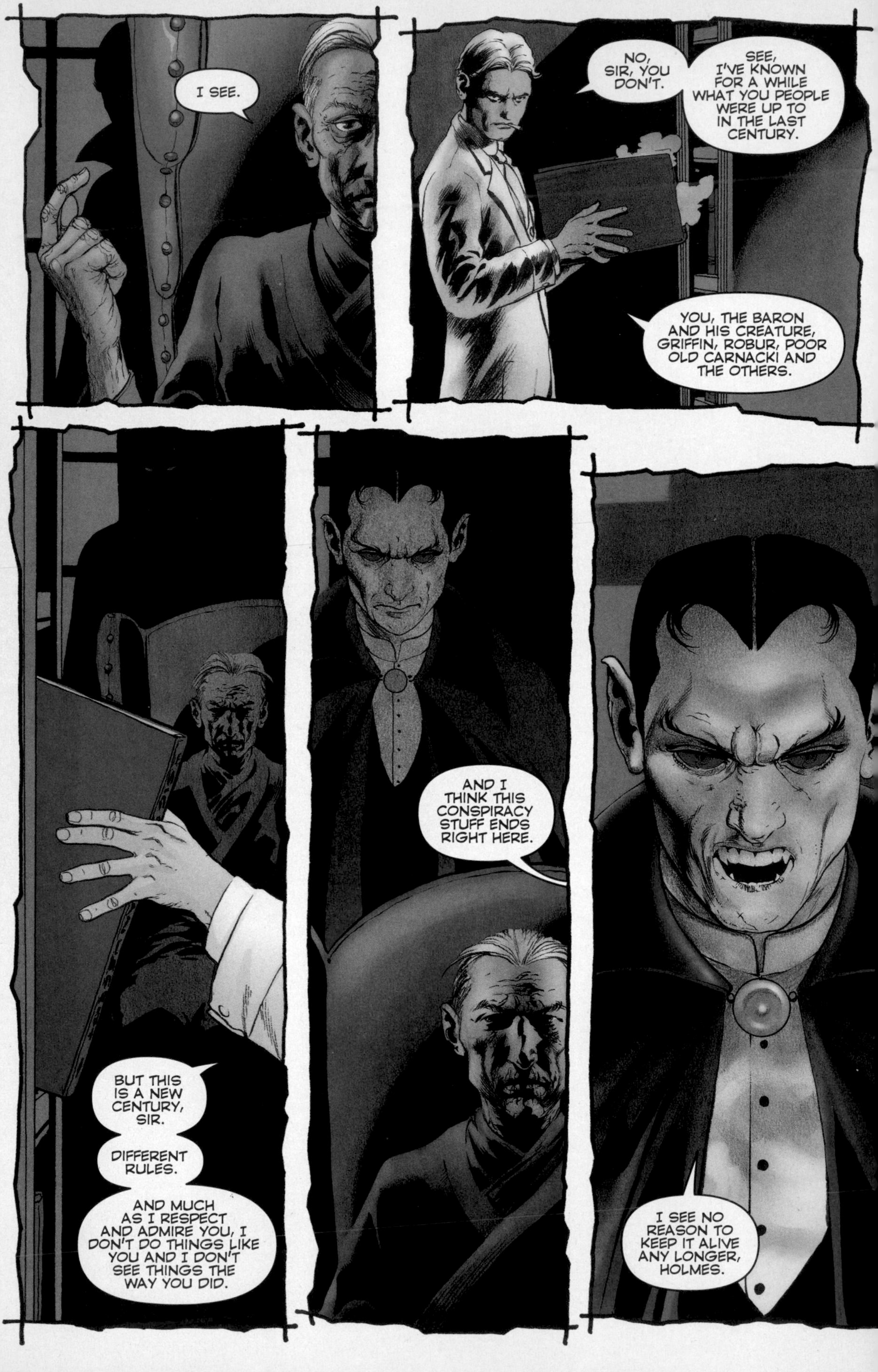
I SEE.
NO, SIR, YOU DON'T.
SEE, I'VE KNOWN FOR A WHILE WHAT YOU PEOPLE WERE UP TO IN THE LAST CENTURY.
YOU, THE BARON AND HIS CREATURE, GRIFFIN, ROBUR, POOR OLD CARNACKI AND THE OTHERS.
BUT THIS IS A NEW CENTURY, SIR.
DIFFERENT RULES.
AND MUCH AS I RESPECT AND ADMIRE YOU, I DON'T DO THINGS LIKE YOU AND I DON'T SEE THINGS THE WAY YOU DID.
AND I THINK THIS CONSPIRACY STUFF ENDS RIGHT HERE.
I SEE NO REASON TO KEEP IT ALIVE ANY LONGER, HOLMES.

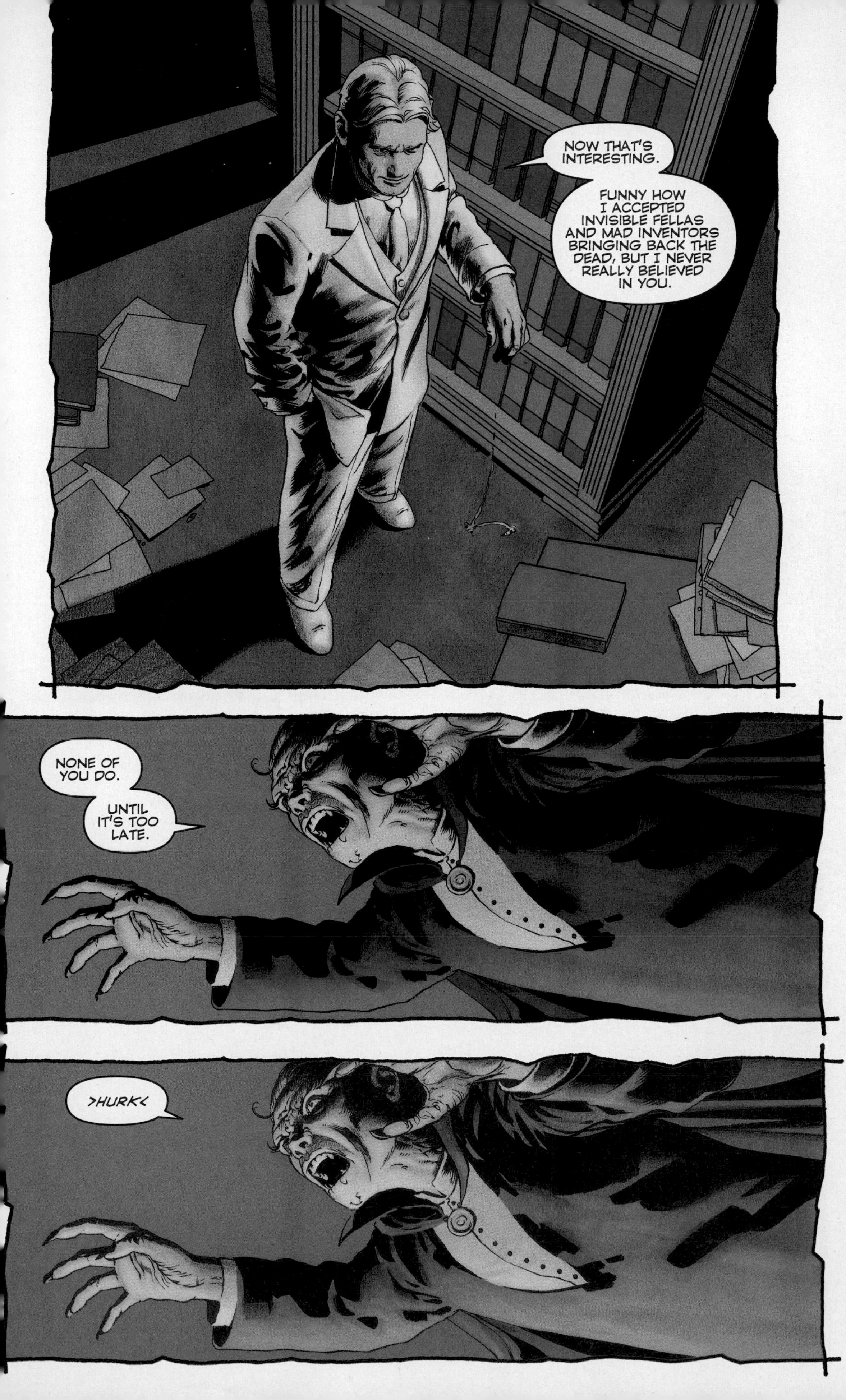
NOW THAT'S INTERESTING.
FUNNY HOW I ACCEPTED INVISIBLE FELLAS AND MAD INVENTORS BRINGING BACK THE DEAD, BUT I NEVER REALLY BELIEVED IN YOU.
NONE OF YOU DO.
UNTIL IT'S TOO LATE.
>HURK<

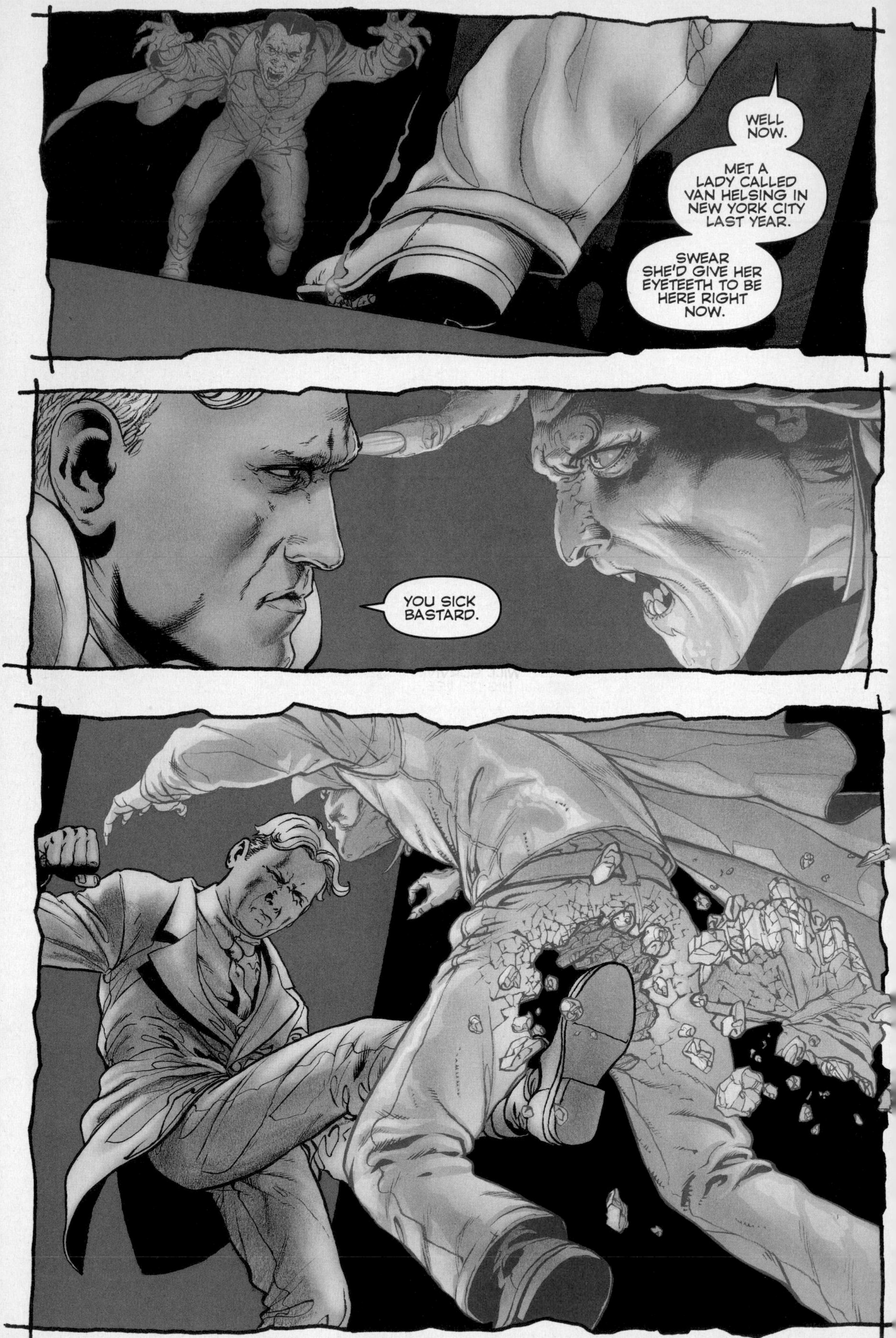
WELL NOW.
MET A LADY CALLED VAN HELSING IN NEW YORK CITY LAST YEAR.
SWEAR SHE'D GIVE HER EYETEETH TO BE HERE RIGHT NOW.
YOU SICK BASTARD.

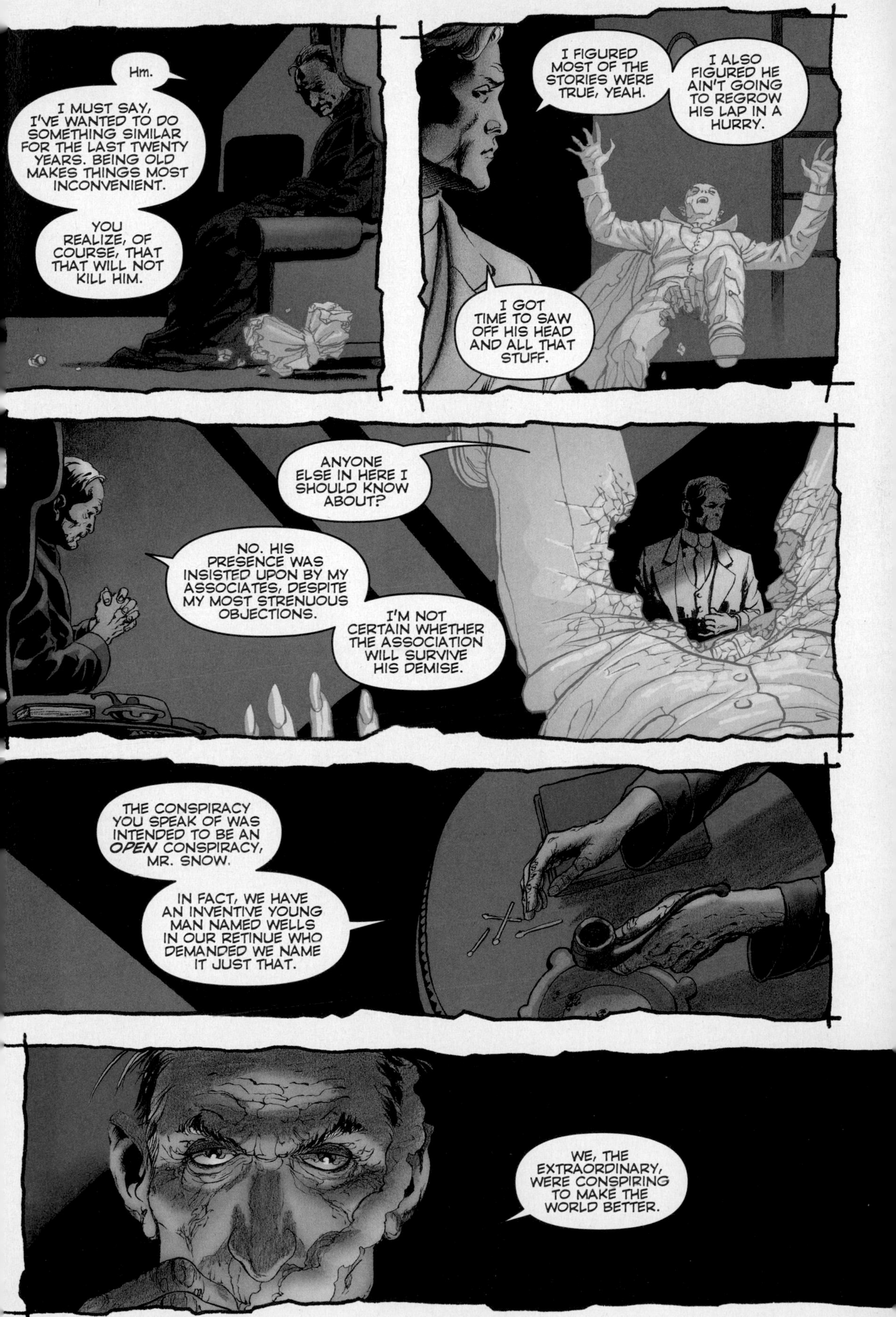
Hm.
I MUST SAY, I'VE WANTED TO DO SOMETHING SIMILAR FOR THE LAST TWENTY YEARS. BEING OLD MAKES THINGS MOST INCONVENIENT.
YOU REALIZE, OF COURSE, THAT THAT WILL NOT KILL HIM.
I FIGURED MOST OF THE STORIES WERE TRUE, YEAH.
I ALSO FIGURED HE AIN'T GOING TO REGROW HIS LAP IN A HURRY.
I GOT TIME TO SAW OFF HIS HEAD AND ALL THAT STUFF.
ANYONE ELSE IN HERE I SHOULD KNOW ABOUT?
NO. HIS PRESENCE WAS INSISTED UPON BY MY ASSOCIATES, DESPITE MY MOST STRENUOUS OBJECTIONS.
I'M NOT CERTAIN WHETHER THE ASSOCIATION WILL SURVIVE HIS DEMISE.
THE CONSPIRACY YOU SPEAK OF WAS INTENDED TO BE AN *OPEN* CONSPIRACY, MR. SNOW.
IN FACT, WE HAVE AN INVENTIVE YOUNG MAN NAMED WELLS IN OUR RETINUE WHO DEMANDED WE NAME IT JUST THAT.
WE, THE EXTRAORDINARY, WERE CONSPIRING TO MAKE THE WORLD BETTER.

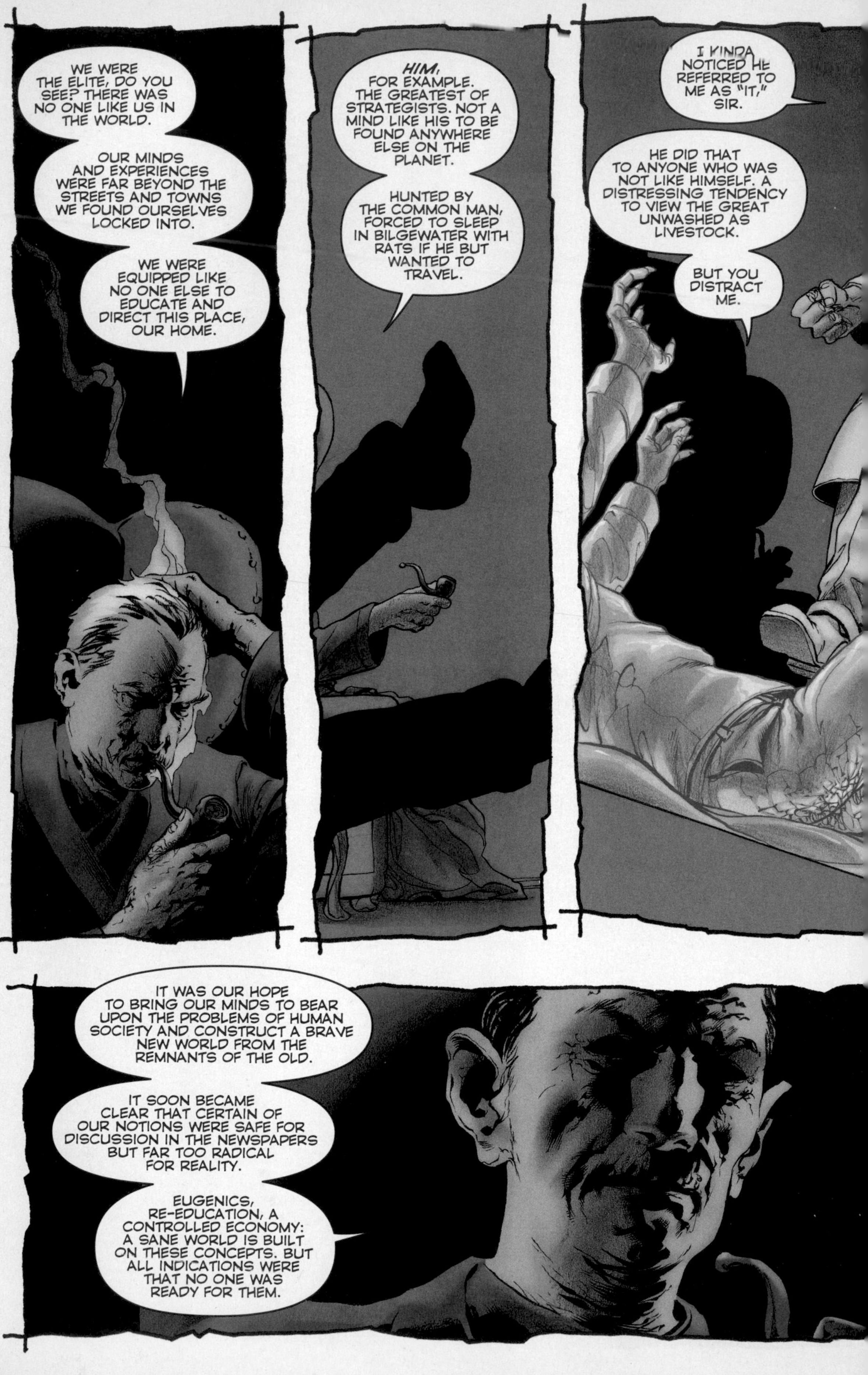

WE WERE THE ELITE, DO YOU SEE? THERE WAS NO ONE LIKE US IN THE WORLD.
OUR MINDS AND EXPERIENCES WERE FAR BEYOND THE STREETS AND TOWNS WE FOUND OURSELVES LOCKED INTO.
WE WERE EQUIPPED LIKE NO ONE ELSE TO EDUCATE AND DIRECT THIS PLACE, OUR HOME.
HIM, FOR EXAMPLE. THE GREATEST OF STRATEGISTS. NOT A MIND LIKE HIS TO BE FOUND ANYWHERE ELSE ON THE PLANET.
HUNTED BY THE COMMON MAN, FORCED TO SLEEP IN BILGEWATER WITH RATS IF HE BUT WANTED TO TRAVEL.
I KINDA NOTICED HE REFERRED TO ME AS "IT," SIR.
HE DID THAT TO ANYONE WHO WAS NOT LIKE HIMSELF. A DISTRESSING TENDENCY TO VIEW THE GREAT UNWASHED AS LIVESTOCK.
BUT YOU DISTRACT ME.
IT WAS OUR HOPE TO BRING OUR MINDS TO BEAR UPON THE PROBLEMS OF HUMAN SOCIETY AND CONSTRUCT A BRAVE NEW WORLD FROM THE REMNANTS OF THE OLD.
IT SOON BECAME CLEAR THAT CERTAIN OF OUR NOTIONS WERE SAFE FOR DISCUSSION IN THE NEWSPAPERS BUT FAR TOO RADICAL FOR REALITY.
EUGENICS, RE-EDUCATION, A CONTROLLED ECONOMY: A SANE WORLD IS BUILT ON THESE CONCEPTS. BUT ALL INDICATIONS WERE THAT NO ONE WAS READY FOR THEM.

AND SO WE TOOK TO THE DARKNESS.

AND AS WE REMAINED IN THE DARKNESS... SO WE GREW DARKER.

I KINDA NOTICED, YEAH.

I DON'T LIKE THE THINGS I'M SEEING AS A RESULT OF YOUR OPEN CONSPIRACY, SIR. NEEDS TO STOP.

I AGREE.

YOU HAVE NO IDEA HOW OFTEN I HAVE WISHED THAT I WERE ALLOWED TO DIE MANY YEARS AGO, SIR.

THIS SECOND LIFE OF MINE HAS NOT BEEN FULFILLING.

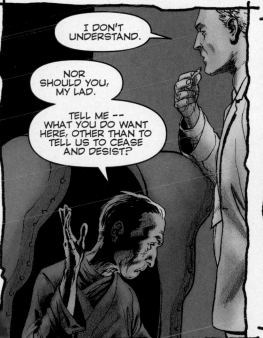

I DON'T UNDERSTAND.

NOR SHOULD YOU, MY LAD.

TELL ME -- WHAT YOU DO WANT HERE, OTHER THAN TO TELL US TO CEASE AND DESIST?

I WANT TO KNOW WHAT YOU KNOW.

I WANT TO KNOW SECRETS.

I'VE SEEN THE SHAPE OF THE SECRET HISTORY OF THE WORLD, AND I NEED TO FOLLOW ITS TRACES.

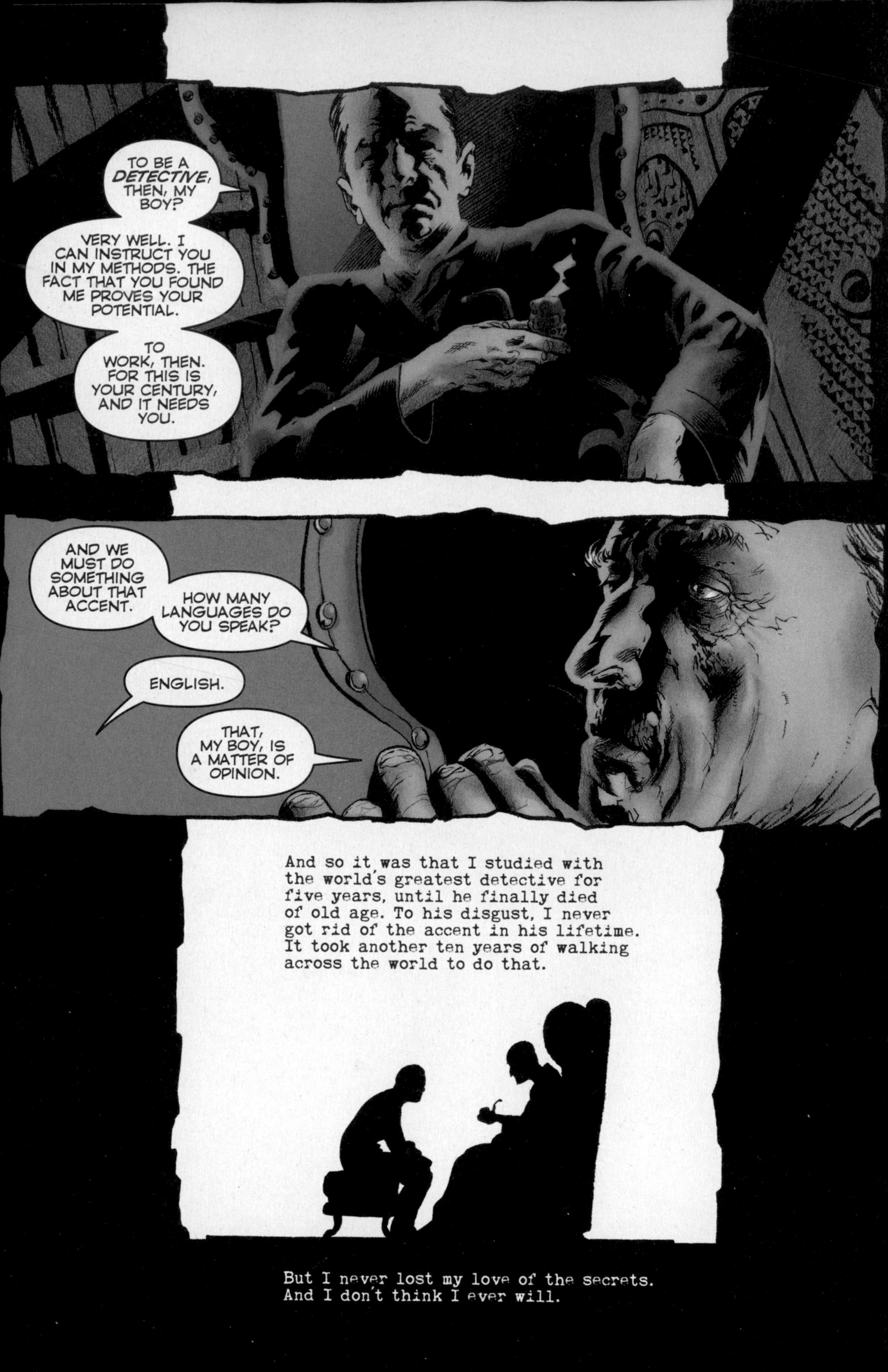
TO BE A *DETECTIVE*, THEN, MY BOY?
VERY WELL. I CAN INSTRUCT YOU IN MY METHODS. THE FACT THAT YOU FOUND ME PROVES YOUR POTENTIAL.
TO WORK, THEN. FOR THIS IS YOUR CENTURY, AND IT NEEDS YOU.
AND WE MUST DO SOMETHING ABOUT THAT ACCENT.
HOW MANY LANGUAGES DO YOU SPEAK?
ENGLISH.
THAT, MY BOY, IS A MATTER OF OPINION.
And so it was that I studied with the world's greatest detective for five years, until he finally died of old age. To his disgust, I never got rid of the accent in his lifetime. It took another ten years of walking across the world to do that.
But I never lost my love of the secrets. And I don't think I ever will.

Century

Elllis Cassaday DePuy O'Neil Layman

Planetary created by Warren Ellis and John Cassaday

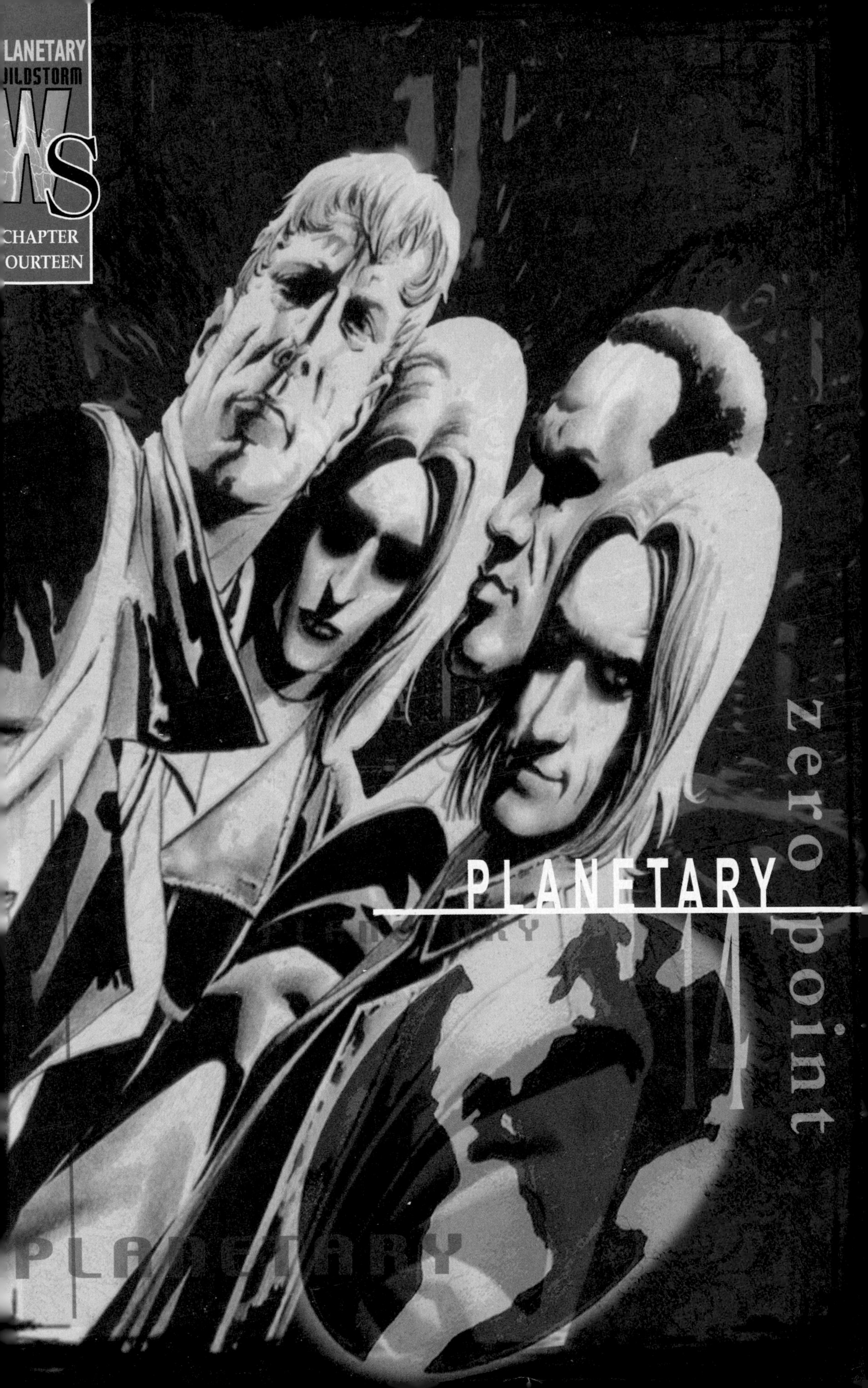

LANETARY
ILDSTORM
WS
CHAPTER
OURTEEN
PLANETARY
zero point
PLANETARY

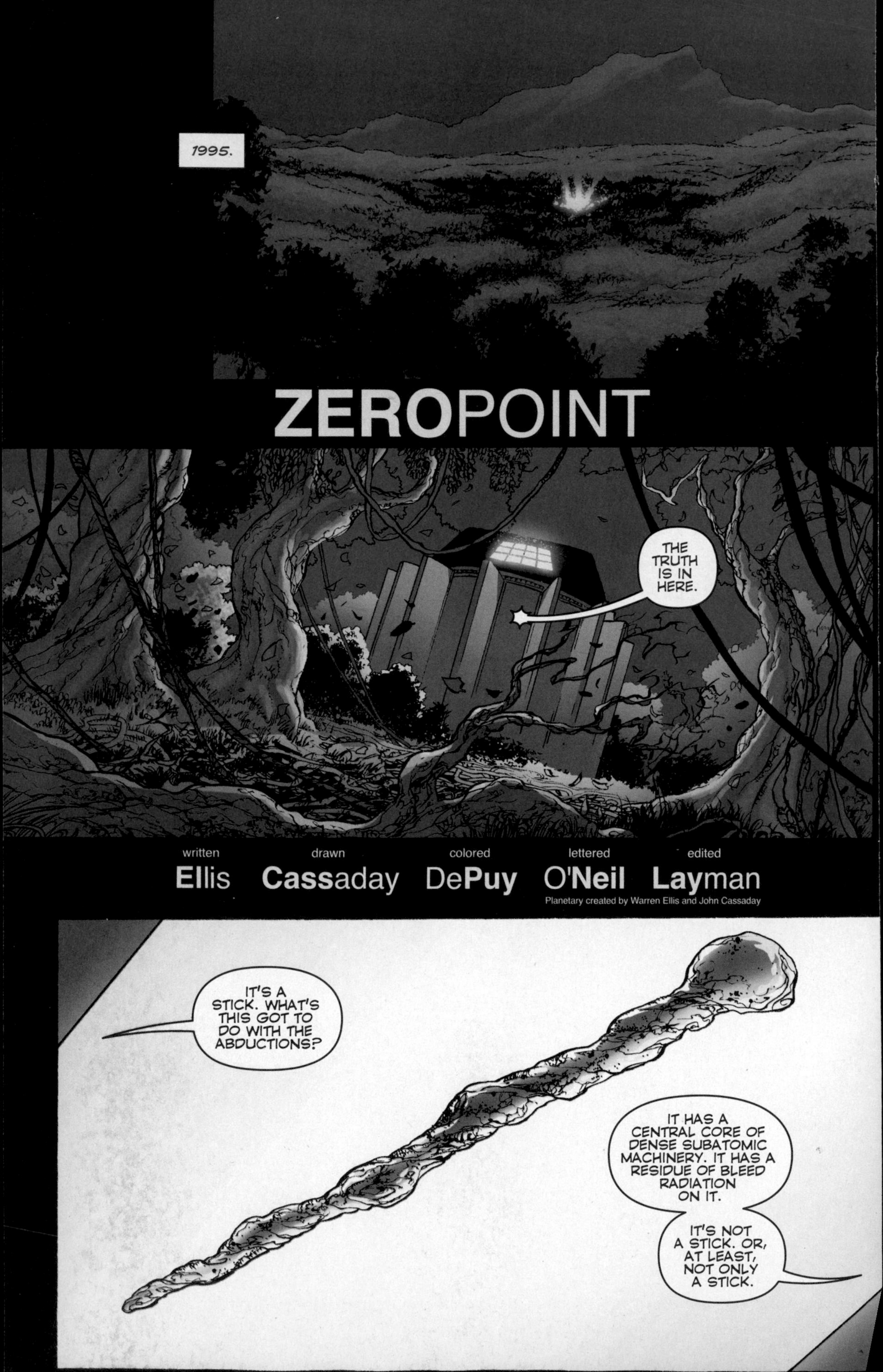
1995.
ZEROPOINT
THE TRUTH IS IN HERE.
written Ellis drawn Cassaday colored DePuy lettered O'Neil edited Layman
Planetary created by Warren Ellis and John Cassaday
IT'S A STICK. WHAT'S THIS GOT TO DO WITH THE ABDUCTIONS?
IT HAS A CENTRAL CORE OF DENSE SUBATOMIC MACHINERY. IT HAS A RESIDUE OF BLEED RADIATION ON IT.
IT'S NOT A STICK. OR, AT LEAST, NOT ONLY A STICK.

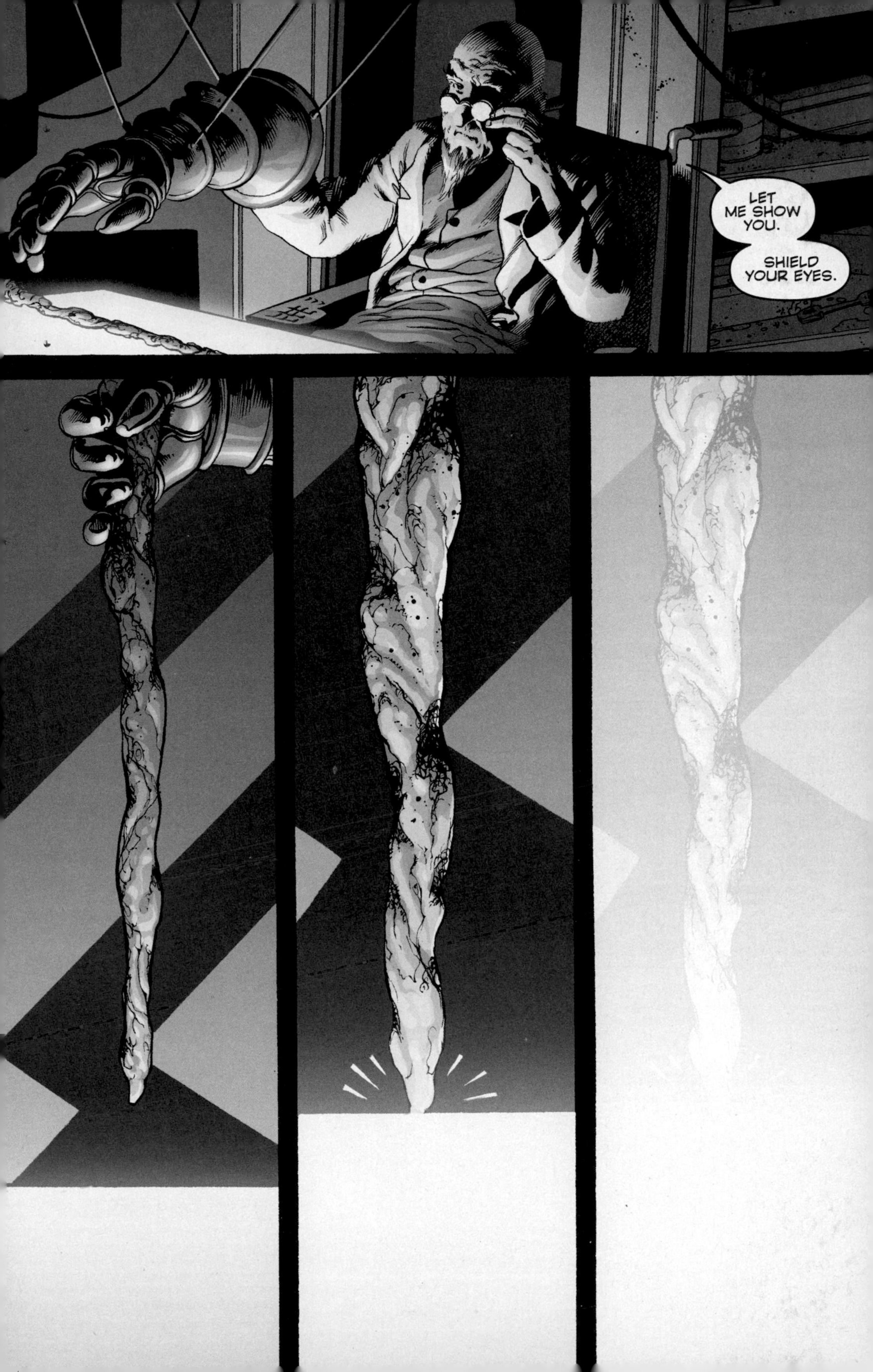

LET ME SHOW YOU.
SHIELD YOUR EYES.

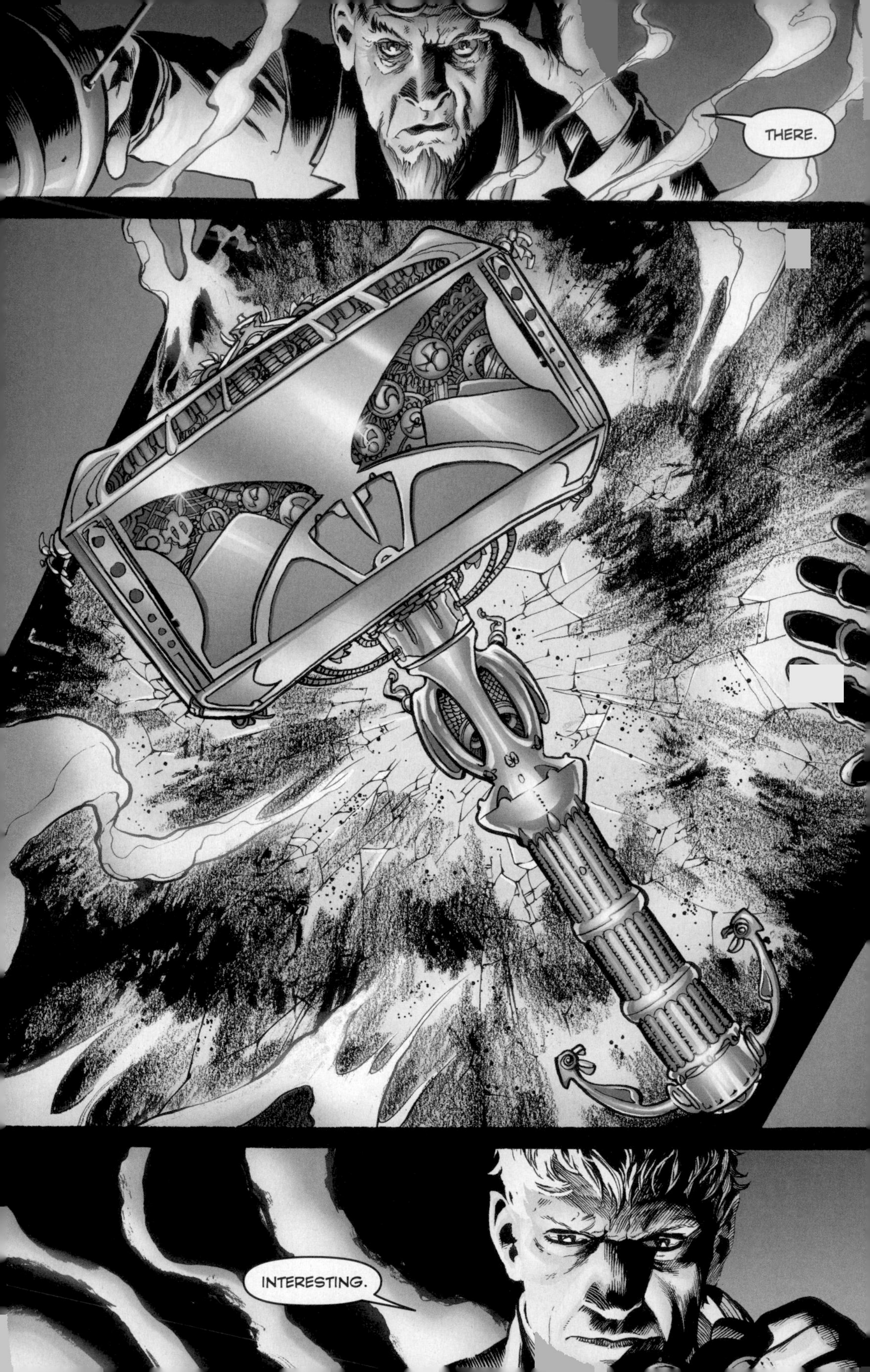
THERE.
INTERESTING.

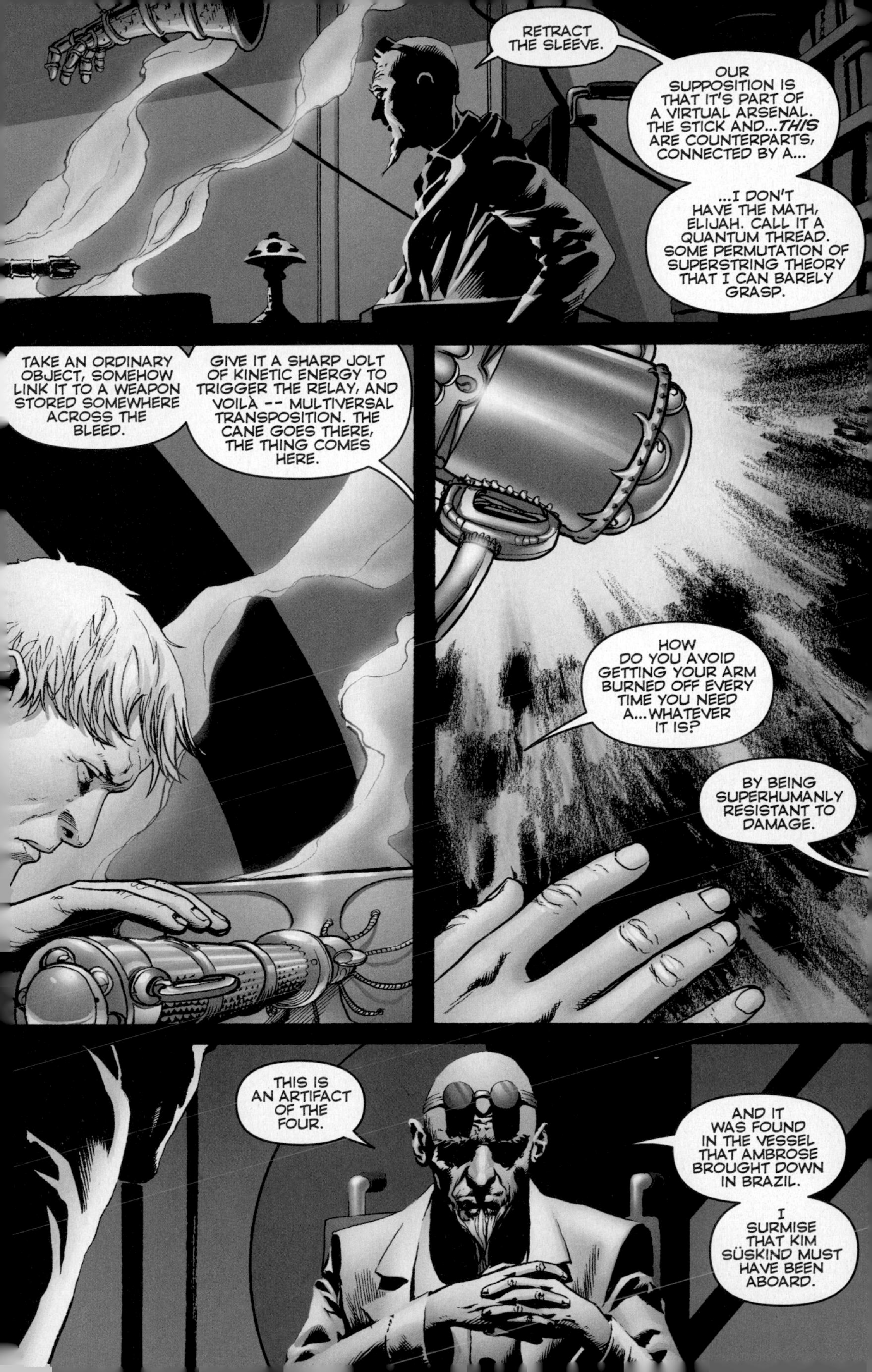
RETRACT THE SLEEVE.
OUR SUPPOSITION IS THAT IT'S PART OF A VIRTUAL ARSENAL. THE STICK AND...*THIS* ARE COUNTERPARTS, CONNECTED BY A...
...I DON'T HAVE THE MATH, ELIJAH. CALL IT A QUANTUM THREAD. SOME PERMUTATION OF SUPERSTRING THEORY THAT I CAN BARELY GRASP.
TAKE AN ORDINARY OBJECT, SOMEHOW LINK IT TO A WEAPON STORED SOMEWHERE ACROSS THE BLEED.
GIVE IT A SHARP JOLT OF KINETIC ENERGY TO TRIGGER THE RELAY, AND VOILÀ -- MULTIVERSAL TRANSPOSITION. THE CANE GOES THERE, THE THING COMES HERE.
HOW DO YOU AVOID GETTING YOUR ARM BURNED OFF EVERY TIME YOU NEED A...WHATEVER IT IS?
BY BEING SUPERHUMANLY RESISTANT TO DAMAGE.
THIS IS AN ARTIFACT OF THE FOUR.
AND IT WAS FOUND IN THE VESSEL THAT AMBROSE BROUGHT DOWN IN BRAZIL.
I SURMISE THAT KIM SÜSKIND MUST HAVE BEEN ABOARD.

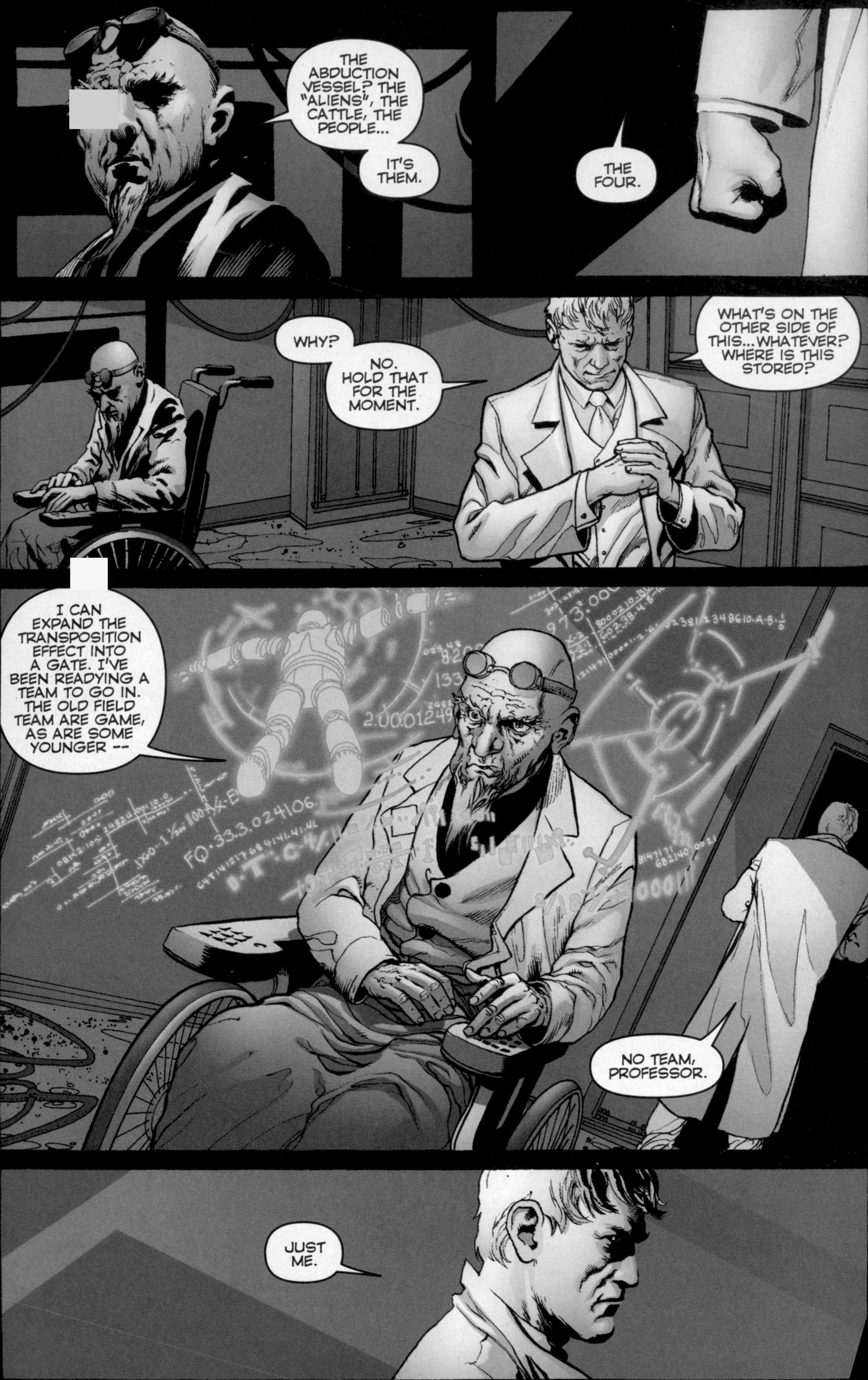
THE ABDUCTION VESSEL? THE "ALIENS", THE CATTLE, THE PEOPLE...
IT'S THEM.
THE FOUR.
WHY?
NO. HOLD THAT FOR THE MOMENT.
WHAT'S ON THE OTHER SIDE OF THIS...WHATEVER? WHERE IS THIS STORED?
I CAN EXPAND THE TRANSPOSITION EFFECT INTO A GATE. I'VE BEEN READYING A TEAM TO GO IN. THE OLD FIELD TEAM ARE GAME, AS ARE SOME YOUNGER --
NO TEAM, PROFESSOR.
JUST ME.

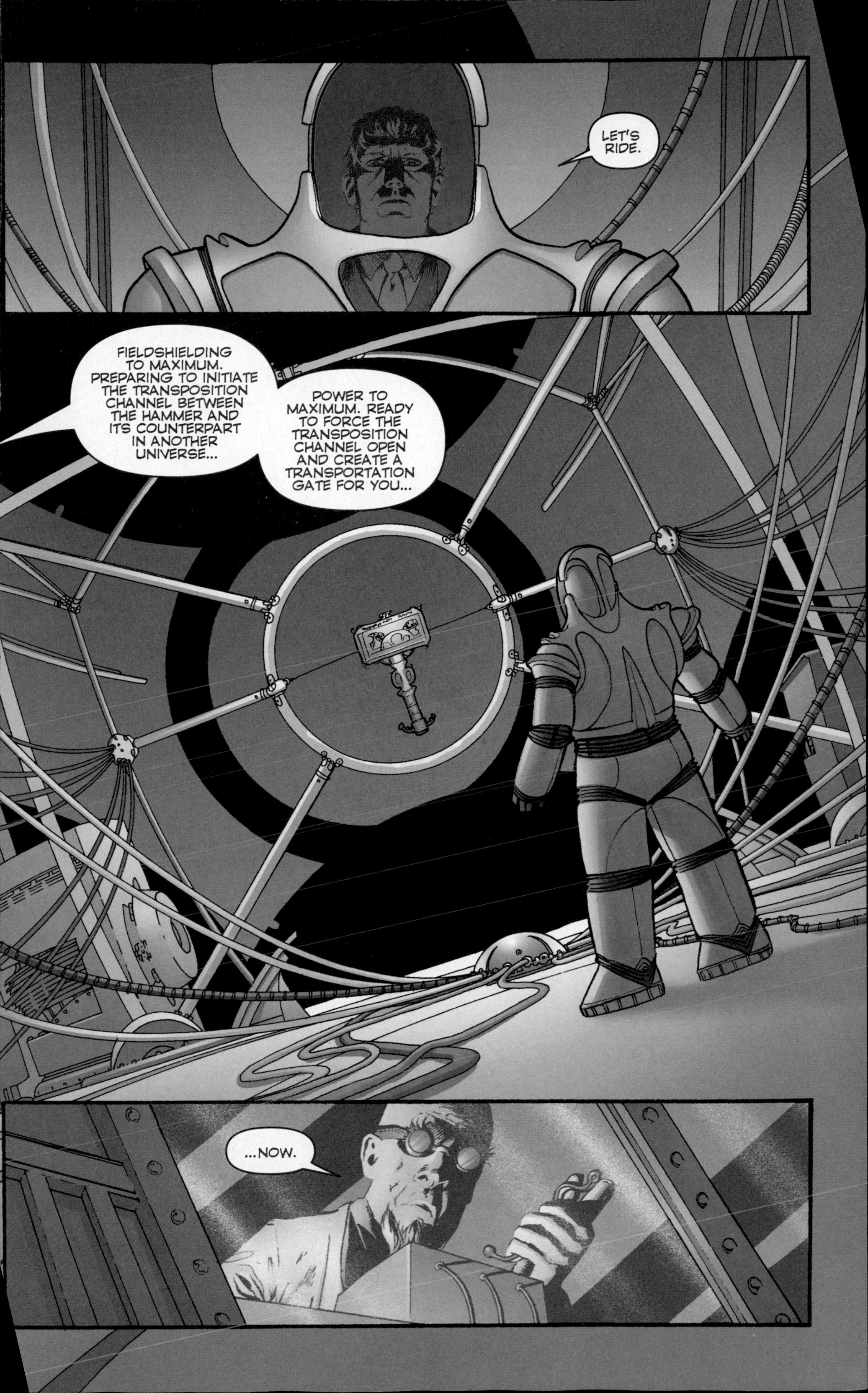
LET'S RIDE.
FIELDSHIELDING TO MAXIMUM. PREPARING TO INITIATE THE TRANSPOSITION CHANNEL BETWEEN THE HAMMER AND ITS COUNTERPART IN ANOTHER UNIVERSE...
POWER TO MAXIMUM. READY TO FORCE THE TRANSPOSITION CHANNEL OPEN AND CREATE A TRANSPORTATION GATE FOR YOU...
...NOW.

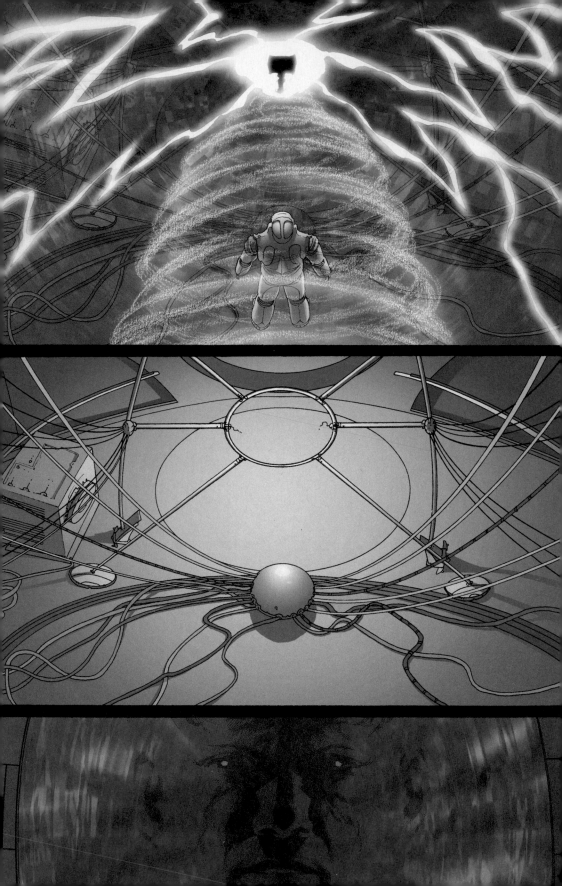

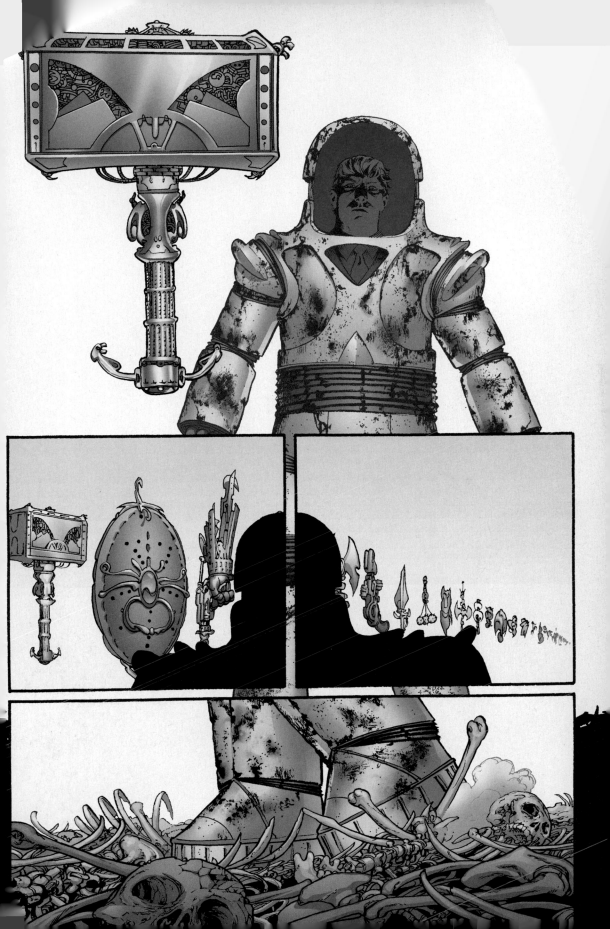

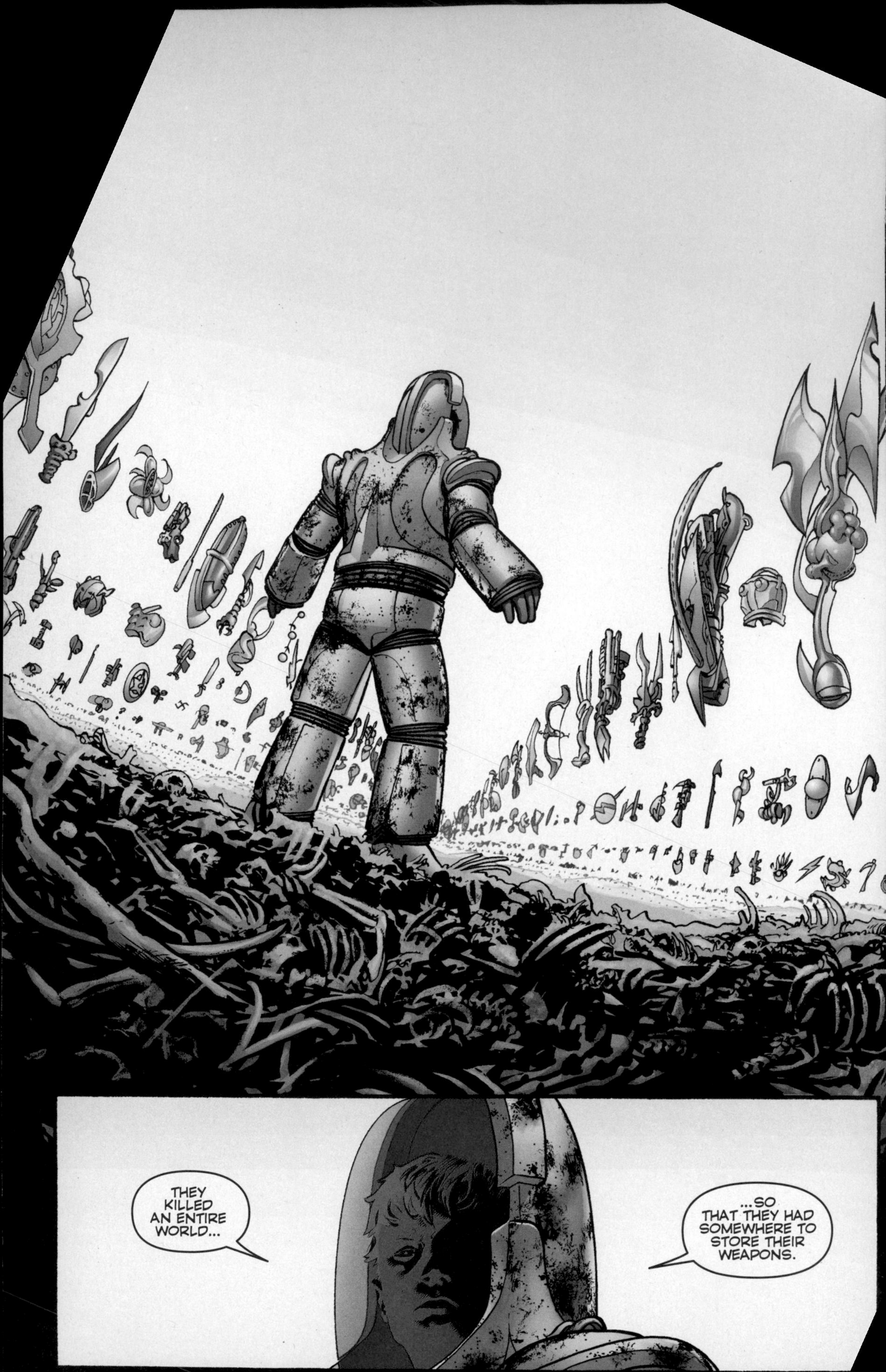
THEY KILLED AN ENTIRE WORLD...
...SO THAT THEY HAD SOMEWHERE TO STORE THEIR WEAPONS.

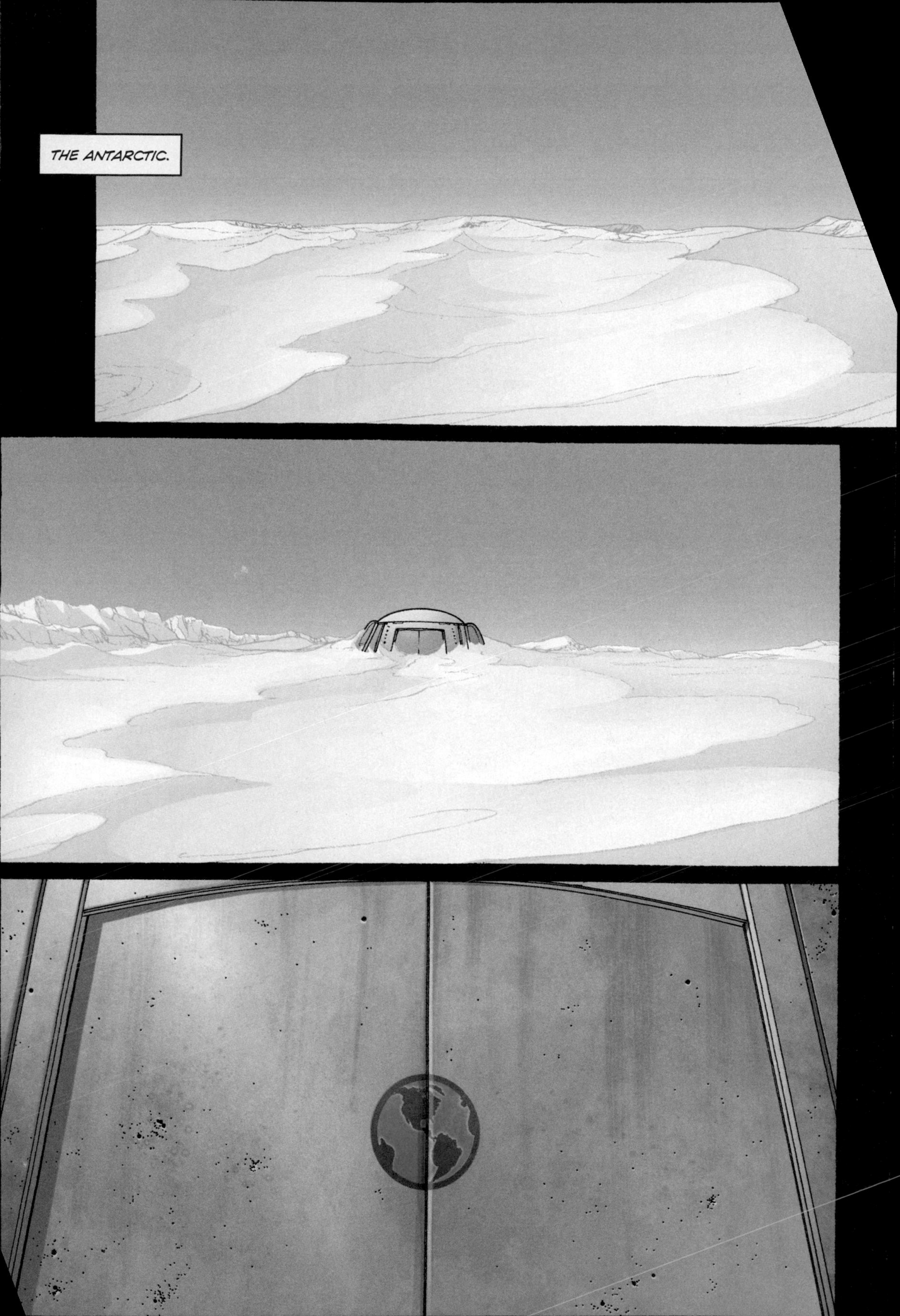
THE ANTARCTIC.

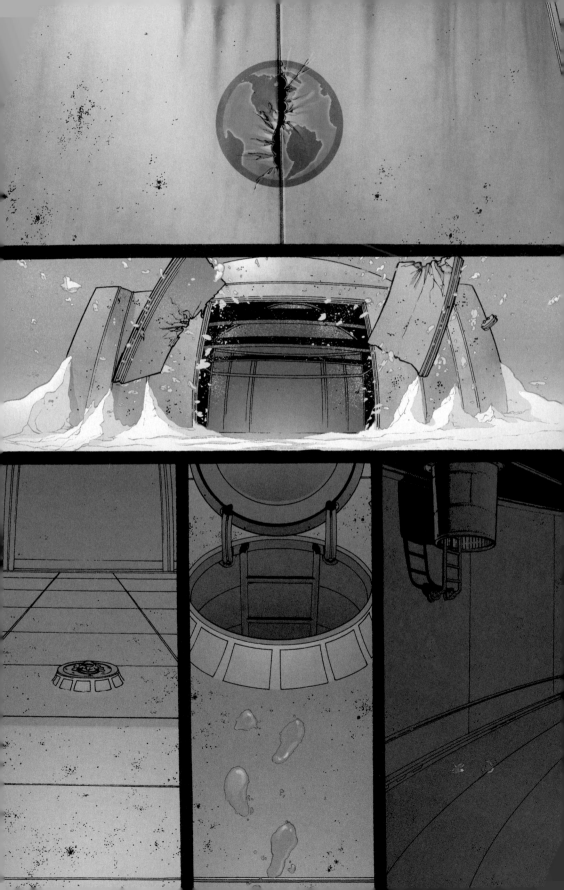

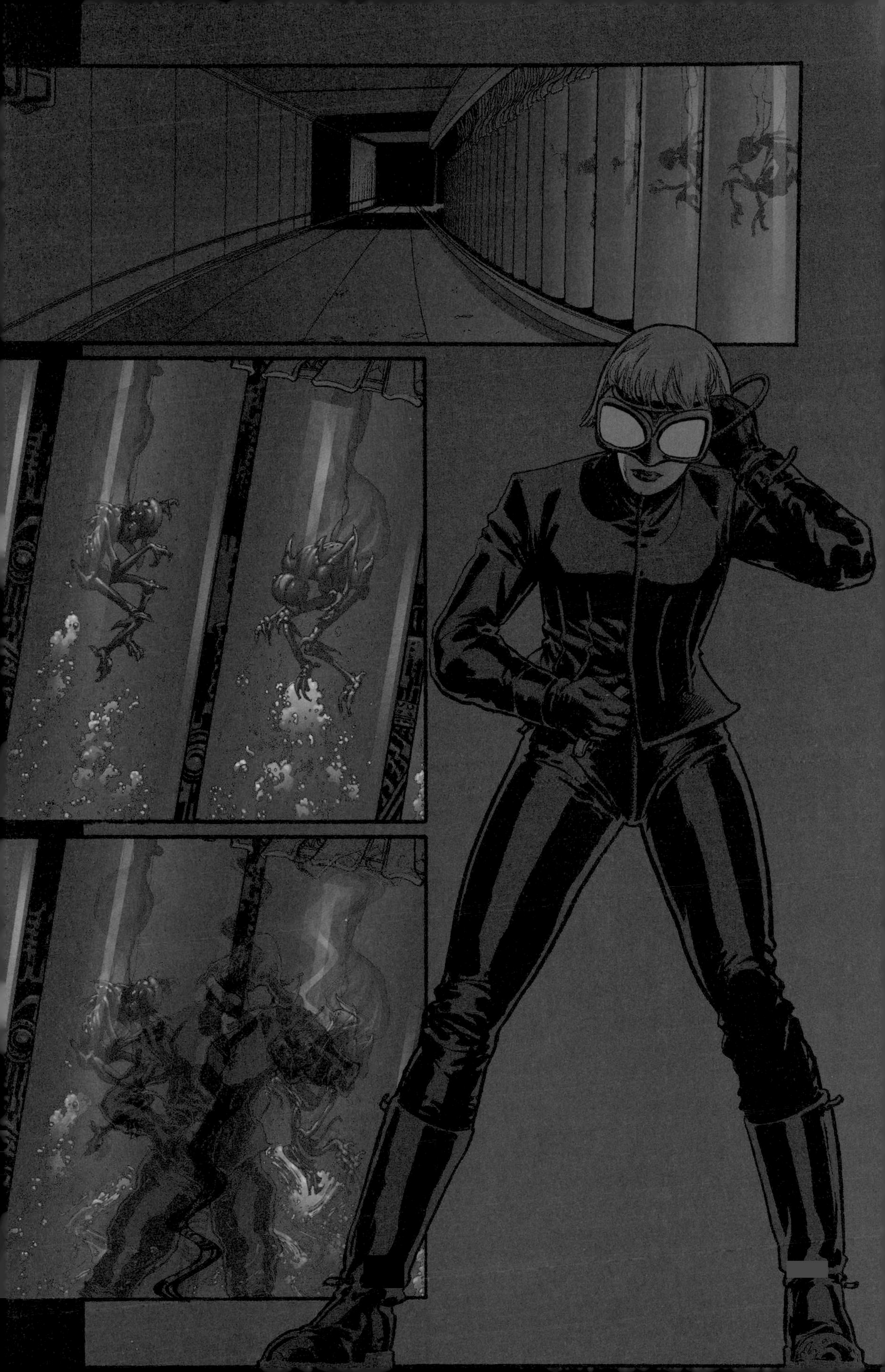

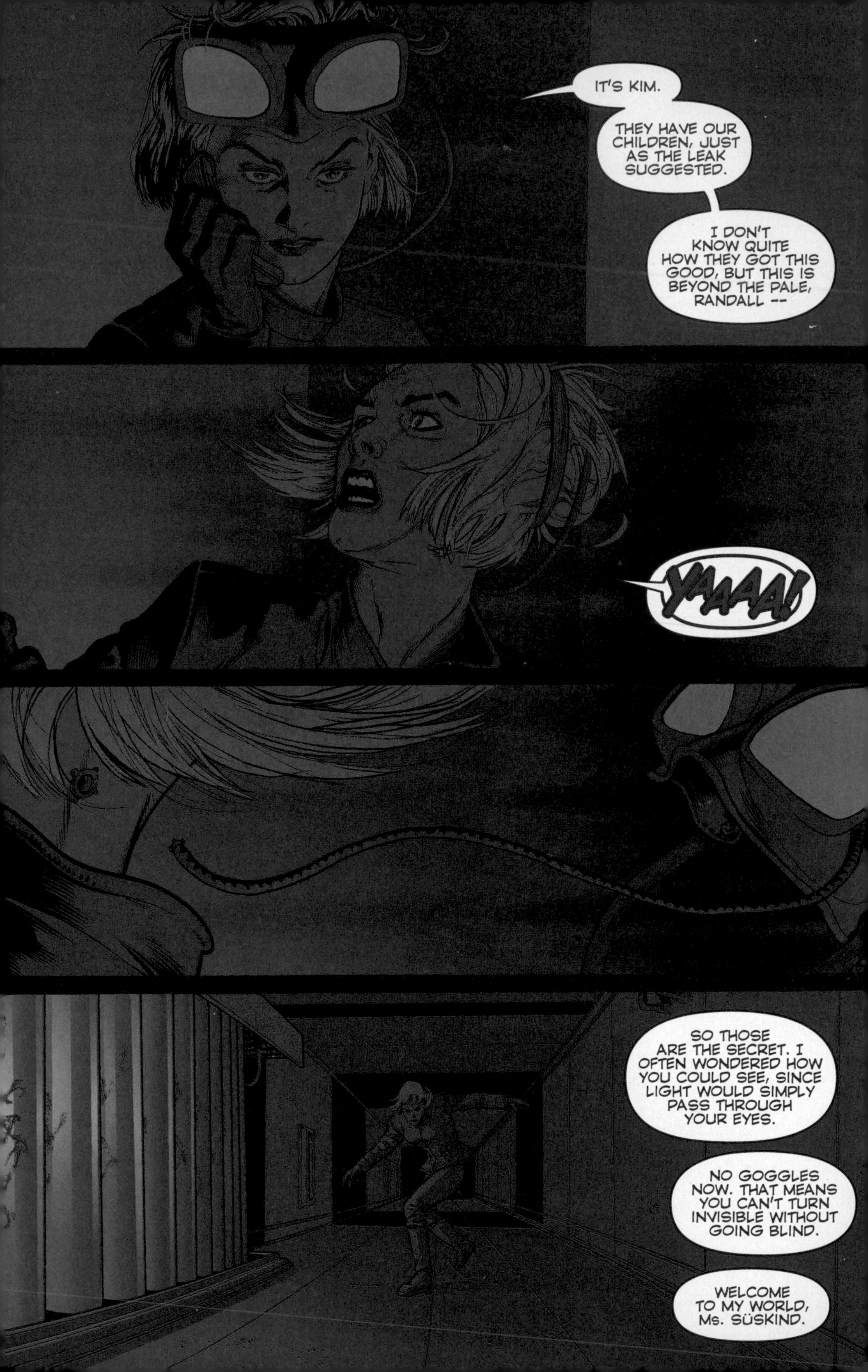
IT'S KIM.
THEY HAVE OUR CHILDREN, JUST AS THE LEAK SUGGESTED.
I DON'T KNOW QUITE HOW THEY GOT THIS GOOD, BUT THIS IS BEYOND THE PALE, RANDALL --
YAAAA!
SO THOSE ARE THE SECRET. I OFTEN WONDERED HOW YOU COULD SEE, SINCE LIGHT WOULD SIMPLY PASS THROUGH YOUR EYES.
NO GOGGLES NOW. THAT MEANS YOU CAN'T TURN INVISIBLE WITHOUT GOING BLIND.
WELCOME TO MY WORLD, Ms. SÜSKIND.

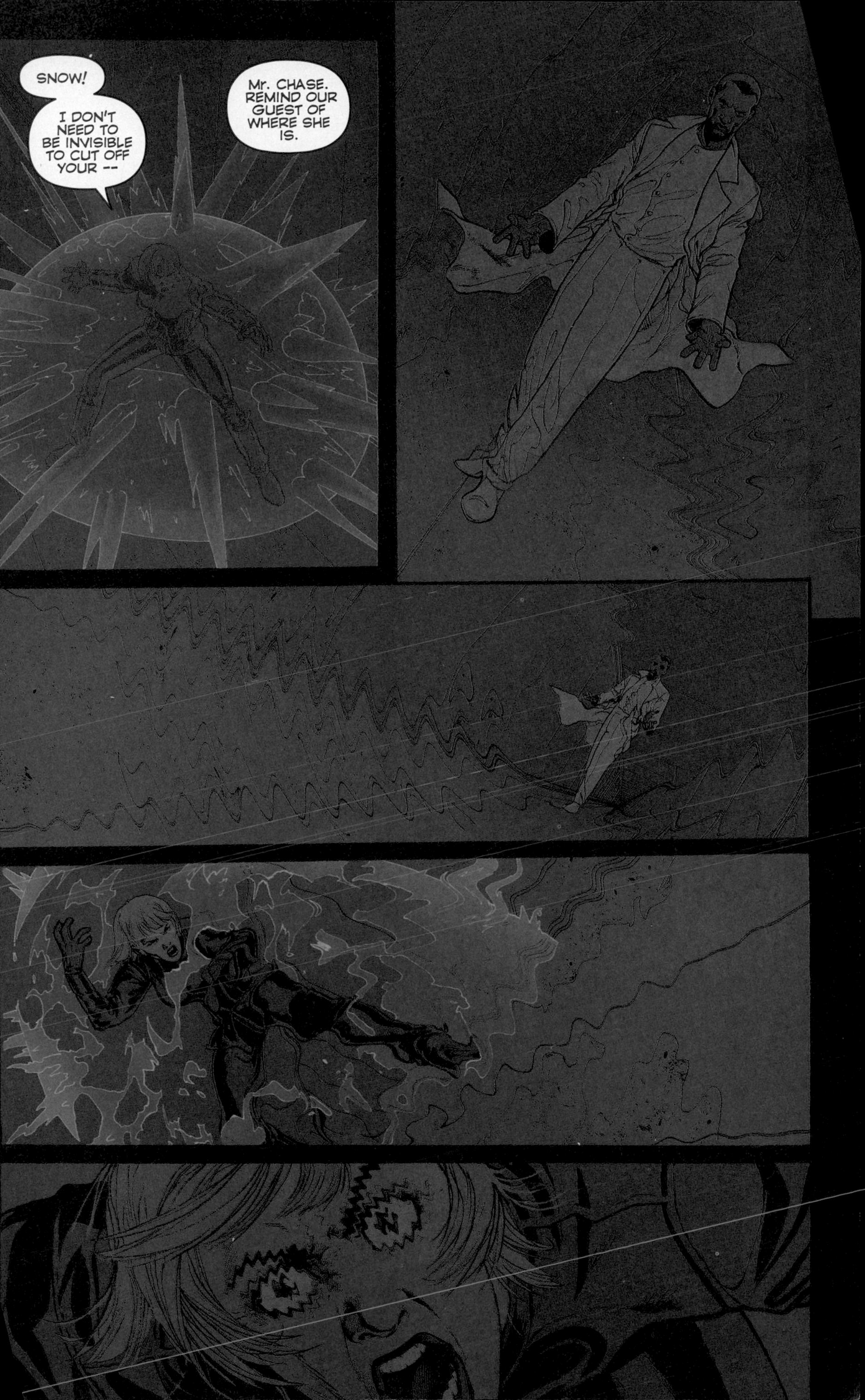
SNOW!
I DON'T NEED TO BE INVISIBLE TO CUT OFF YOUR --
Mr. CHASE. REMIND OUR GUEST OF WHERE SHE IS.

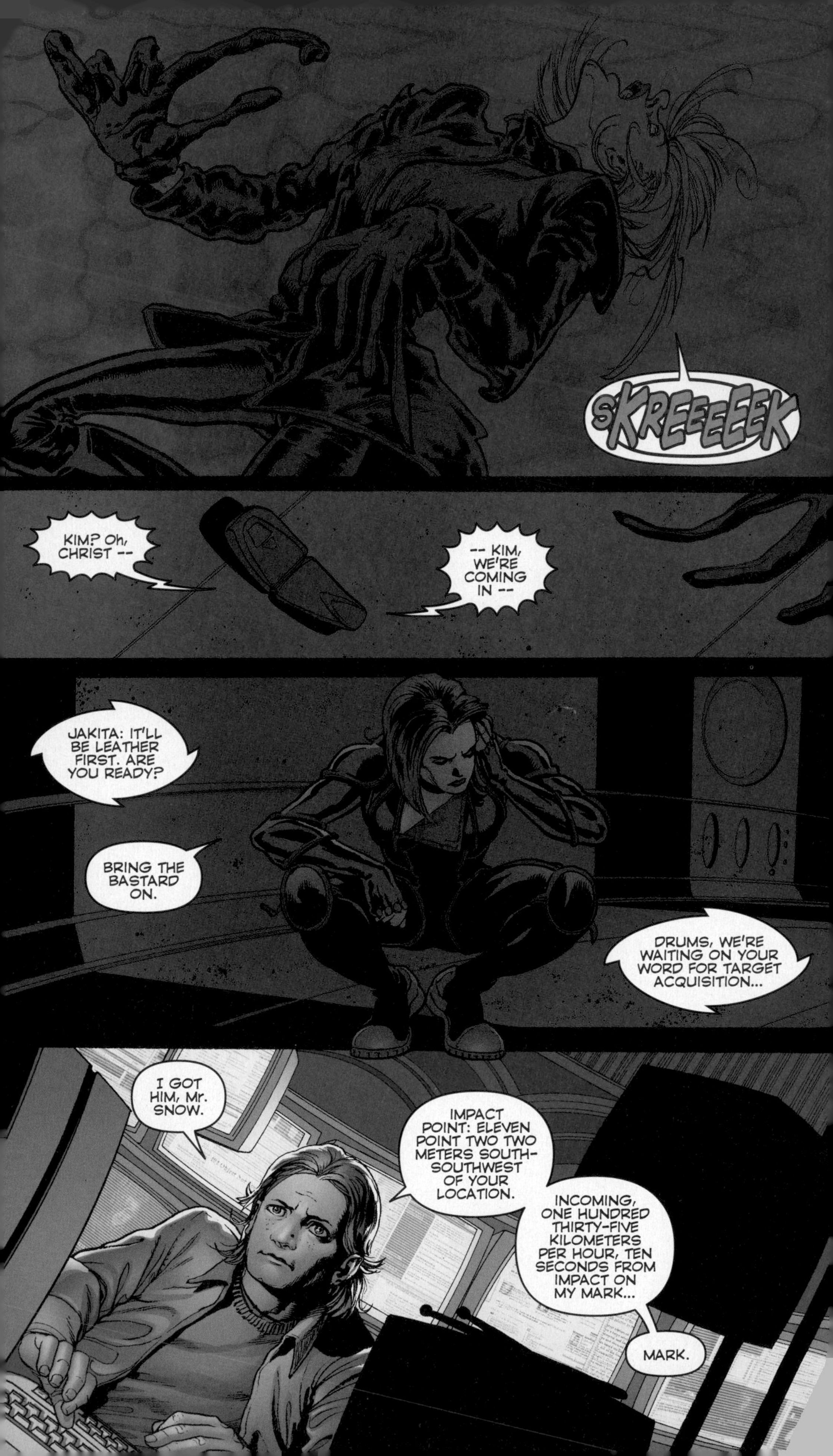
sKREEEEEK
KIM? Oh, CHRIST --
-- KIM, WE'RE COMING IN --
JAKITA: IT'LL BE LEATHER FIRST. ARE YOU READY?
BRING THE BASTARD ON.
DRUMS, WE'RE WAITING ON YOUR WORD FOR TARGET ACQUISITION...
I GOT HIM, Mr. SNOW.
IMPACT POINT: ELEVEN POINT TWO TWO METERS SOUTH-SOUTHWEST OF YOUR LOCATION.
INCOMING, ONE HUNDRED THIRTY-FIVE KILOMETERS PER HOUR, TEN SECONDS FROM IMPACT ON MY MARK...
MARK.

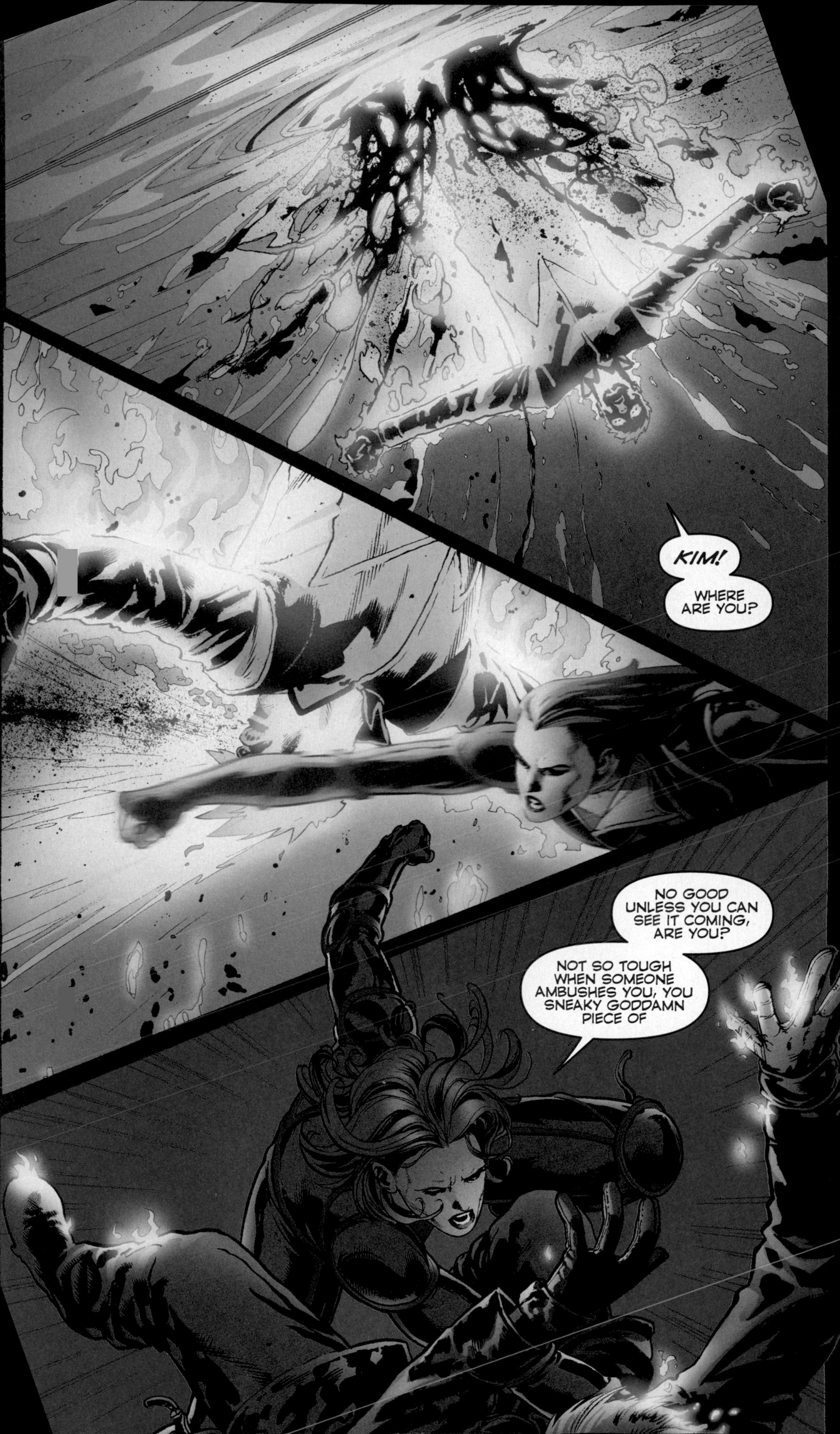
KIM!
WHERE ARE YOU?
NO GOOD UNLESS YOU CAN SEE IT COMING, ARE YOU?
NOT SO TOUGH WHEN SOMEONE AMBUSHES YOU, YOU SNEAKY GODDAMN PIECE OF

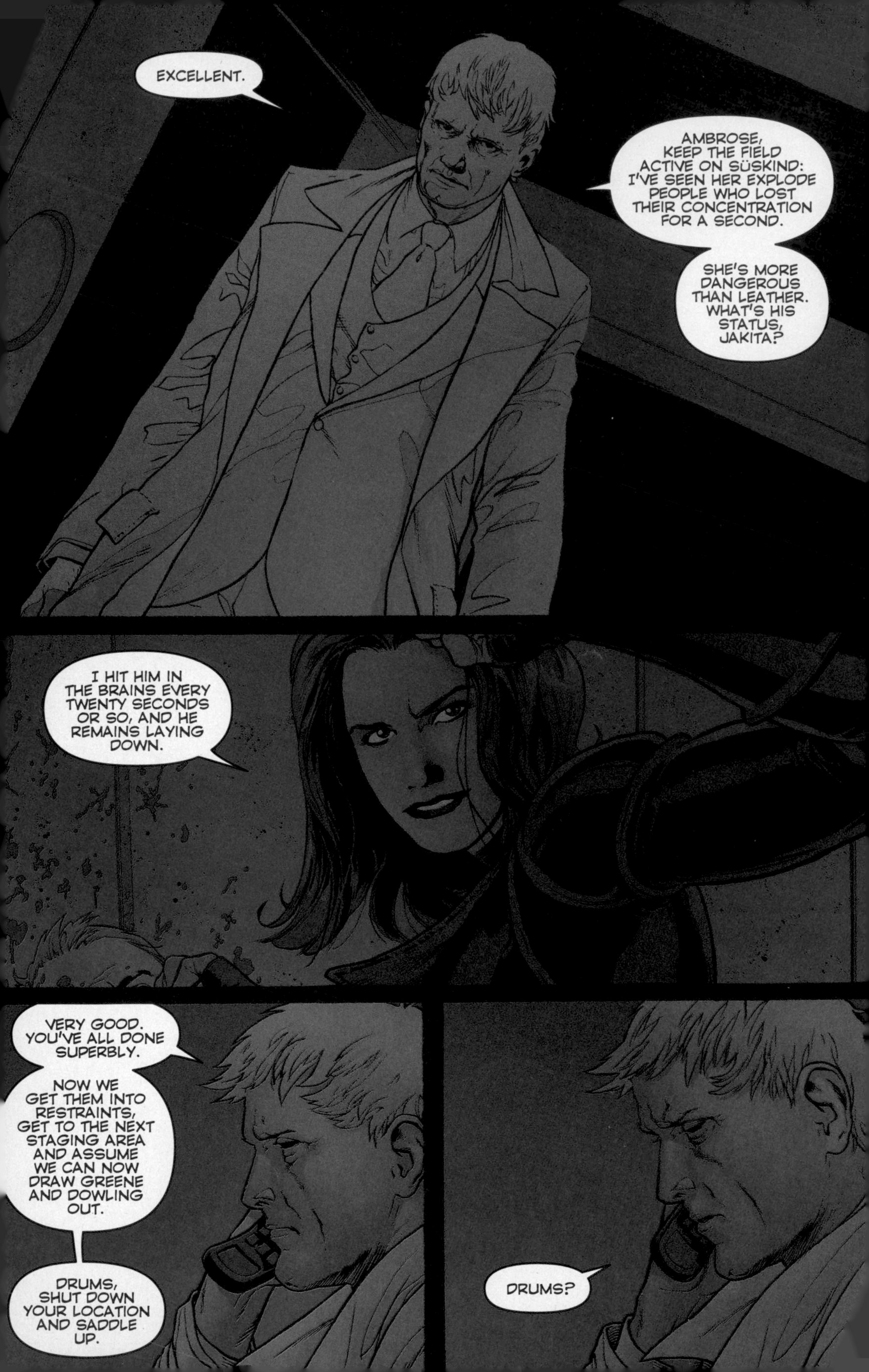
EXCELLENT.
AMBROSE, KEEP THE FIELD ACTIVE ON SÜSKIND: I'VE SEEN HER EXPLODE PEOPLE WHO LOST THEIR CONCENTRATION FOR A SECOND.
SHE'S MORE DANGEROUS THAN LEATHER. WHAT'S HIS STATUS, JAKITA?
I HIT HIM IN THE BRAINS EVERY TWENTY SECONDS OR SO, AND HE REMAINS LAYING DOWN.
VERY GOOD. YOU'VE ALL DONE SUPERBLY.
NOW WE GET THEM INTO RESTRAINTS, GET TO THE NEXT STAGING AREA AND ASSUME WE CAN NOW DRAW GREENE AND DOWLING OUT.
DRUMS, SHUT DOWN YOUR LOCATION AND SADDLE UP.
DRUMS?

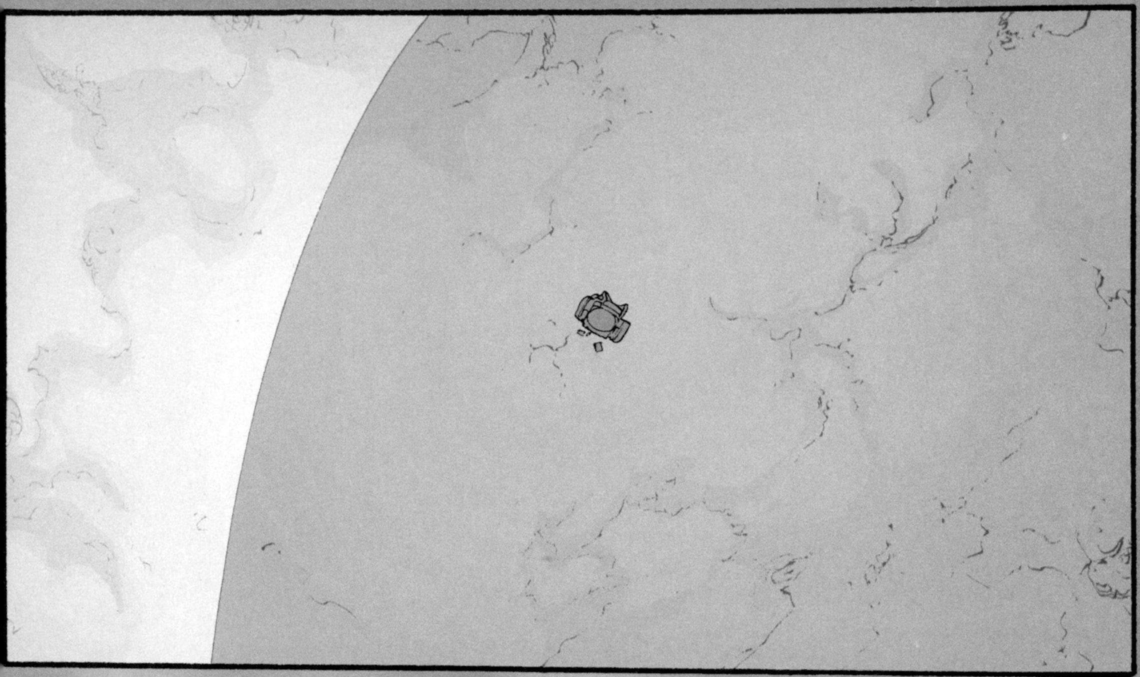
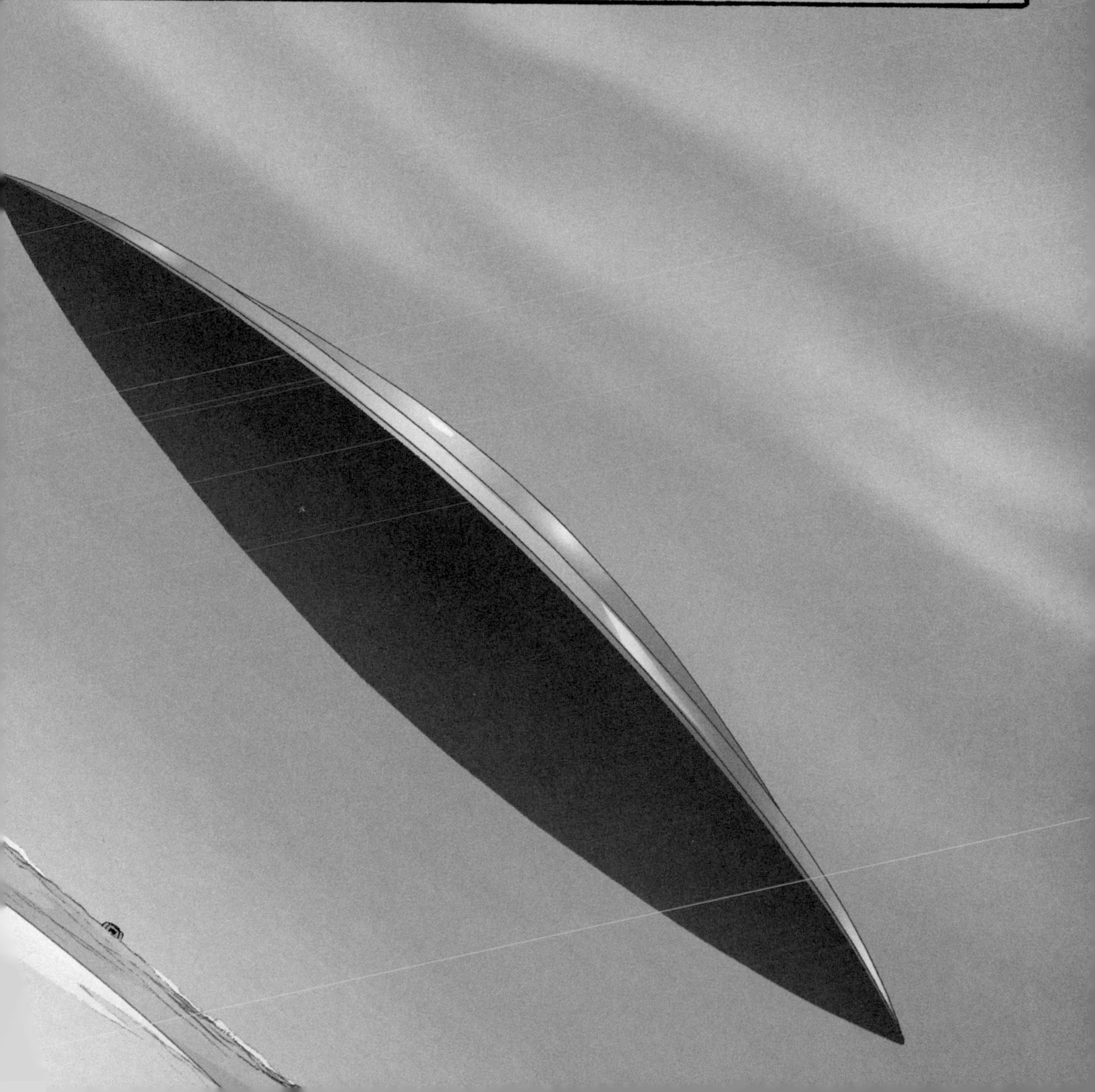

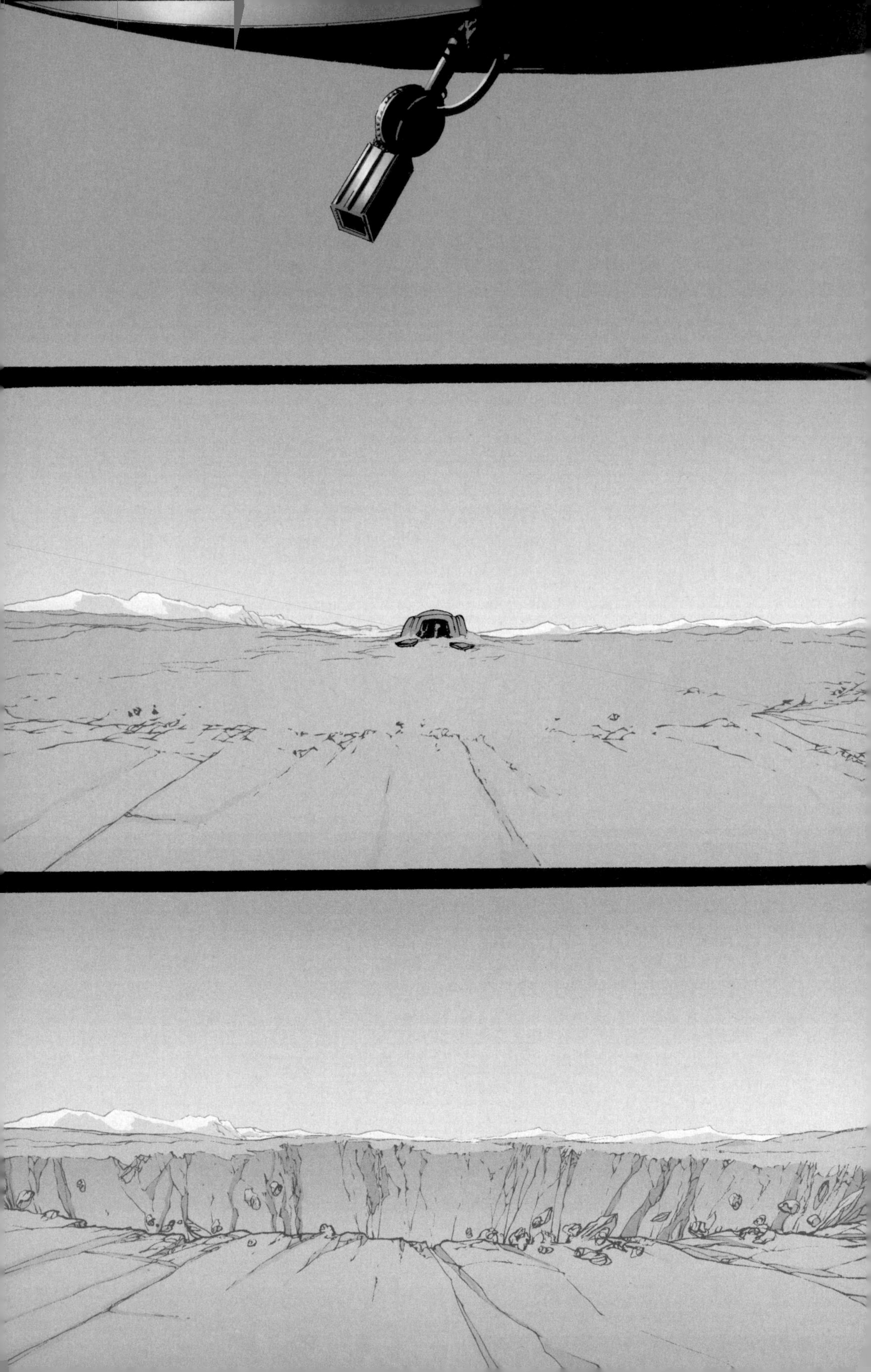

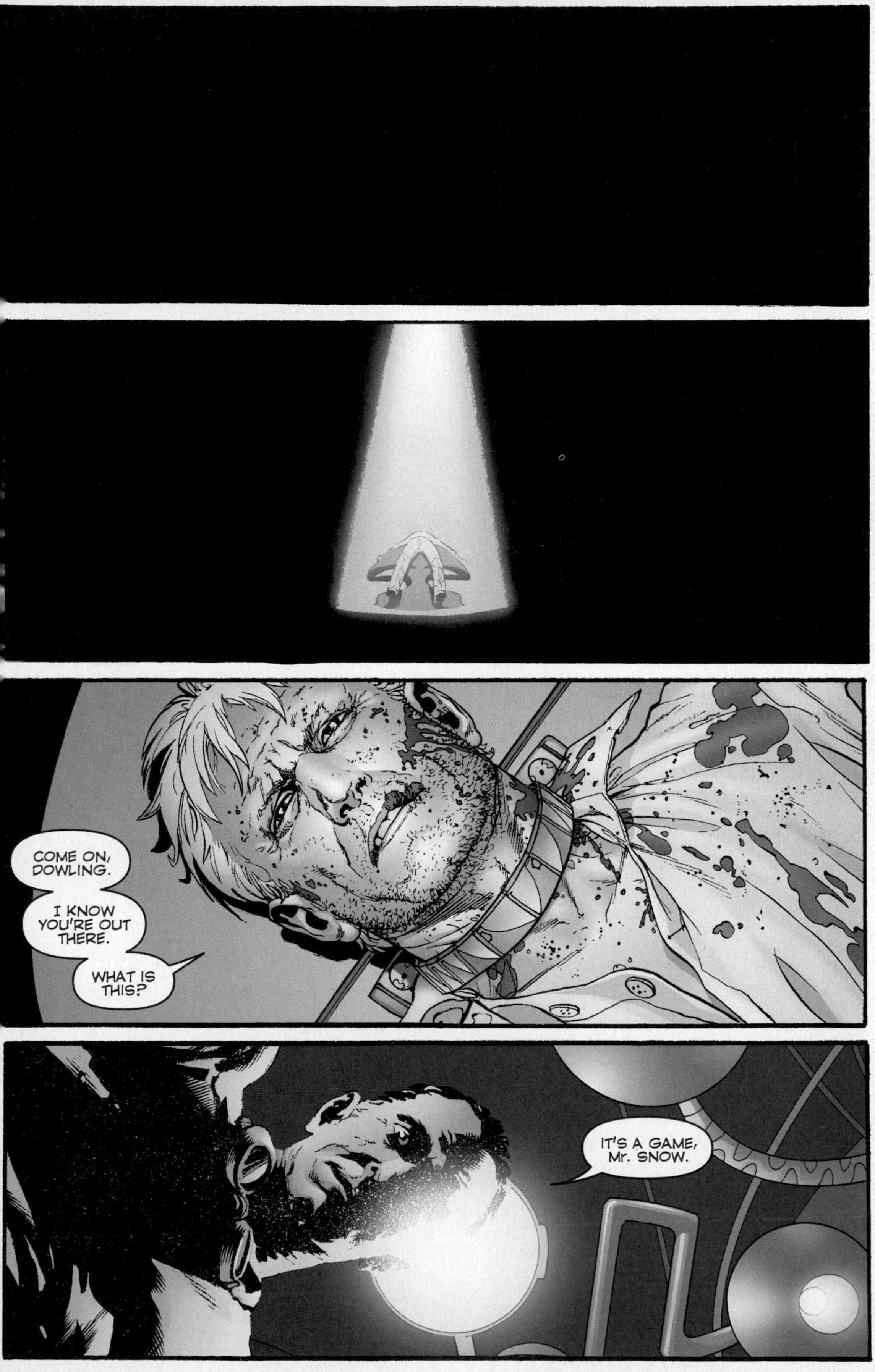
COME ON, DOWLING.
I KNOW YOU'RE OUT THERE.
WHAT IS THIS?
IT'S A GAME, Mr. SNOW.

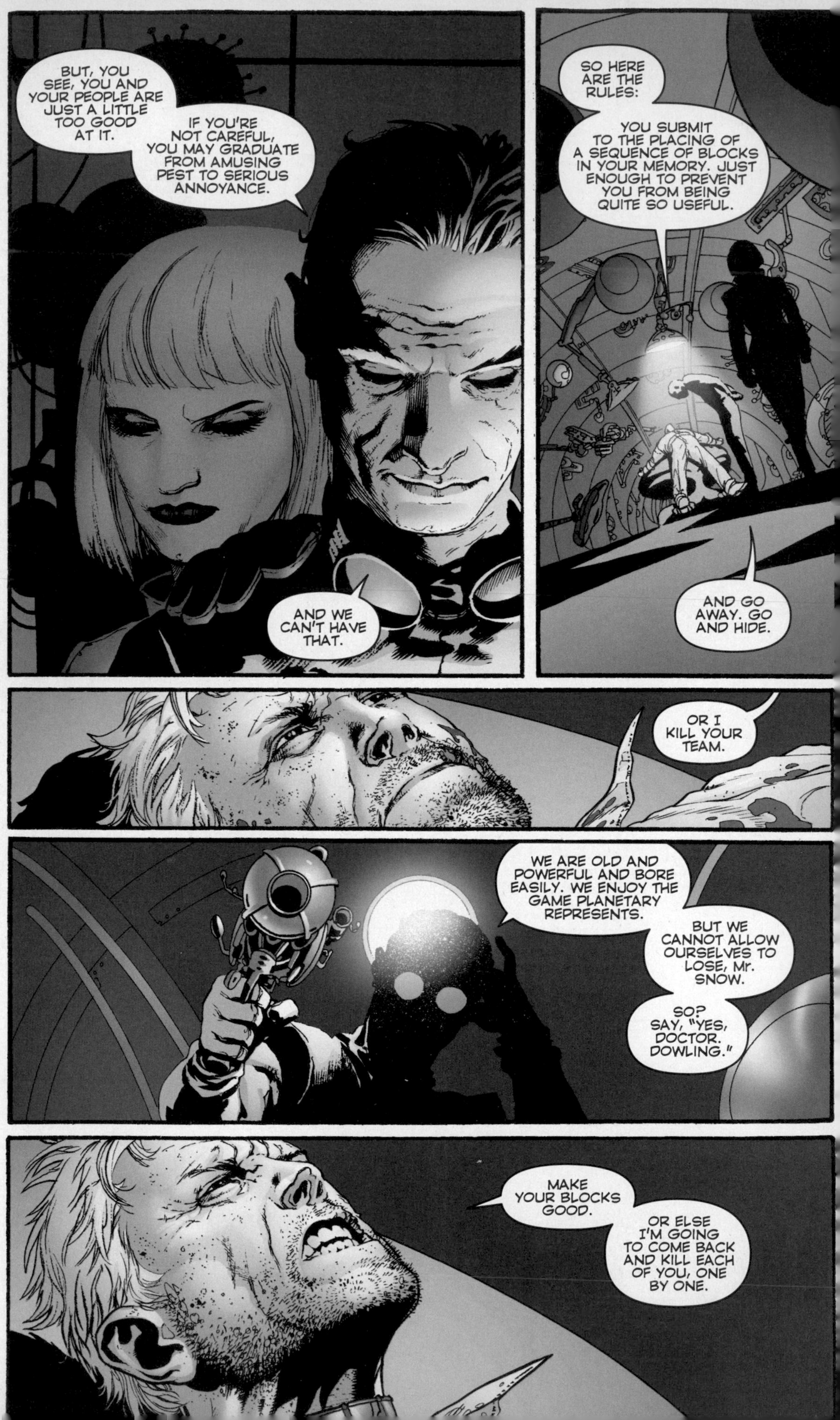
BUT, YOU SEE, YOU AND YOUR PEOPLE ARE JUST A LITTLE TOO GOOD AT IT.
IF YOU'RE NOT CAREFUL, YOU MAY GRADUATE FROM AMUSING PEST TO SERIOUS ANNOYANCE.
AND WE CAN'T HAVE THAT.
SO HERE ARE THE RULES:
YOU SUBMIT TO THE PLACING OF A SEQUENCE OF BLOCKS IN YOUR MEMORY. JUST ENOUGH TO PREVENT YOU FROM BEING QUITE SO USEFUL.
AND GO AWAY. GO AND HIDE.
OR I KILL YOUR TEAM.
WE ARE OLD AND POWERFUL AND BORE EASILY. WE ENJOY THE GAME PLANETARY REPRESENTS.
BUT WE CANNOT ALLOW OURSELVES TO LOSE, Mr. SNOW.
SO? SAY, "YES, DOCTOR. DOWLING."
MAKE YOUR BLOCKS GOOD.
OR ELSE I'M GOING TO COME BACK AND KILL EACH OF YOU, ONE BY ONE.

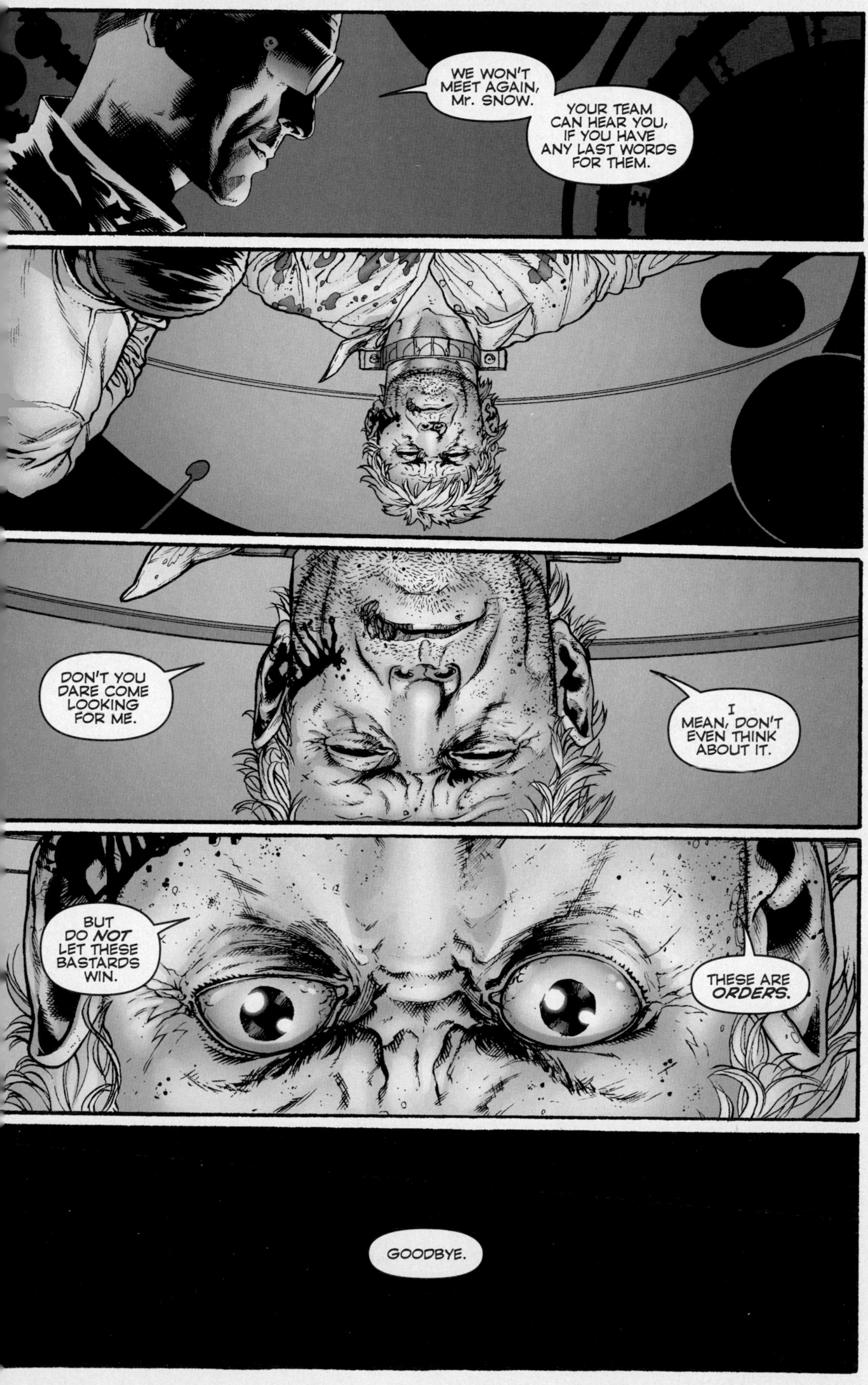
WE WON'T MEET AGAIN, Mr. SNOW.
YOUR TEAM CAN HEAR YOU, IF YOU HAVE ANY LAST WORDS FOR THEM.
DON'T YOU DARE COME LOOKING FOR ME.
I MEAN, DON'T EVEN THINK ABOUT IT.
BUT DO **NOT** LET THESE BASTARDS WIN.
THESE ARE ***ORDERS.***
GOODBYE.

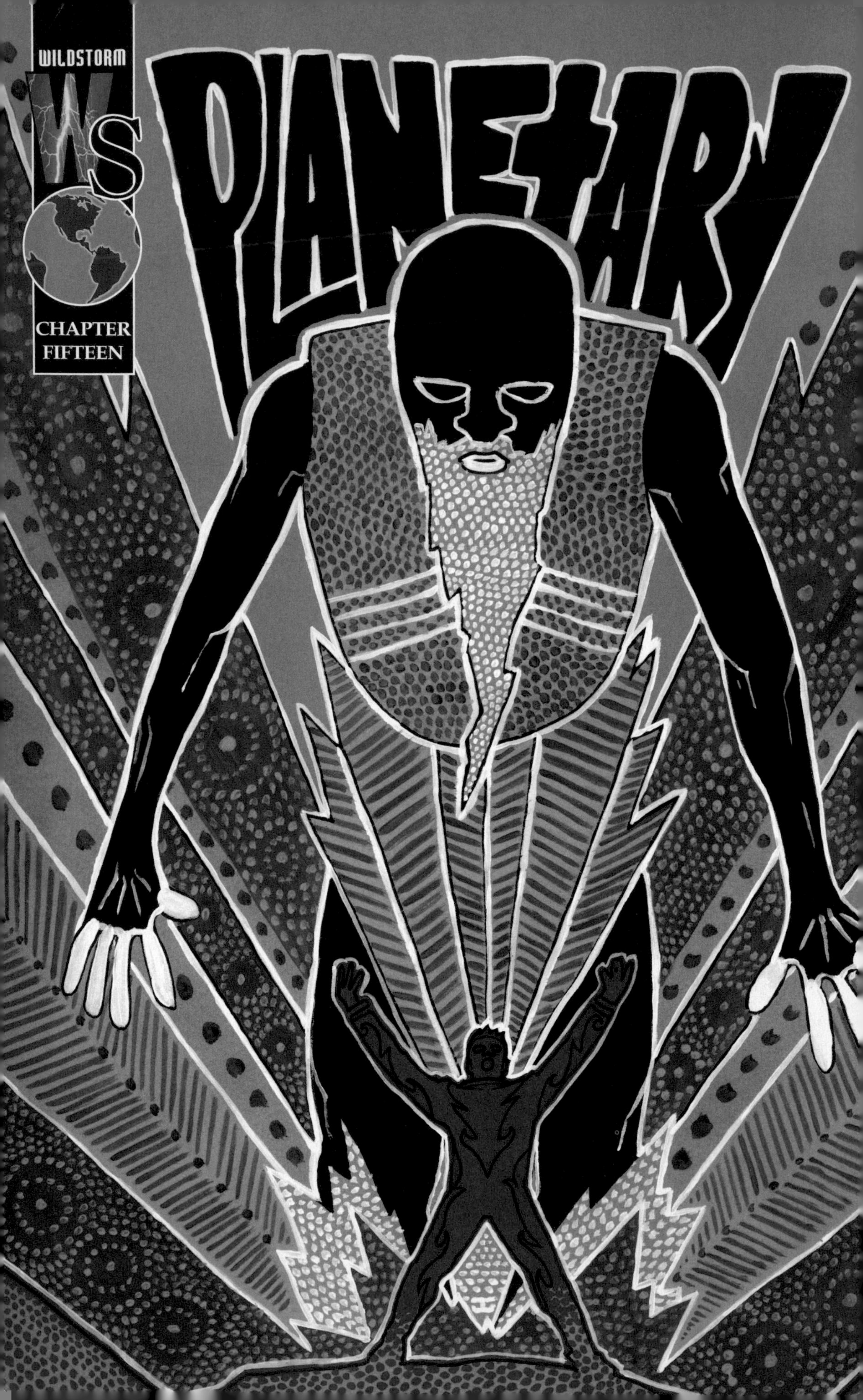
WILDSTORM
WS
PLANETARY
CHAPTER
FIFTEEN

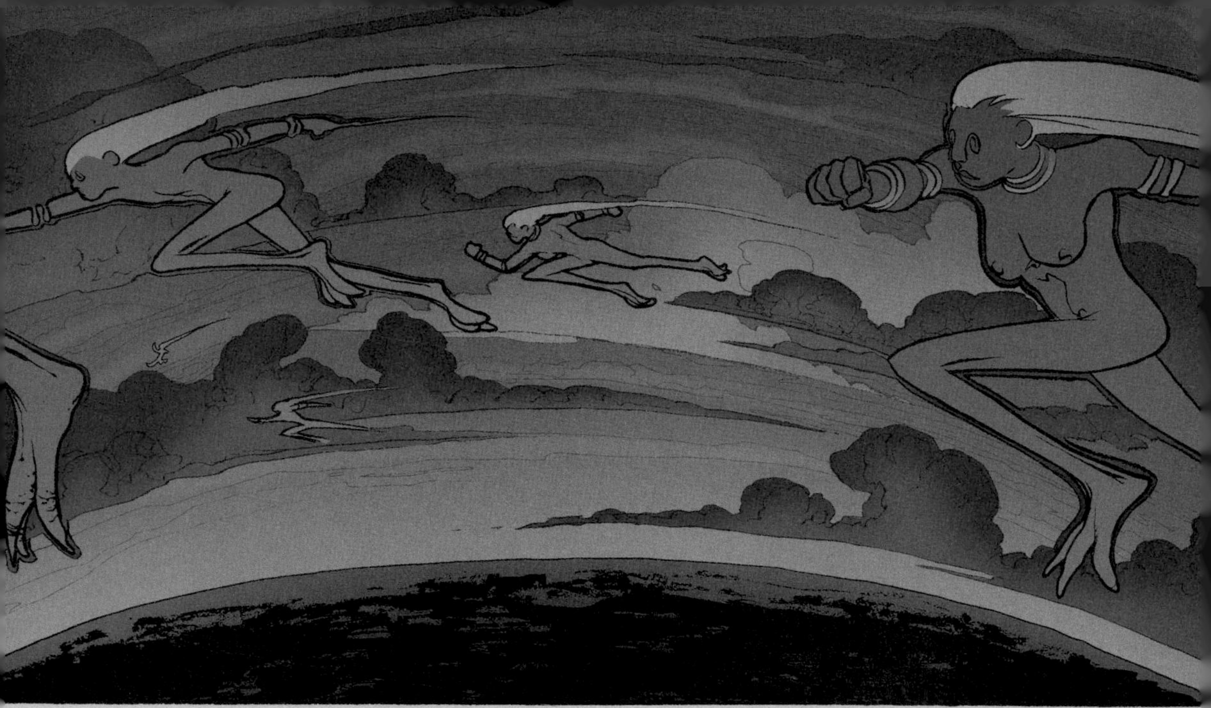

In the Beginning

The Earth was an infinite dark plain, separated from the sky and from the murky sea and enveloped in shadowy twilight.

There were no stars, no sun or moon.

In the sky, there were Sky-dwellers, running beyond the Western Clouds, ageless and sparkling.

On the earth, under the shallow ditches that in the future would become waterholes, laid The Ancients, so old they could do nothing but sleep. Like the ditches, they were pregnant with potential, for each contained the merest breath of aspirational life.

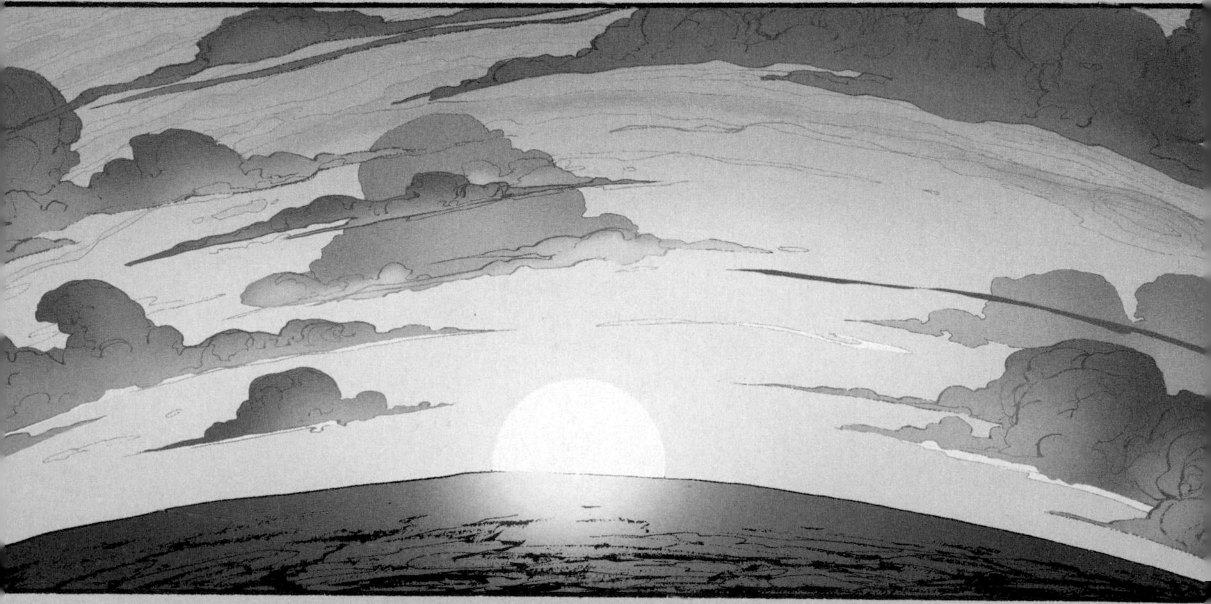

Under the plain were all the constellations, the burning sun, the shining moon. Waiting.

On the morning of the First Day, the Sun finally wanted to be born. It exploded through the surface and up into the sky, casting light and heat all about.

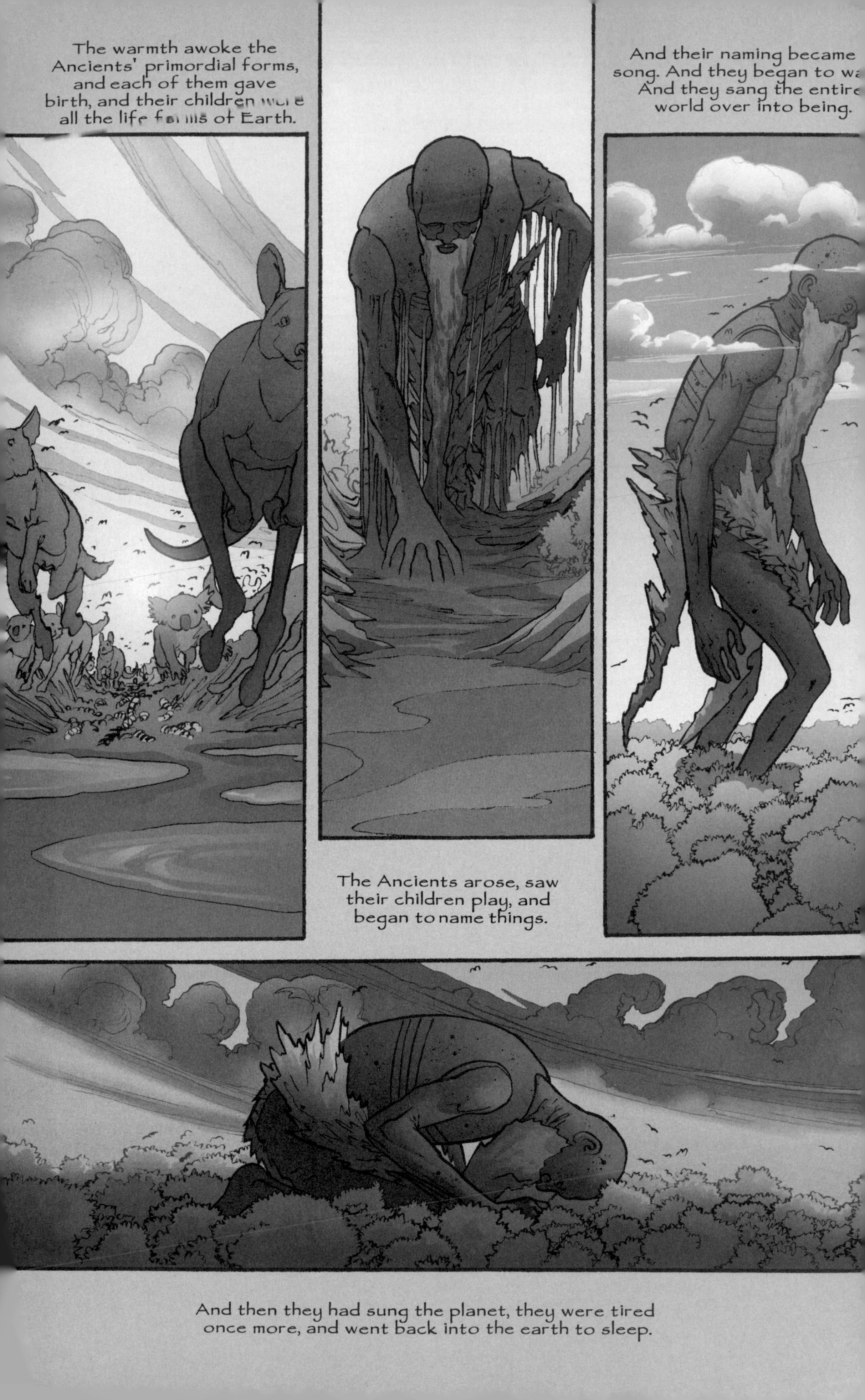
The warmth awoke the Ancients' primordial forms, and each of them gave birth, and their children
all the life
of Earth.
And their naming became song. And they began to
And they sang the
world over into being.
The Ancients arose, saw their children play, and began to name things.
And then they had sung the planet, they were tired once more, and went back into the earth to sleep.

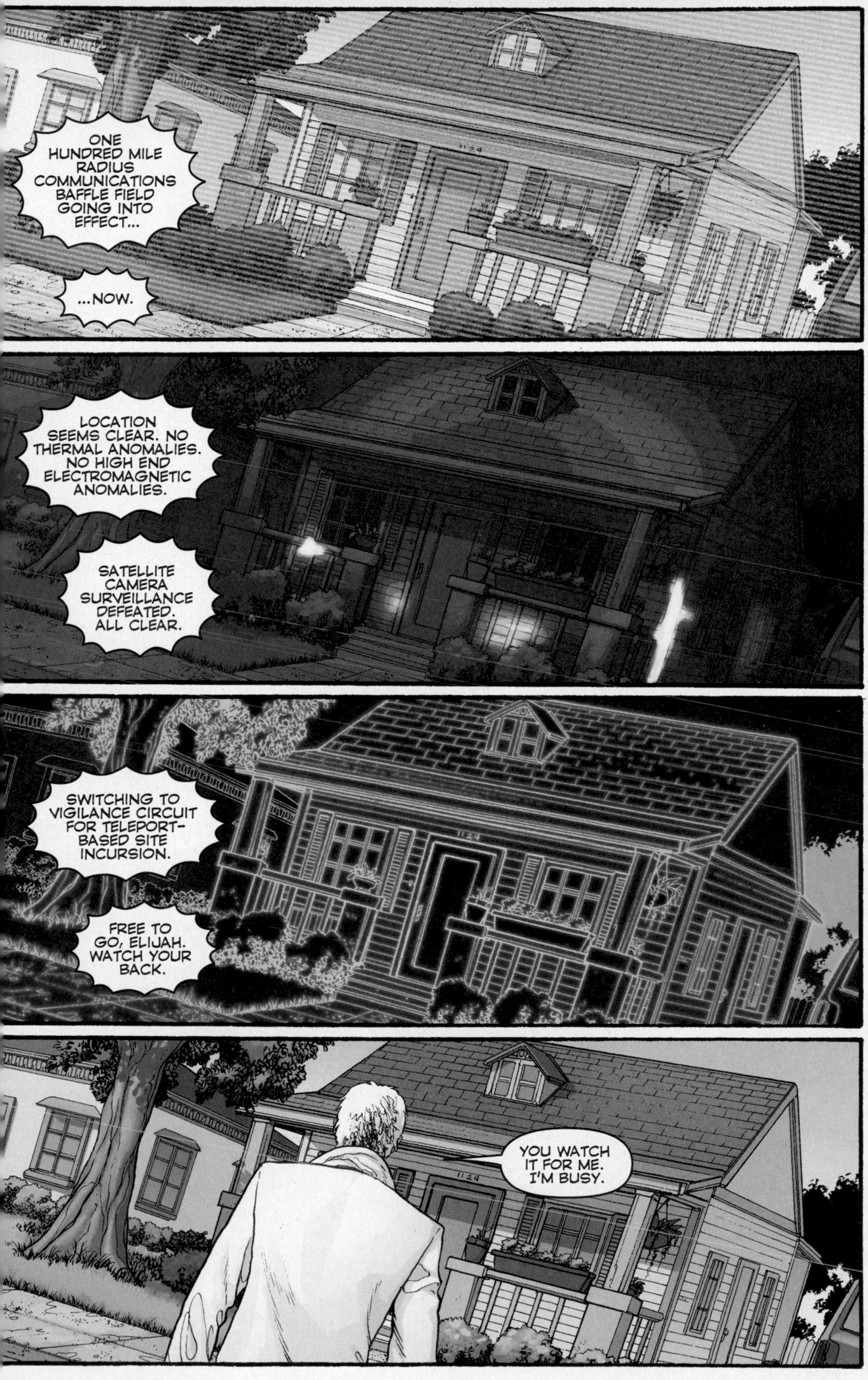
ONE HUNDRED MILE RADIUS COMMUNICATIONS BAFFLE FIELD GOING INTO EFFECT...
...NOW.
LOCATION SEEMS CLEAR. NO THERMAL ANOMALIES. NO HIGH END ELECTROMAGNETIC ANOMALIES.
SATELLITE CAMERA SURVEILLANCE DEFEATED. ALL CLEAR.
SWITCHING TO VIGILANCE CIRCUIT FOR TELEPORT-BASED SITE INCURSION.
FREE TO GO, ELIJAH. WATCH YOUR BACK.
YOU WATCH IT FOR ME. I'M BUSY.

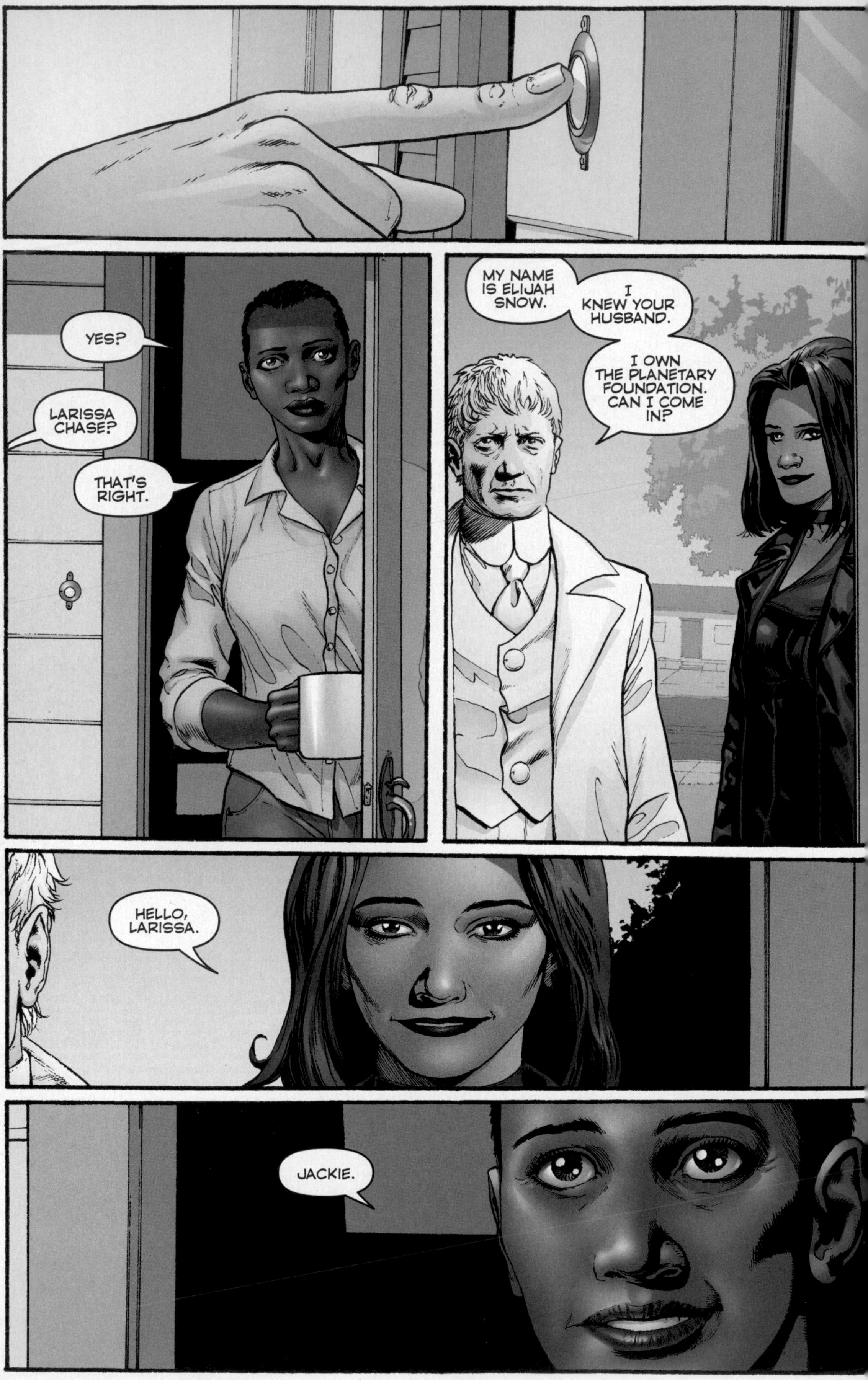
YES?
LARISSA CHASE?
THAT'S RIGHT.
MY NAME IS ELIJAH SNOW.
I KNEW YOUR HUSBAND.
I OWN THE PLANETARY FOUNDATION. CAN I COME IN?
HELLO, LARISSA.
JACKIE.

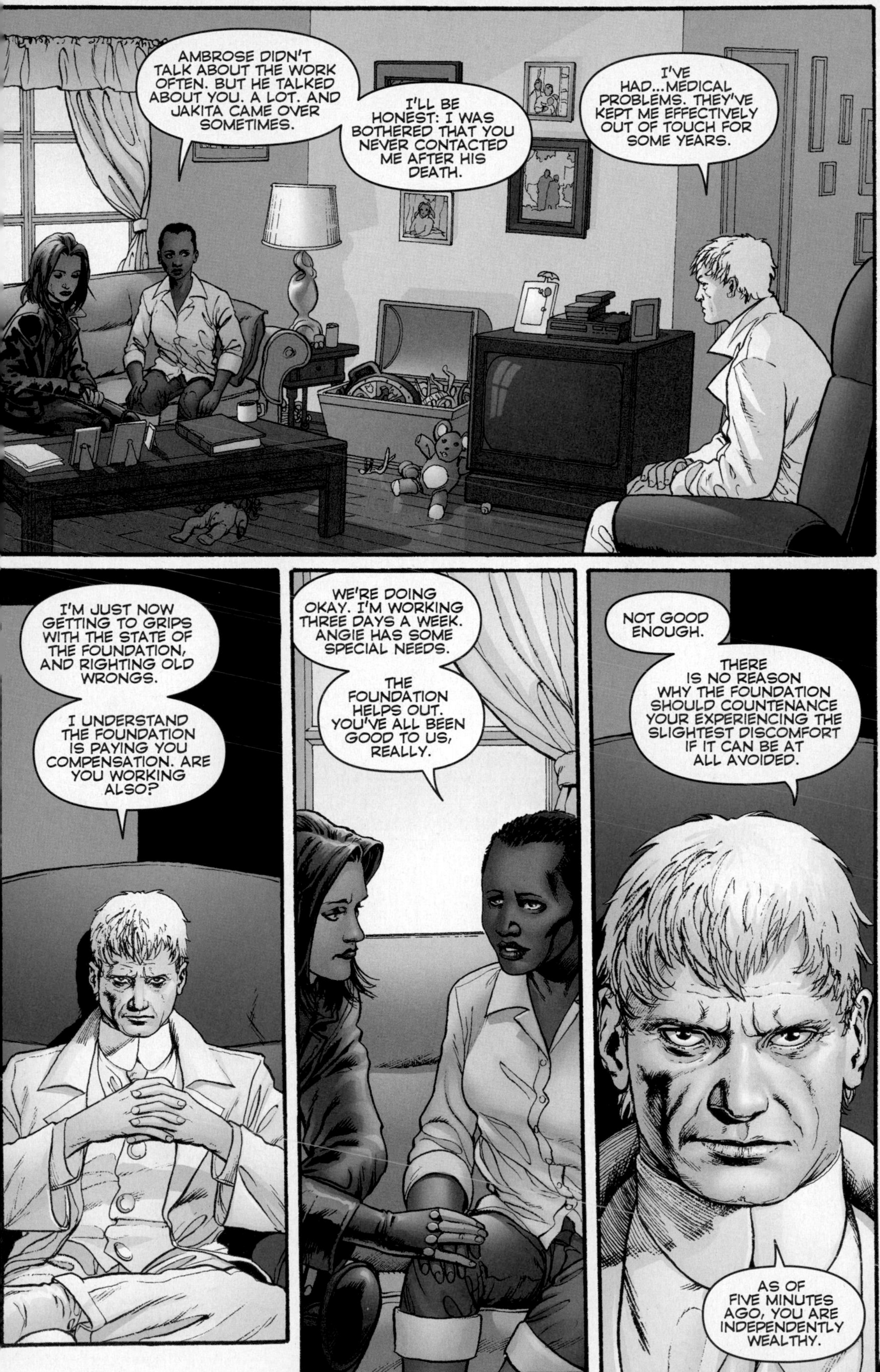
AMBROSE DIDN'T TALK ABOUT THE WORK OFTEN. BUT HE TALKED ABOUT YOU. A LOT. AND JAKITA CAME OVER SOMETIMES.
I'LL BE HONEST: I WAS BOTHERED THAT YOU NEVER CONTACTED ME AFTER HIS DEATH.
I'VE HAD...MEDICAL PROBLEMS. THEY'VE KEPT ME EFFECTIVELY OUT OF TOUCH FOR SOME YEARS.
I'M JUST NOW GETTING TO GRIPS WITH THE STATE OF THE FOUNDATION, AND RIGHTING OLD WRONGS.
I UNDERSTAND THE FOUNDATION IS PAYING YOU COMPENSATION. ARE YOU WORKING ALSO?
WE'RE DOING OKAY. I'M WORKING THREE DAYS A WEEK. ANGIE HAS SOME SPECIAL NEEDS.
THE FOUNDATION HELPS OUT. YOU'VE ALL BEEN GOOD TO US, REALLY.
NOT GOOD ENOUGH.
THERE IS NO REASON WHY THE FOUNDATION SHOULD COUNTENANCE YOUR EXPERIENCING THE SLIGHTEST DISCOMFORT IF IT CAN BE AT ALL AVOIDED.
AS OF FIVE MINUTES AGO, YOU ARE INDEPENDENTLY WEALTHY.

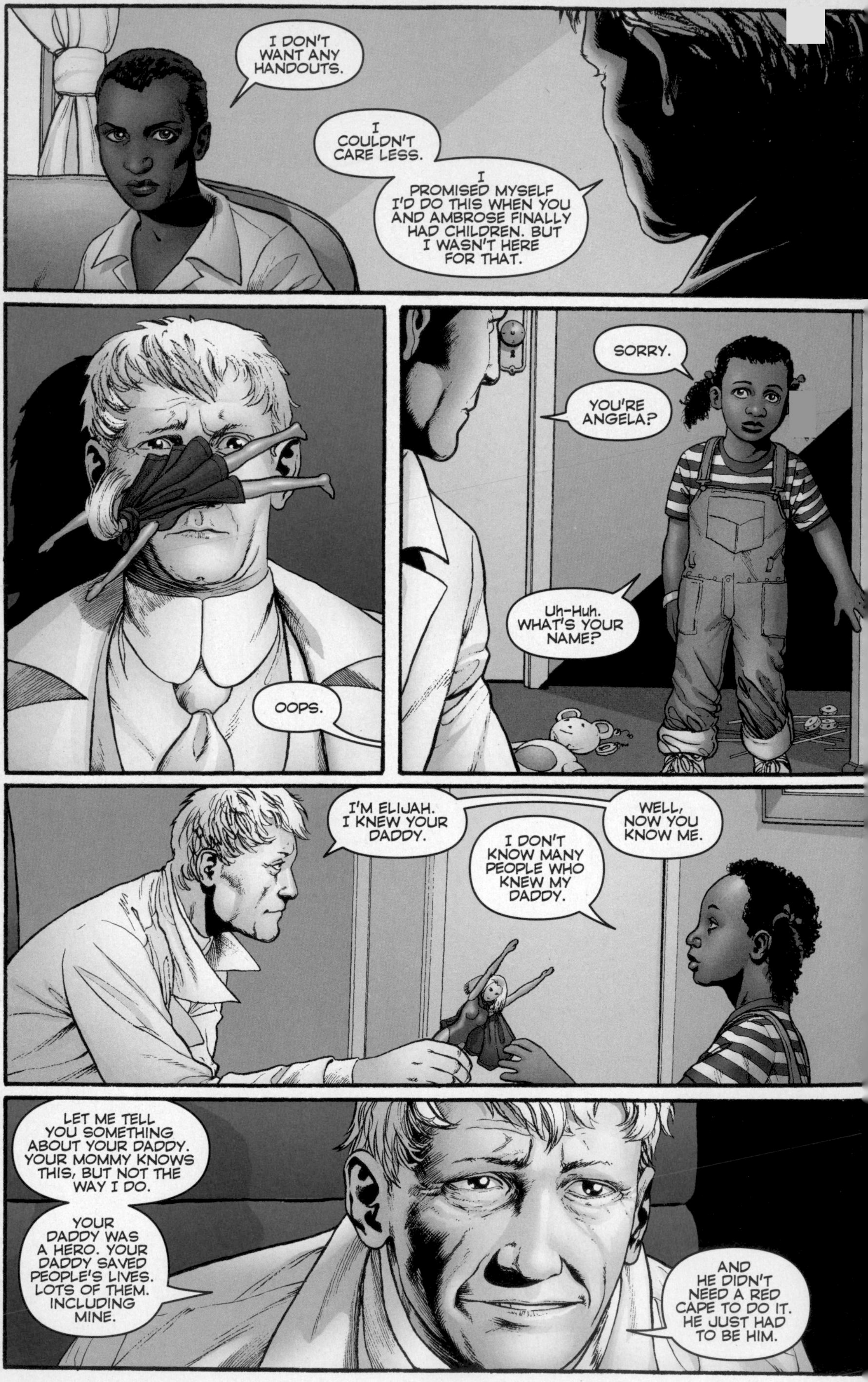
I DON'T WANT ANY HANDOUTS.
I COULDN'T CARE LESS.
I PROMISED MYSELF I'D DO THIS WHEN YOU AND AMBROSE FINALLY HAD CHILDREN. BUT I WASN'T HERE FOR THAT.
OOPS.
SORRY.
YOU'RE ANGELA?
Uh-Huh. WHAT'S YOUR NAME?
I'M ELIJAH. I KNEW YOUR DADDY.
I DON'T KNOW MANY PEOPLE WHO KNEW MY DADDY.
WELL, NOW YOU KNOW ME.
LET ME TELL YOU SOMETHING ABOUT YOUR DADDY. YOUR MOMMY KNOWS THIS, BUT NOT THE WAY I DO.
YOUR DADDY WAS A HERO. YOUR DADDY SAVED PEOPLE'S LIVES. LOTS OF THEM. INCLUDING MINE.
AND HE DIDN'T NEED A RED CAPE TO DO IT. HE JUST HAD TO BE HIM.

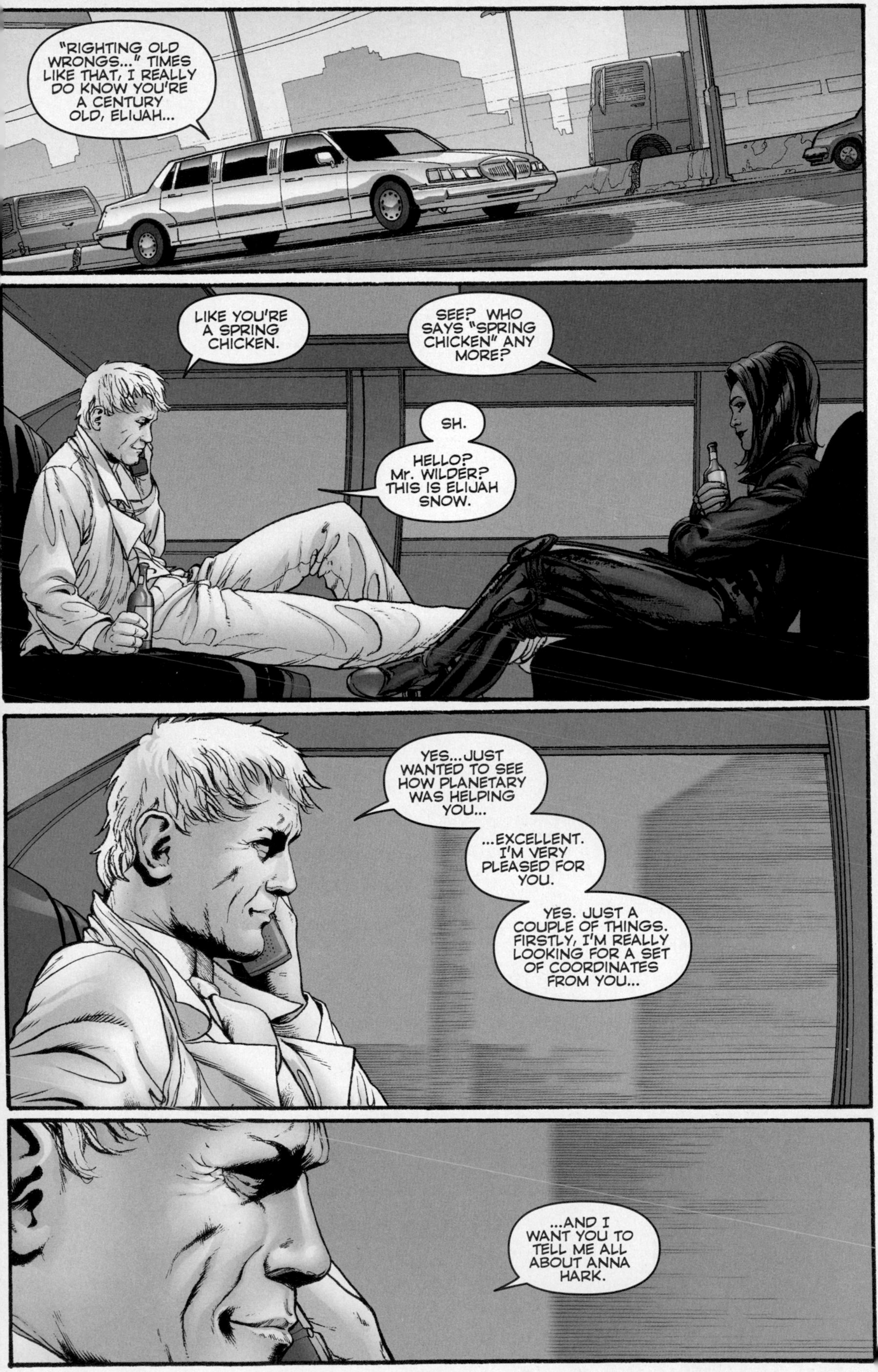
"RIGHTING OLD WRONGS..." TIMES LIKE THAT, I REALLY DO KNOW YOU'RE A CENTURY OLD, ELIJAH...
LIKE YOU'RE A SPRING CHICKEN.
SEE? WHO SAYS "SPRING CHICKEN" ANY MORE?
SH.
HELLO? Mr. WILDER? THIS IS ELIJAH SNOW.
YES...JUST WANTED TO SEE HOW PLANETARY WAS HELPING YOU...
...EXCELLENT. I'M VERY PLEASED FOR YOU.
YES. JUST A COUPLE OF THINGS. FIRSTLY, I'M REALLY LOOKING FOR A SET OF COORDINATES FROM YOU...
...AND I WANT YOU TO TELL ME ALL ABOUT ANNA HARK.

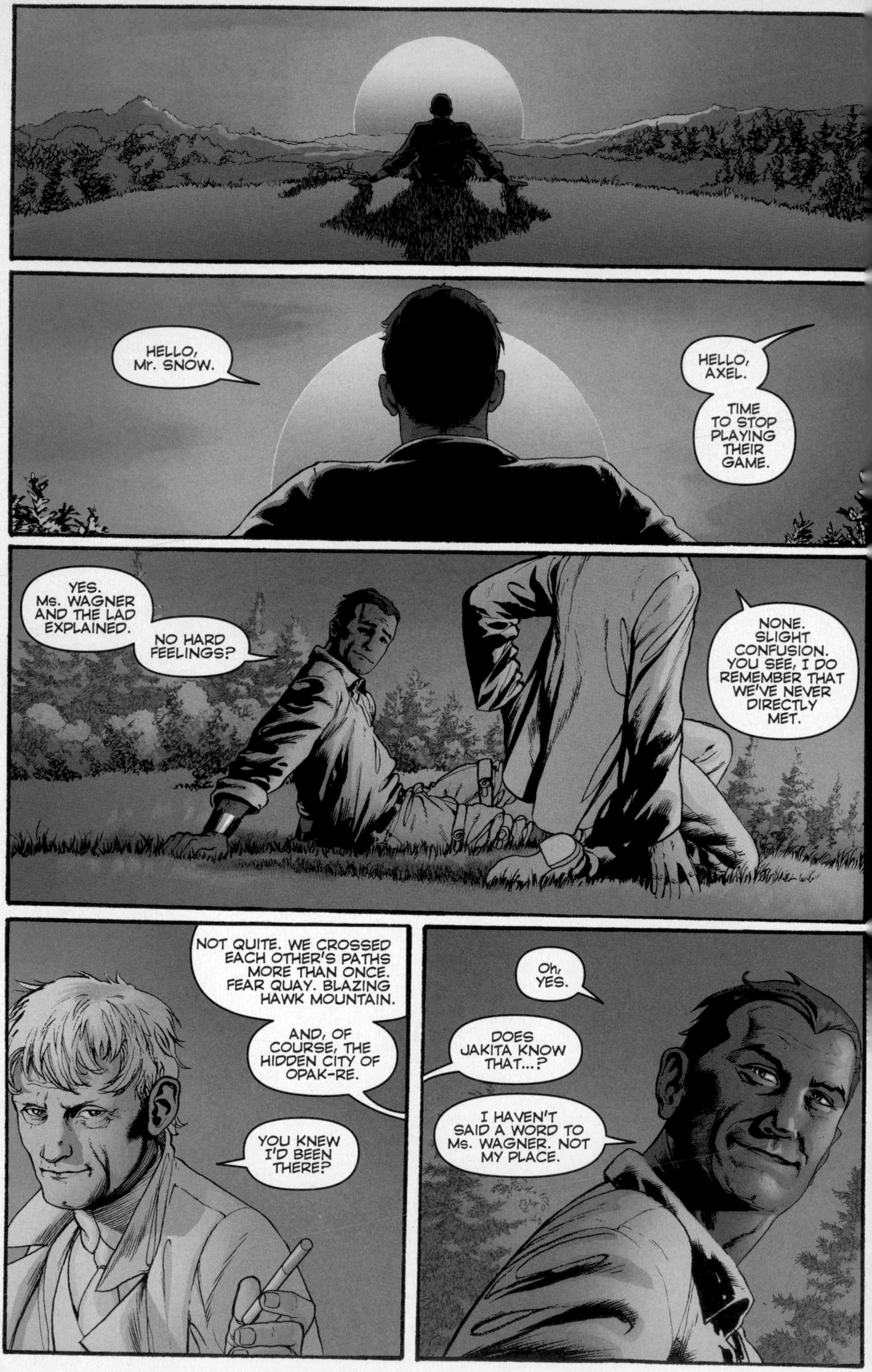

HELLO, Mr. SNOW.
HELLO, AXEL.
TIME TO STOP PLAYING THEIR GAME.
YES. Ms. WAGNER AND THE LAD EXPLAINED.
NO HARD FEELINGS?
NONE. SLIGHT CONFUSION. YOU SEE, I DO REMEMBER THAT WE'VE NEVER DIRECTLY MET.
NOT QUITE. WE CROSSED EACH OTHER'S PATHS MORE THAN ONCE. FEAR QUAY. BLAZING HAWK MOUNTAIN.
AND, OF COURSE, THE HIDDEN CITY OF OPAK-RE.
YOU KNEW I'D BEEN THERE?
Oh, YES.
DOES JAKITA KNOW THAT...?
I HAVEN'T SAID A WORD TO Ms. WAGNER. NOT MY PLACE.

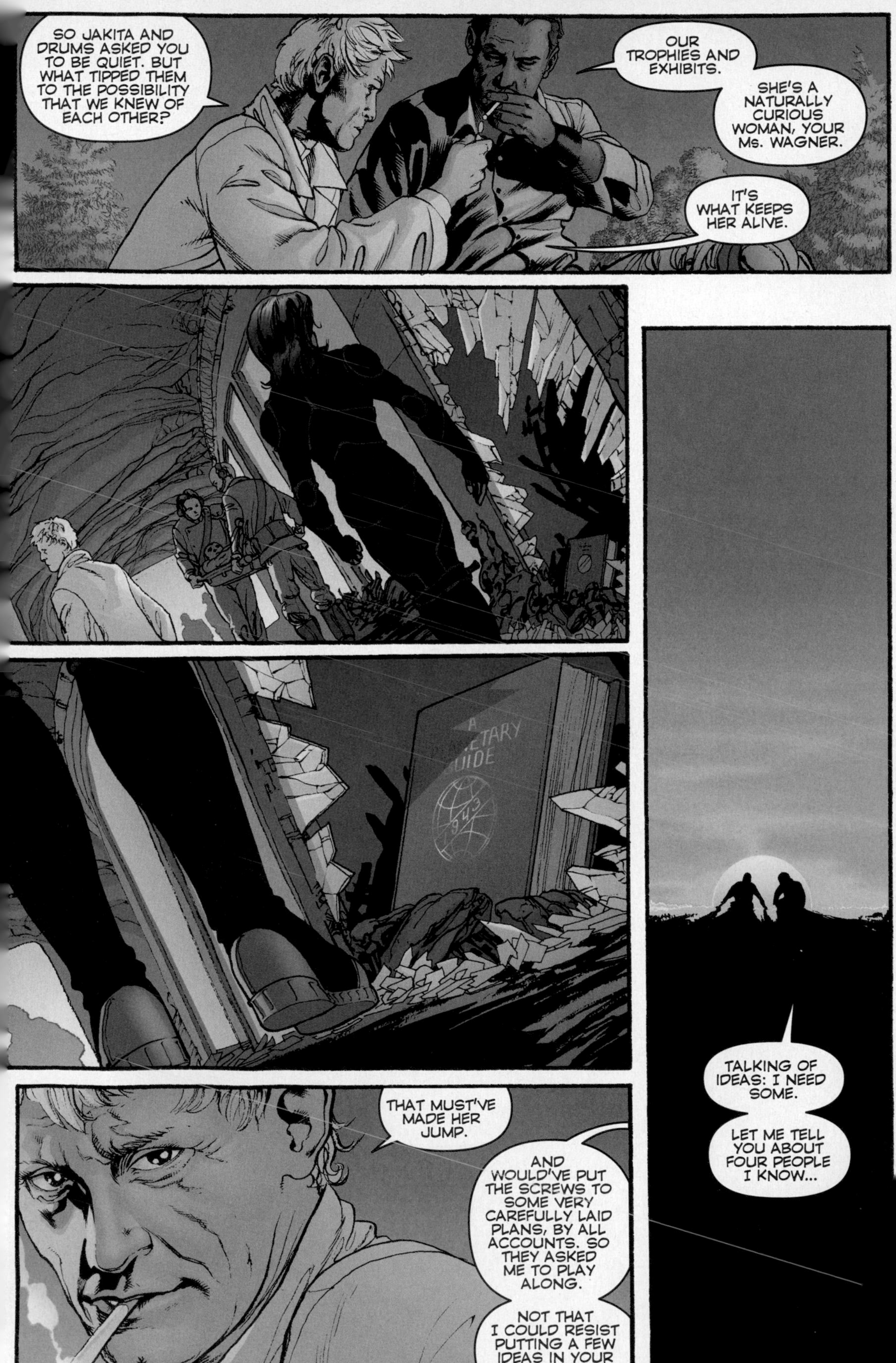
SO JAKITA AND DRUMS ASKED YOU TO BE QUIET. BUT WHAT TIPPED THEM TO THE POSSIBILITY THAT WE KNEW OF EACH OTHER?
OUR TROPHIES AND EXHIBITS.
SHE'S A NATURALLY CURIOUS WOMAN, YOUR Ms. WAGNER.
IT'S WHAT KEEPS HER ALIVE.
A PLANETARY GUIDE
1943
THAT MUST'VE MADE HER JUMP.
AND WOULD'VE PUT THE SCREWS TO SOME VERY CAREFULLY LAID PLANS, BY ALL ACCOUNTS. SO THEY ASKED ME TO PLAY ALONG.
NOT THAT I COULD RESIST PUTTING A FEW IDEAS IN YOUR HEAD ANYWAY.
TALKING OF IDEAS: I NEED SOME.
LET ME TELL YOU ABOUT FOUR PEOPLE I KNOW...

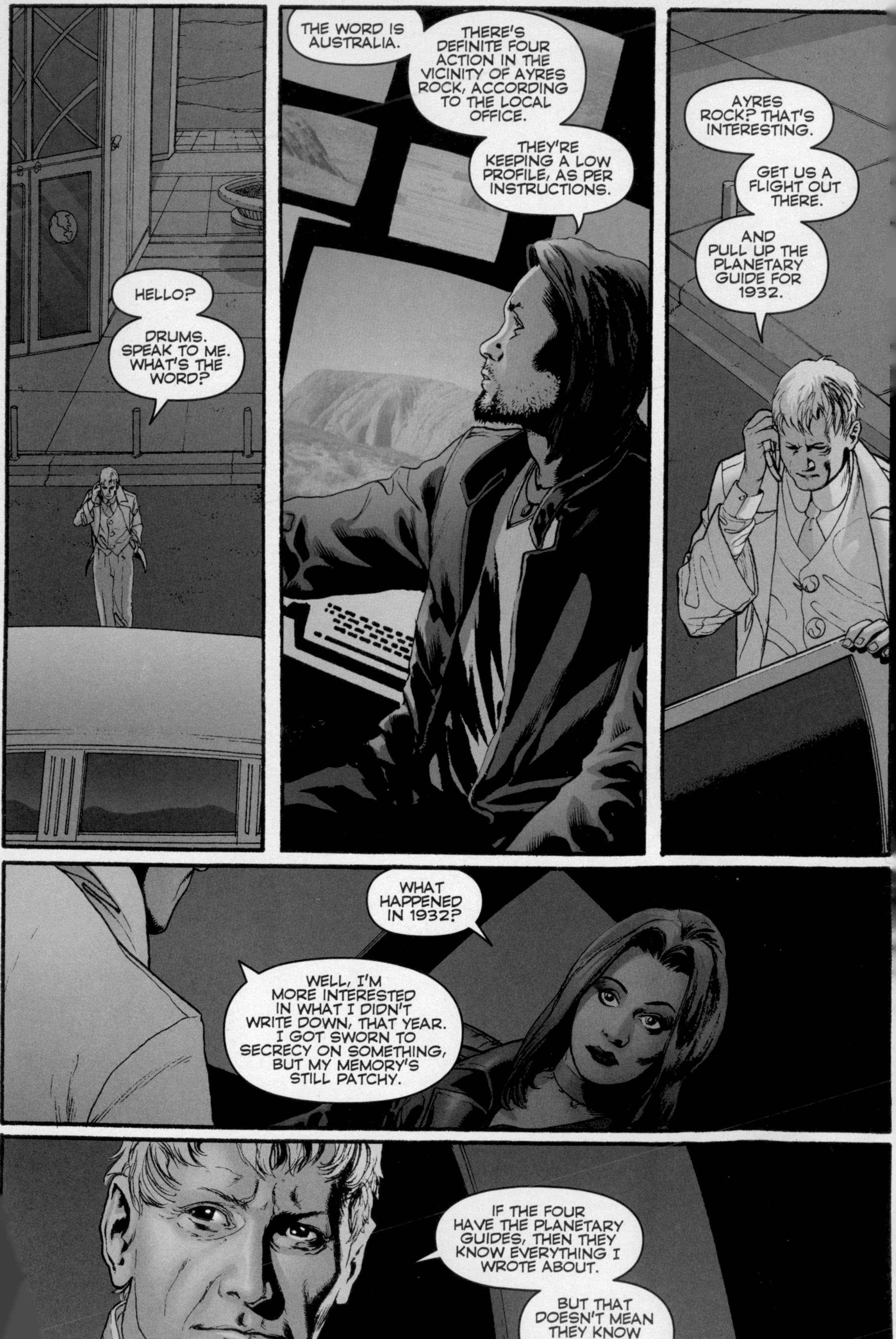
HELLO?
DRUMS. SPEAK TO ME. WHAT'S THE WORD?
THE WORD IS AUSTRALIA.
THERE'S DEFINITE FOUR ACTION IN THE VICINITY OF AYRES ROCK, ACCORDING TO THE LOCAL OFFICE.
THEY'RE KEEPING A LOW PROFILE, AS PER INSTRUCTIONS.
AYRES ROCK? THAT'S INTERESTING.
GET US A FLIGHT OUT THERE.
AND PULL UP THE PLANETARY GUIDE FOR 1932.
WHAT HAPPENED IN 1932?
WELL, I'M MORE INTERESTED IN WHAT I DIDN'T WRITE DOWN, THAT YEAR. I GOT SWORN TO SECRECY ON SOMETHING, BUT MY MEMORY'S STILL PATCHY.
IF THE FOUR HAVE THE PLANETARY GUIDES, THEN THEY KNOW EVERYTHING I WROTE ABOUT.
BUT THAT DOESN'T MEAN THEY KNOW EVERYTHING I KNOW.

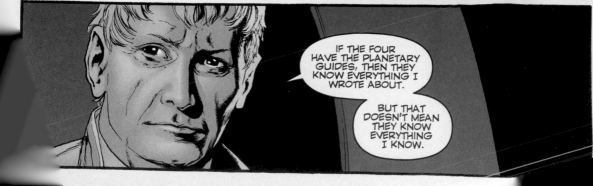

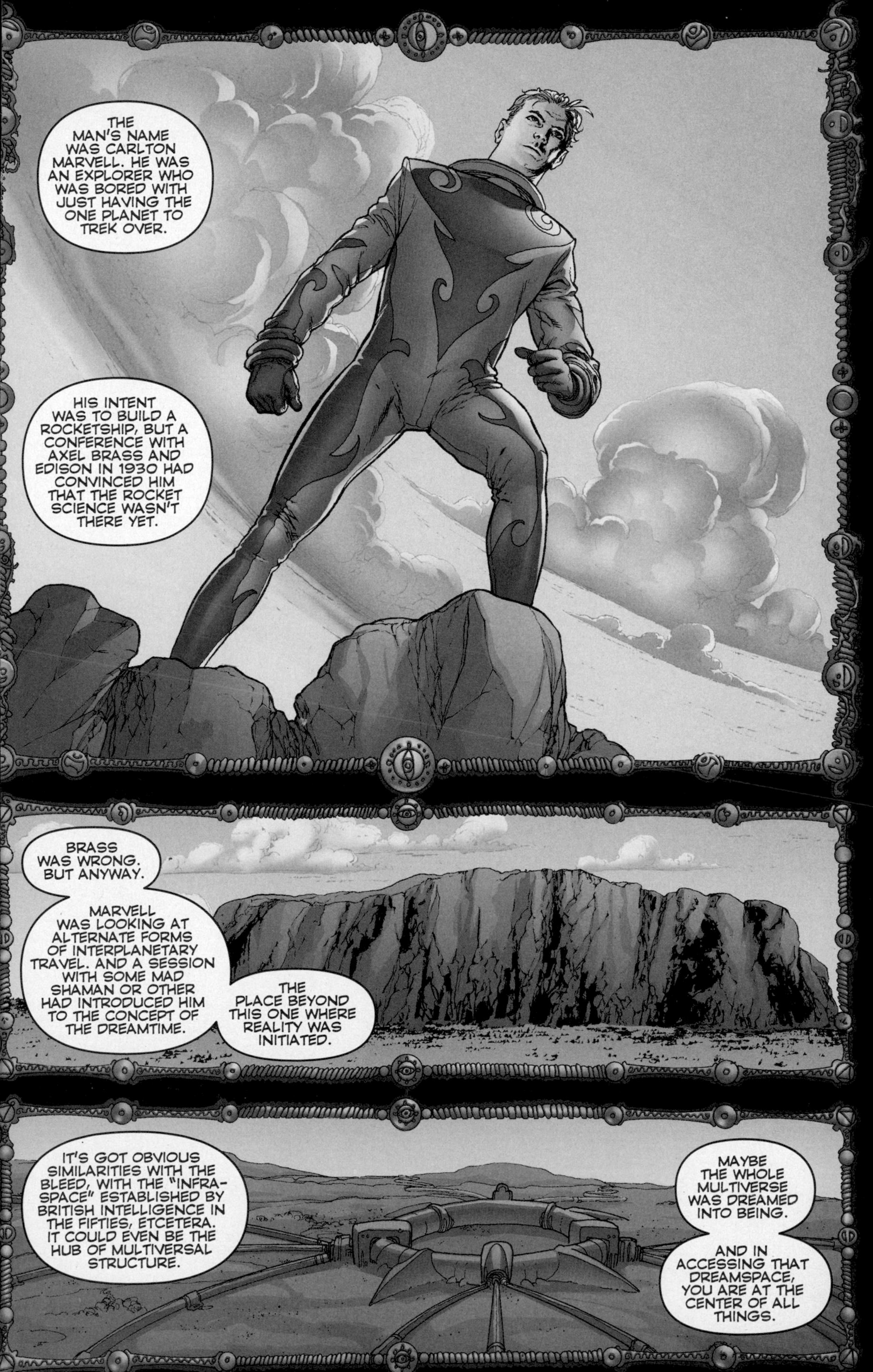
THE MAN'S NAME WAS CARLTON MARVELL. HE WAS AN EXPLORER WHO WAS BORED WITH JUST HAVING THE ONE PLANET TO TREK OVER.
HIS INTENT WAS TO BUILD A ROCKETSHIP, BUT A CONFERENCE WITH AXEL BRASS AND EDISON IN 1930 HAD CONVINCED HIM THAT THE ROCKET SCIENCE WASN'T THERE YET.
BRASS WAS WRONG. BUT ANYWAY.
MARVELL WAS LOOKING AT ALTERNATE FORMS OF INTERPLANETARY TRAVEL. AND A SESSION WITH SOME MAD SHAMAN OR OTHER HAD INTRODUCED HIM TO THE CONCEPT OF THE DREAMTIME.
THE PLACE BEYOND THIS ONE WHERE REALITY WAS INITIATED.
IT'S GOT OBVIOUS SIMILARITIES WITH THE BLEED, WITH THE "INFRA-SPACE" ESTABLISHED BY BRITISH INTELLIGENCE IN THE FIFTIES, ETCETERA. IT COULD EVEN BE THE HUB OF MULTIVERSAL STRUCTURE.
MAYBE THE WHOLE MULTIVERSE WAS DREAMED INTO BEING.
AND IN ACCESSING THAT DREAMSPACE, YOU ARE AT THE CENTER OF ALL THINGS.

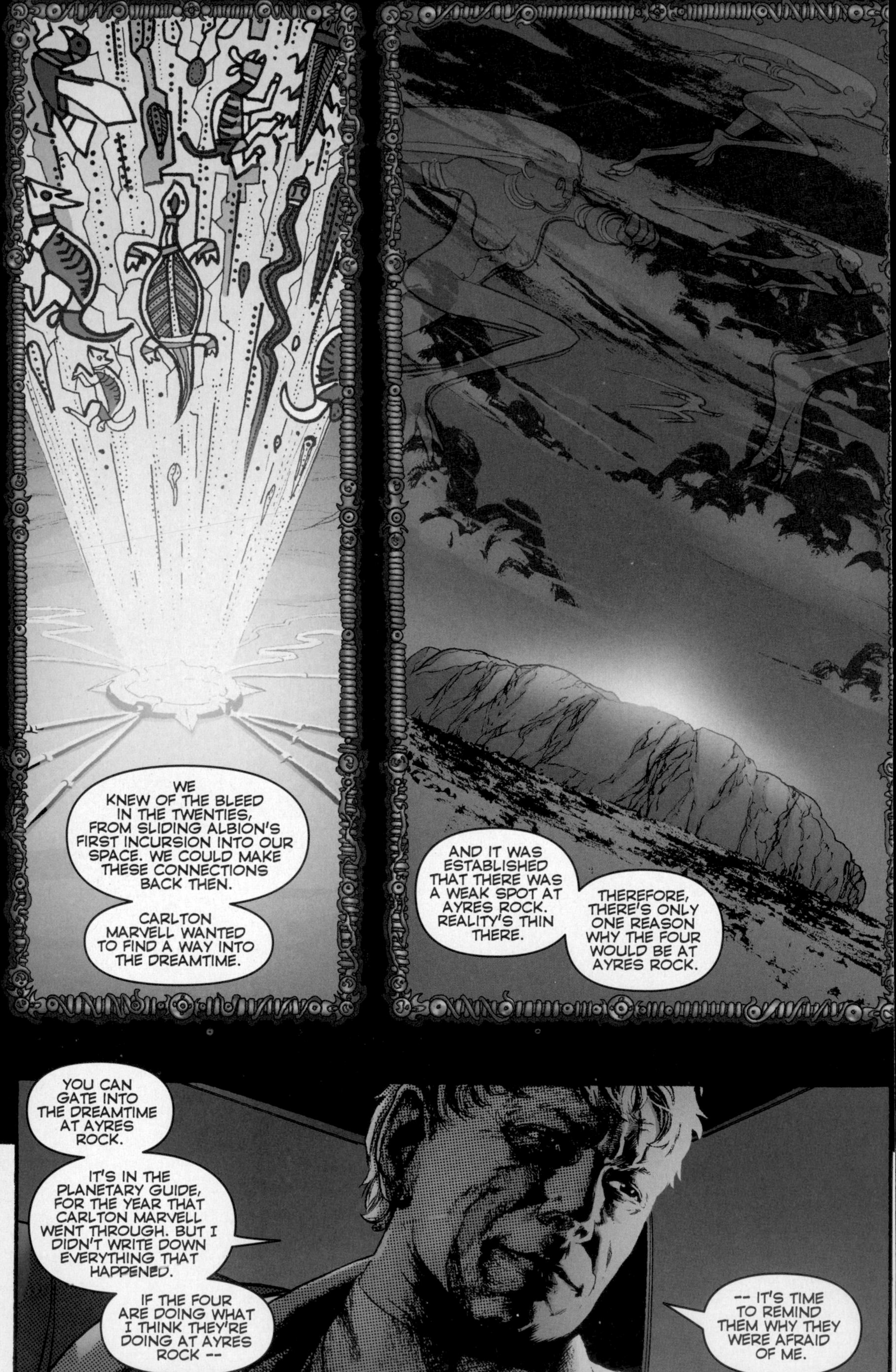
WE KNEW OF THE BLEED IN THE TWENTIES, FROM SLIDING ALBION'S FIRST INCURSION INTO OUR SPACE. WE COULD MAKE THESE CONNECTIONS BACK THEN.
CARLTON MARVELL WANTED TO FIND A WAY INTO THE DREAMTIME.
AND IT WAS ESTABLISHED THAT THERE WAS A WEAK SPOT AT AYRES ROCK. REALITY'S THIN THERE.
THEREFORE, THERE'S ONLY ONE REASON WHY THE FOUR WOULD BE AT AYRES ROCK.
YOU CAN GATE INTO THE DREAMTIME AT AYRES ROCK.
IT'S IN THE PLANETARY GUIDE, FOR THE YEAR THAT CARLTON MARVELL WENT THROUGH. BUT I DIDN'T WRITE DOWN EVERYTHING THAT HAPPENED.
IF THE FOUR ARE DOING WHAT I THINK THEY'RE DOING AT AYRES ROCK --
-- IT'S TIME TO REMIND THEM WHY THEY WERE AFRAID OF ME.

CREATION SONGS

BY WARREN ELLIS AND JOHN CASSADAY
WITH LAURA DEPUY
LETTERING - BILL O'NEIL   EDITOR - JOHN LAYMAN
Planetary created by Warren Ellis and John Cassaday

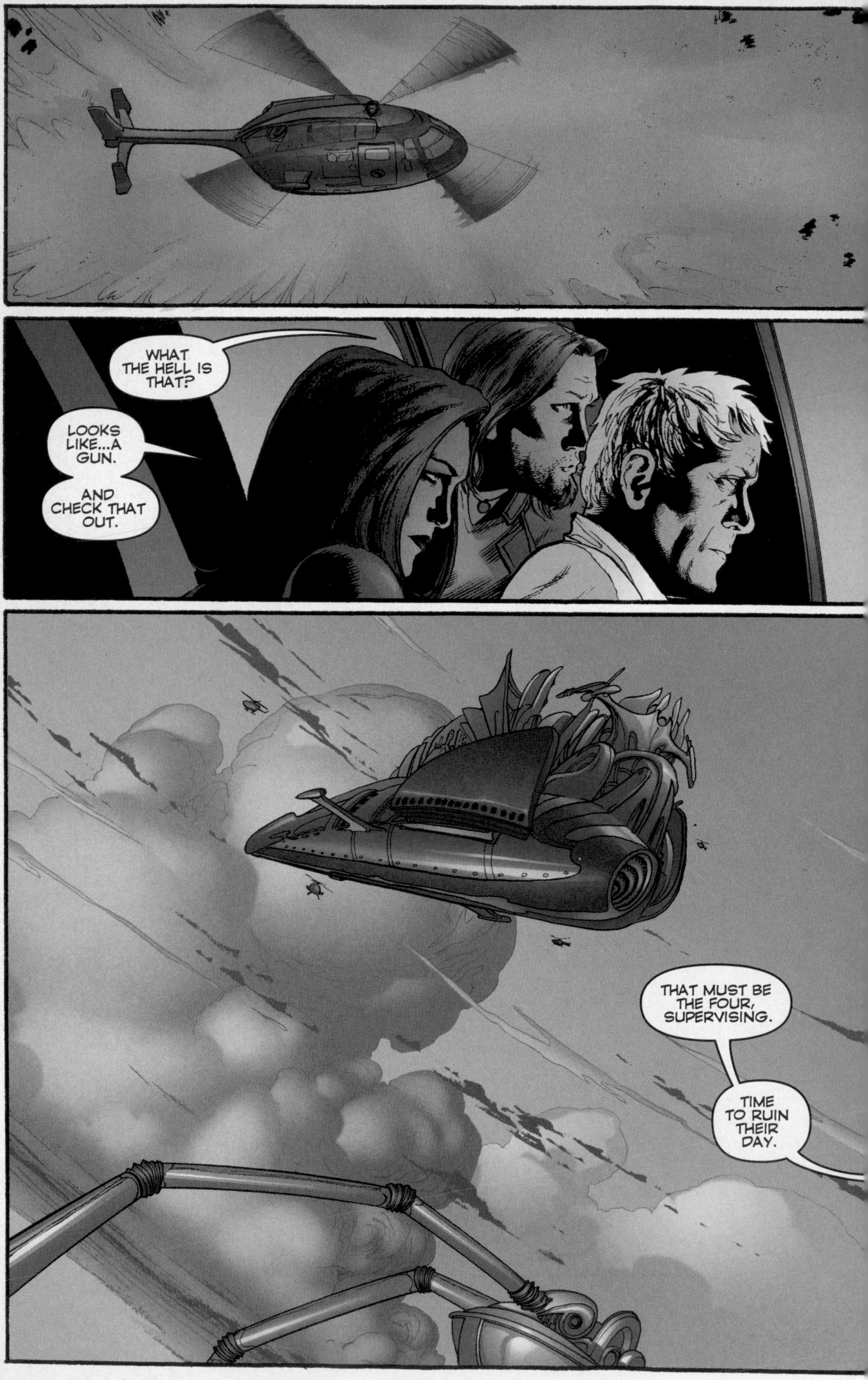
WHAT THE HELL IS THAT?
LOOKS LIKE...A GUN.
AND CHECK THAT OUT.
THAT MUST BE THE FOUR, SUPERVISING.
TIME TO RUIN THEIR DAY.

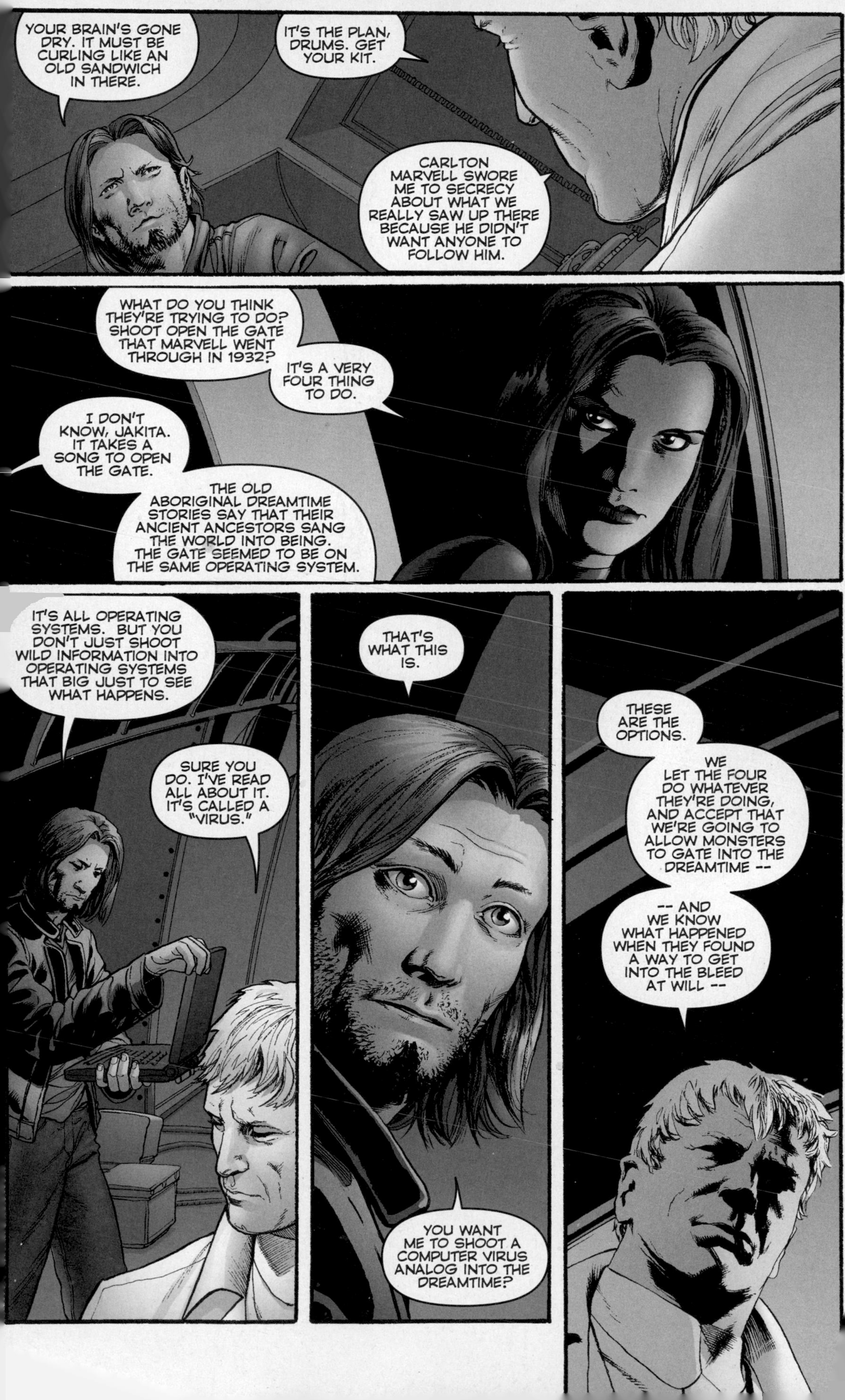
YOUR BRAIN'S GONE DRY. IT MUST BE CURLING LIKE AN OLD SANDWICH IN THERE.
IT'S THE PLAN, DRUMS. GET YOUR KIT.
CARLTON MARVELL SWORE ME TO SECRECY ABOUT WHAT WE REALLY SAW UP THERE BECAUSE HE DIDN'T WANT ANYONE TO FOLLOW HIM.
WHAT DO YOU THINK THEY'RE TRYING TO DO? SHOOT OPEN THE GATE THAT MARVELL WENT THROUGH IN 1932?
IT'S A VERY FOUR THING TO DO.
I DON'T KNOW, JAKITA. IT TAKES A SONG TO OPEN THE GATE.
THE OLD ABORIGINAL DREAMTIME STORIES SAY THAT THEIR ANCIENT ANCESTORS SANG THE WORLD INTO BEING. THE GATE SEEMED TO BE ON THE SAME OPERATING SYSTEM.
IT'S ALL OPERATING SYSTEMS. BUT YOU DON'T JUST SHOOT WILD INFORMATION INTO OPERATING SYSTEMS THAT BIG JUST TO SEE WHAT HAPPENS.
SURE YOU DO. I'VE READ ALL ABOUT IT. IT'S CALLED A "VIRUS."
THAT'S WHAT THIS IS.
YOU WANT ME TO SHOOT A COMPUTER VIRUS ANALOG INTO THE DREAMTIME?
THESE ARE THE OPTIONS.
WE LET THE FOUR DO WHATEVER THEY'RE DOING, AND ACCEPT THAT WE'RE GOING TO ALLOW MONSTERS TO GATE INTO THE DREAMTIME --
-- AND WE KNOW WHAT HAPPENED WHEN THEY FOUND A WAY TO GET INTO THE BLEED AT WILL --

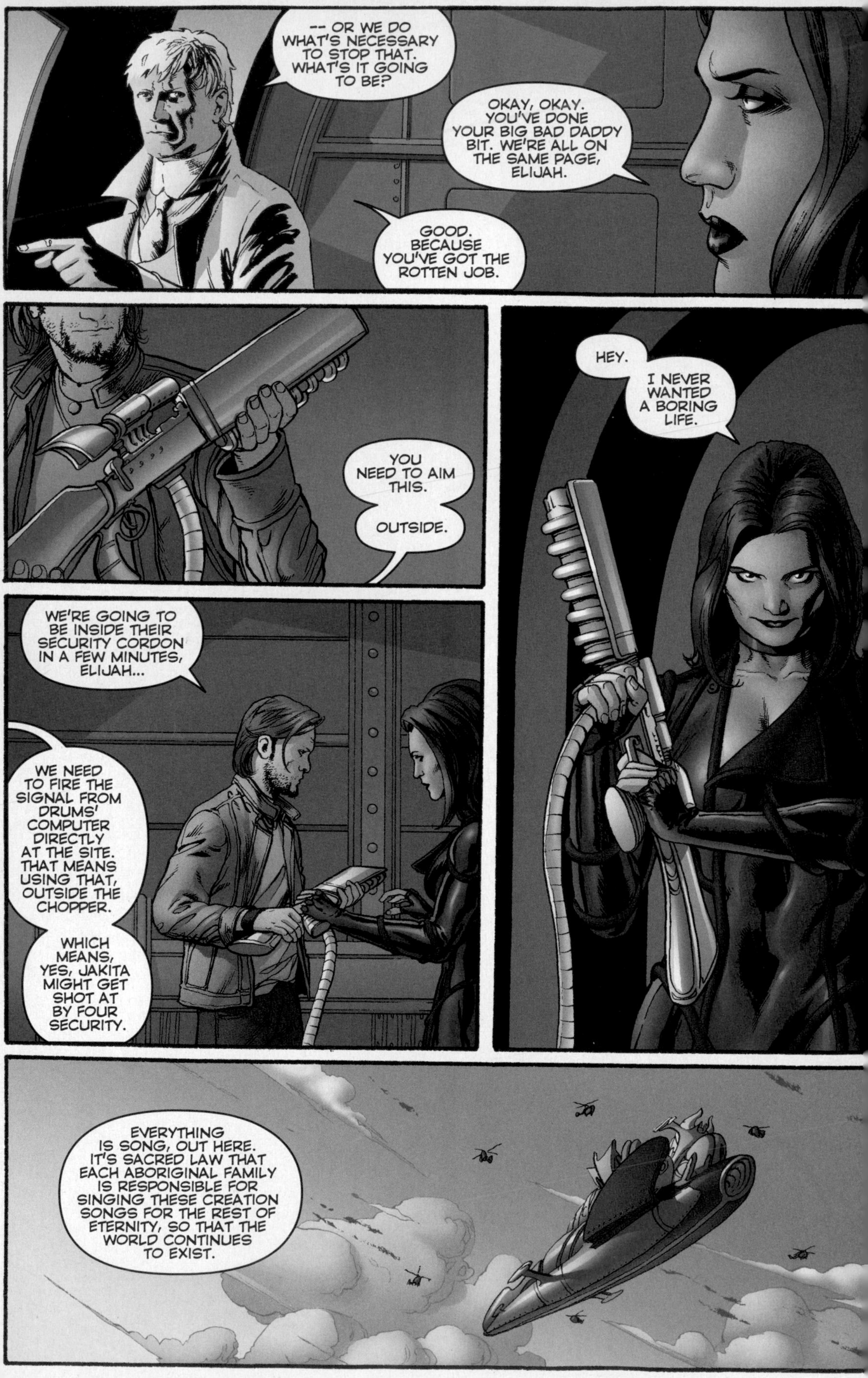
-- OR WE DO WHAT'S NECESSARY TO STOP THAT. WHAT'S IT GOING TO BE?
OKAY, OKAY. YOU'VE DONE YOUR BIG BAD DADDY BIT. WE'RE ALL ON THE SAME PAGE, ELIJAH.
GOOD. BECAUSE YOU'VE GOT THE ROTTEN JOB.
YOU NEED TO AIM THIS.
OUTSIDE.
HEY.
I NEVER WANTED A BORING LIFE.
WE'RE GOING TO BE INSIDE THEIR SECURITY CORDON IN A FEW MINUTES, ELIJAH...
WE NEED TO FIRE THE SIGNAL FROM DRUMS' COMPUTER DIRECTLY AT THE SITE. THAT MEANS USING THAT, OUTSIDE THE CHOPPER.
WHICH MEANS, YES, JAKITA MIGHT GET SHOT AT BY FOUR SECURITY.
EVERYTHING IS SONG, OUT HERE. IT'S SACRED LAW THAT EACH ABORIGINAL FAMILY IS RESPONSIBLE FOR SINGING THESE CREATION SONGS FOR THE REST OF ETERNITY, SO THAT THE WORLD CONTINUES TO EXIST.

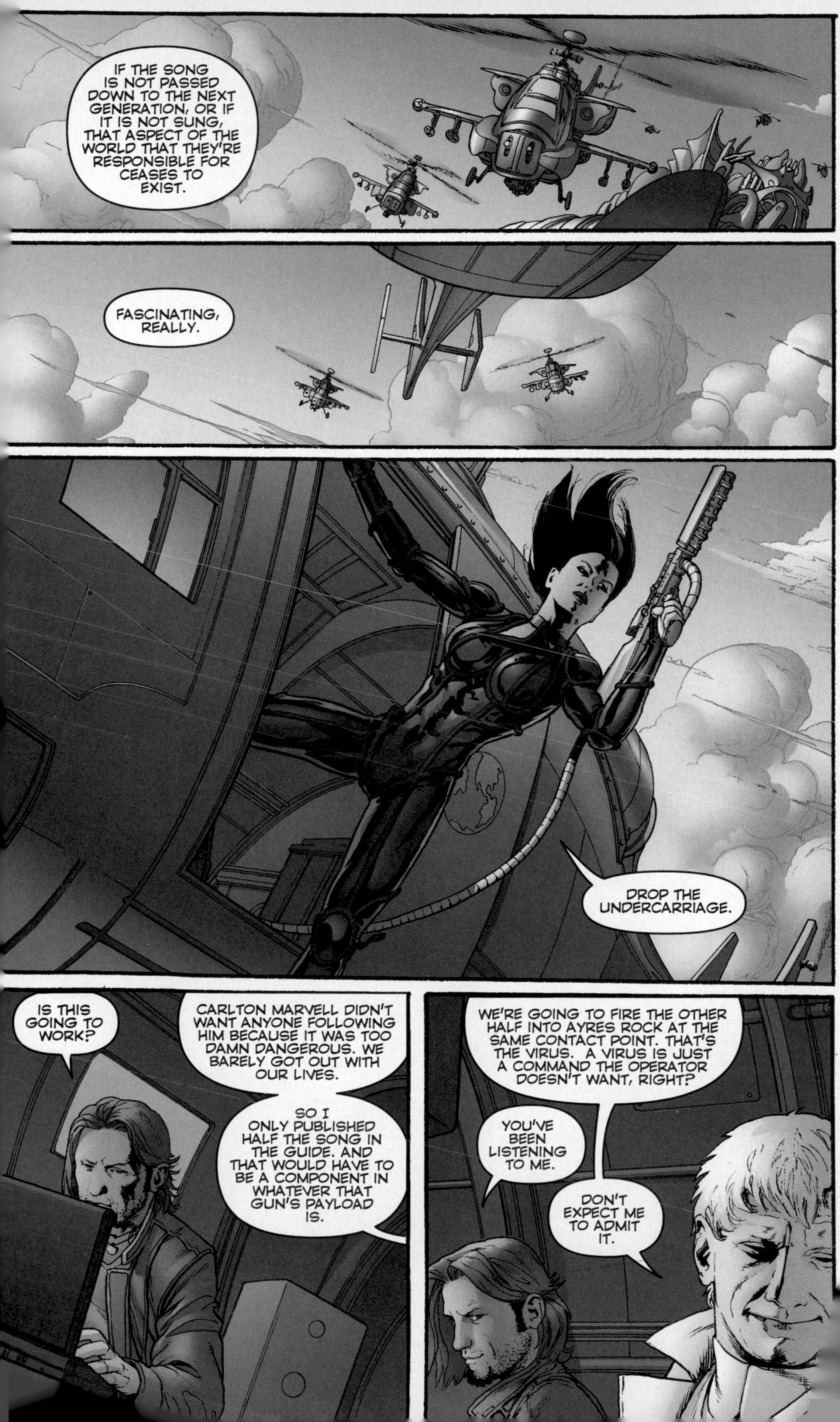
IF THE SONG IS NOT PASSED DOWN TO THE NEXT GENERATION, OR IF IT IS NOT SUNG, THAT ASPECT OF THE WORLD THAT THEY'RE RESPONSIBLE FOR CEASES TO EXIST.
FASCINATING, REALLY.
DROP THE UNDERCARRIAGE.
IS THIS GOING TO WORK?
CARLTON MARVELL DIDN'T WANT ANYONE FOLLOWING HIM BECAUSE IT WAS TOO DAMN DANGEROUS. WE BARELY GOT OUT WITH OUR LIVES.
SO I ONLY PUBLISHED HALF THE SONG IN THE GUIDE. AND THAT WOULD HAVE TO BE A COMPONENT IN WHATEVER THAT GUN'S PAYLOAD IS.
WE'RE GOING TO FIRE THE OTHER HALF INTO AYRES ROCK AT THE SAME CONTACT POINT. THAT'S THE VIRUS. A VIRUS IS JUST A COMMAND THE OPERATOR DOESN'T WANT, RIGHT?
YOU'VE BEEN LISTENING TO ME.
DON'T EXPECT ME TO ADMIT IT.

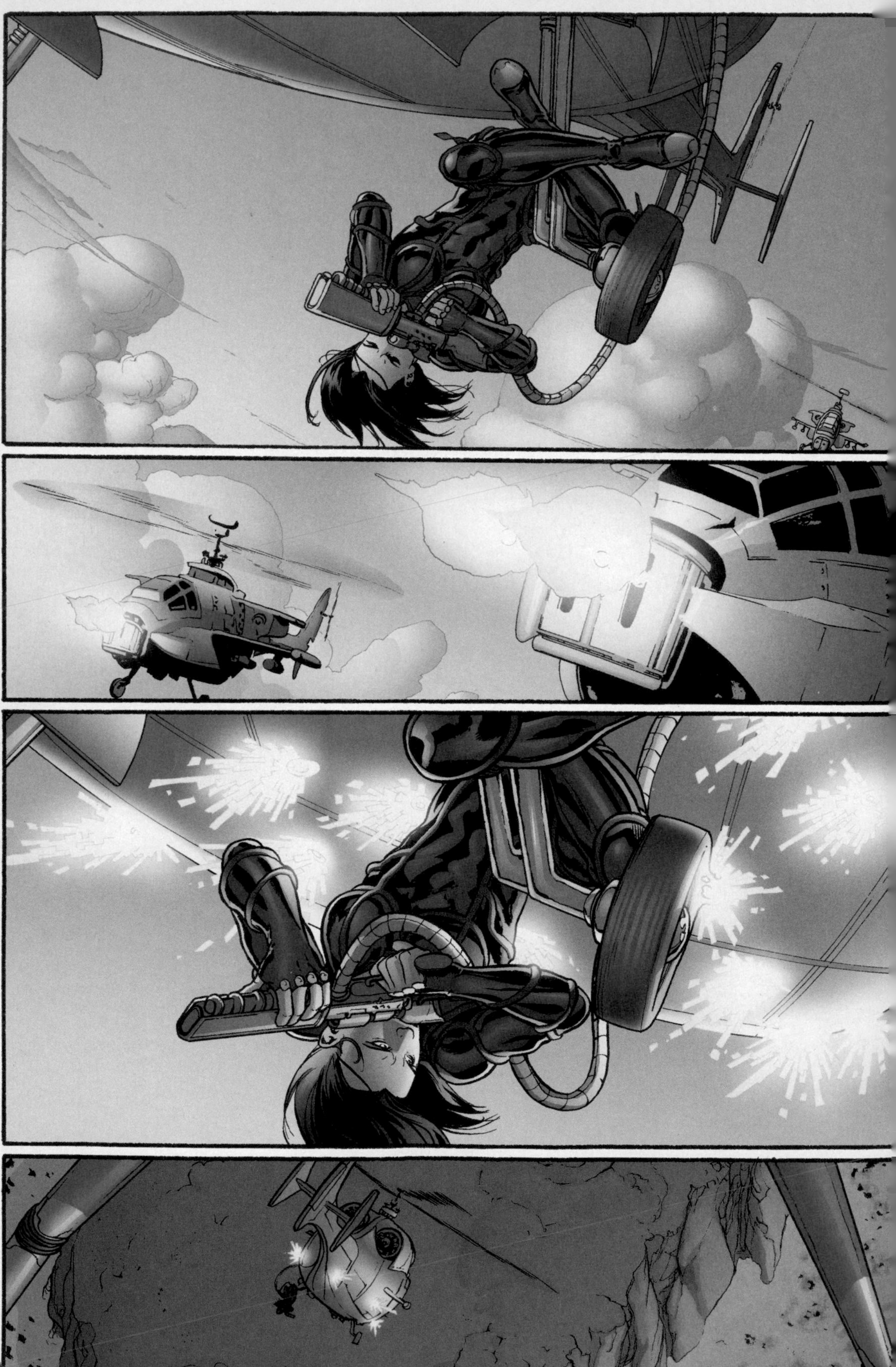

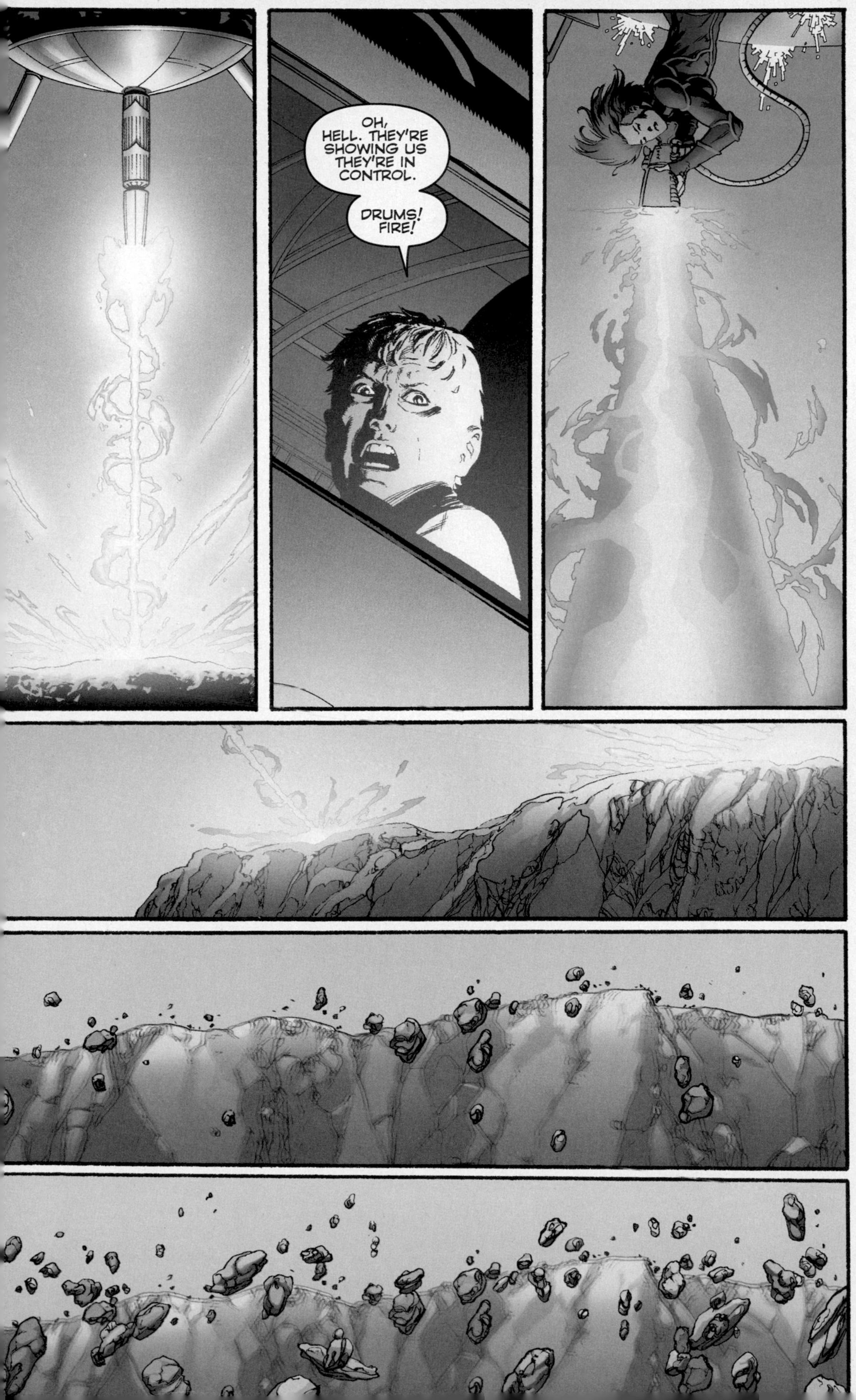
OH, HELL. THEY'RE SHOWING US THEY'RE IN CONTROL.
DRUMS! FIRE!

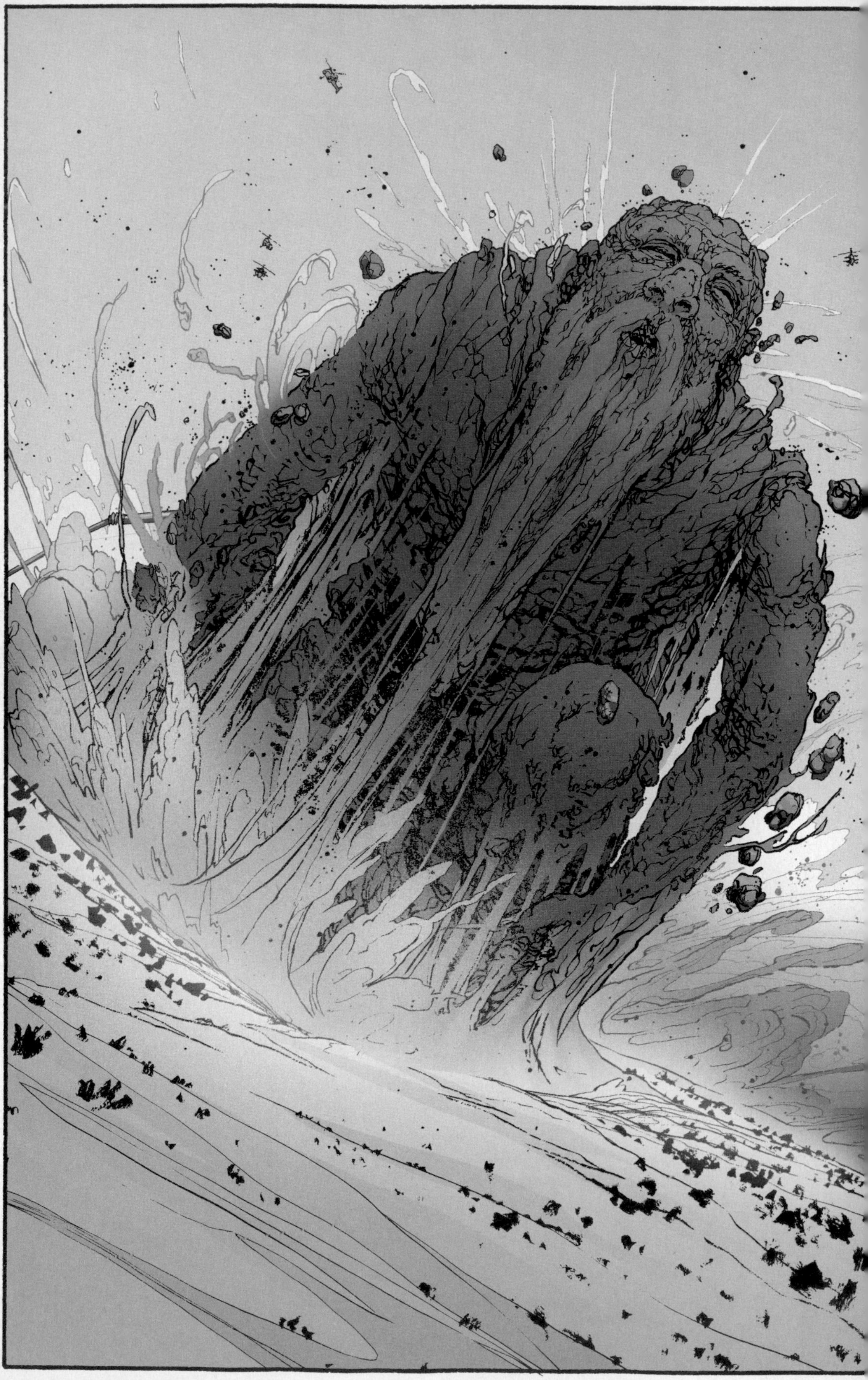

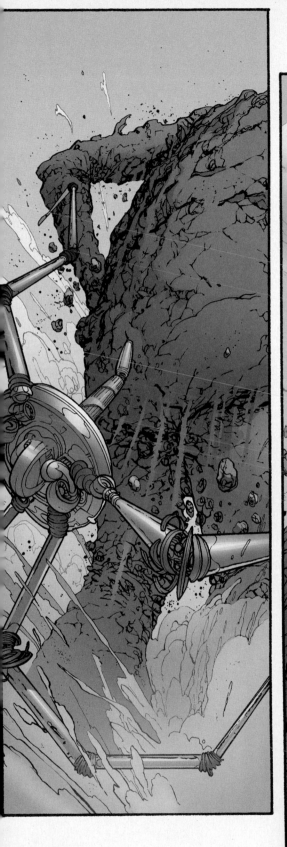

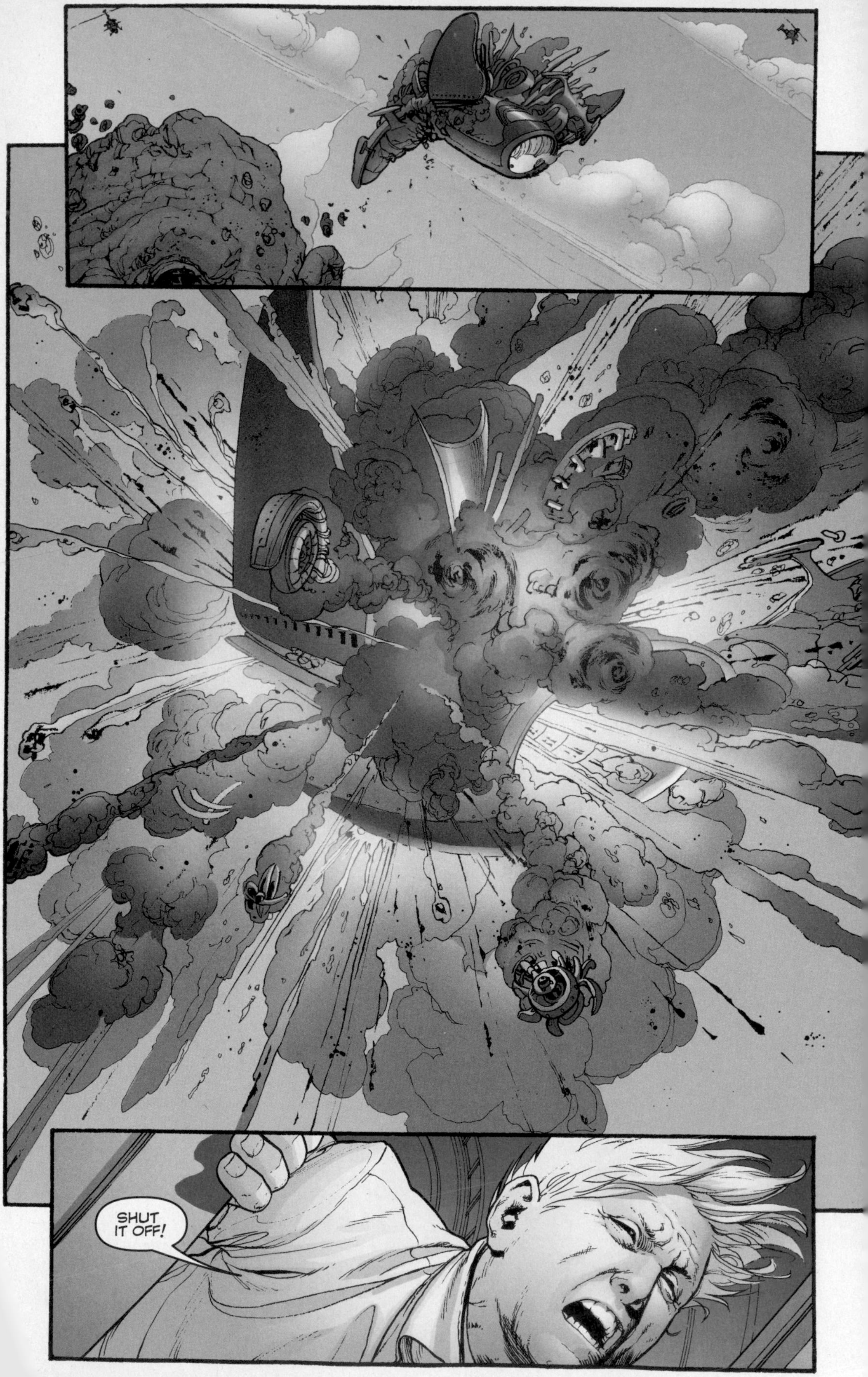
SHUT IT OFF!

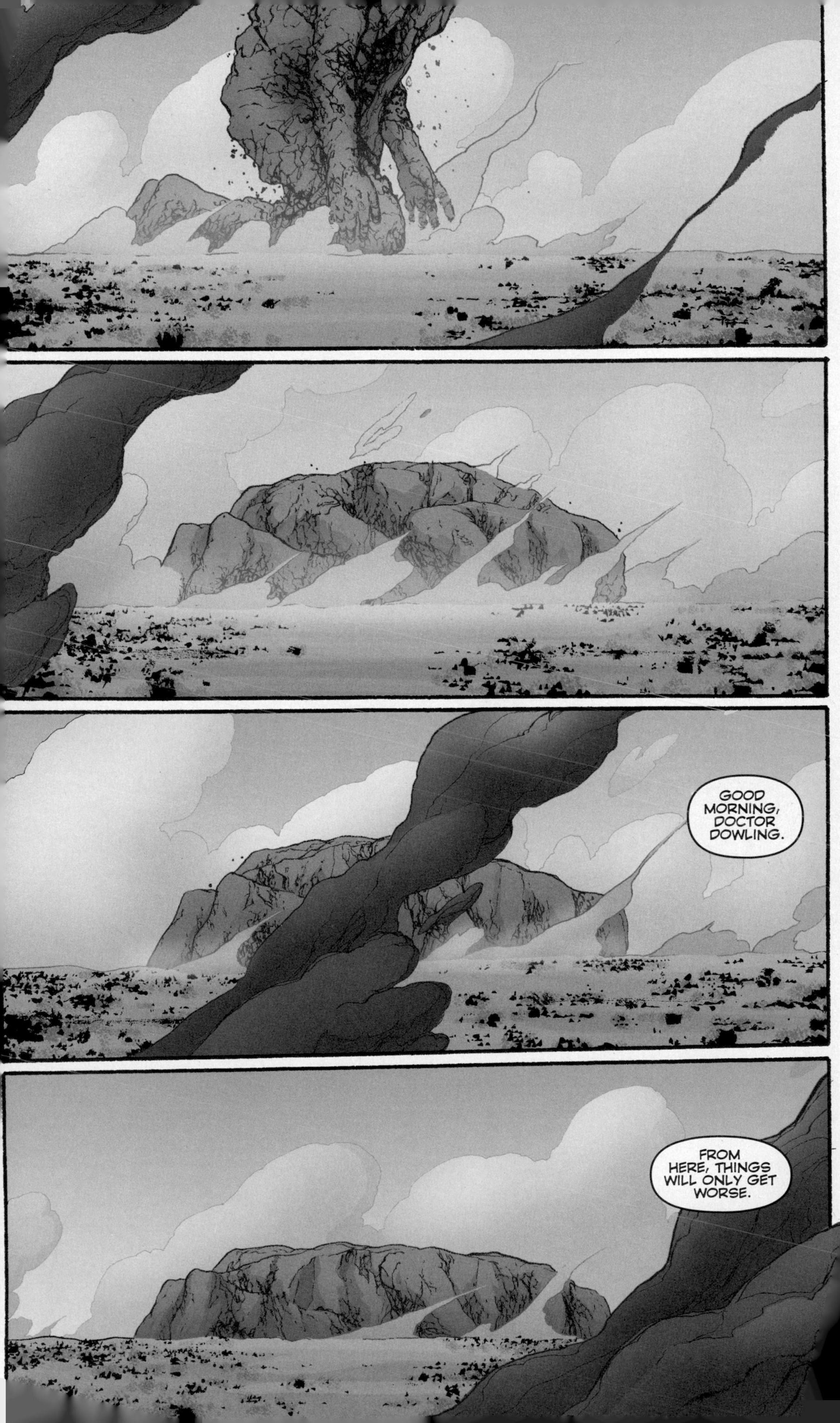
GOOD MORNING, DOCTOR DOWLING.
FROM HERE, THINGS WILL ONLY GET WORSE.

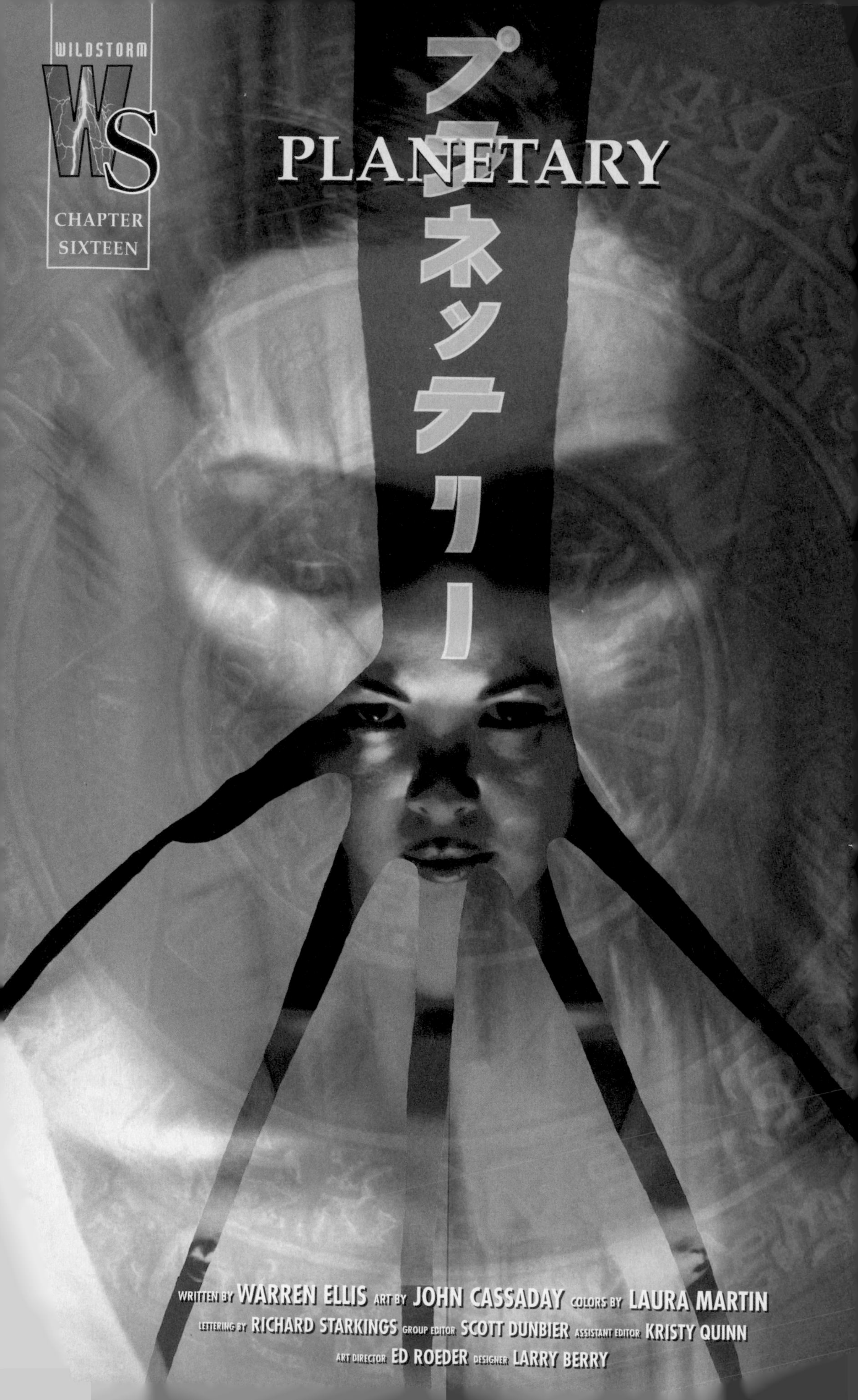
WILDSTORM
CHAPTER SIXTEEN
PLANETARY
プラネッテリー
WRITTEN BY WARREN ELLIS ART BY JOHN CASSADAY COLORS BY LAURA MARTIN
LETTERING BY RICHARD STARKINGS GROUP EDITOR SCOTT DUNBIER ASSISTANT EDITOR KRISTY QUINN
ART DIRECTOR ED ROEDER DESIGNER LARRY BERRY

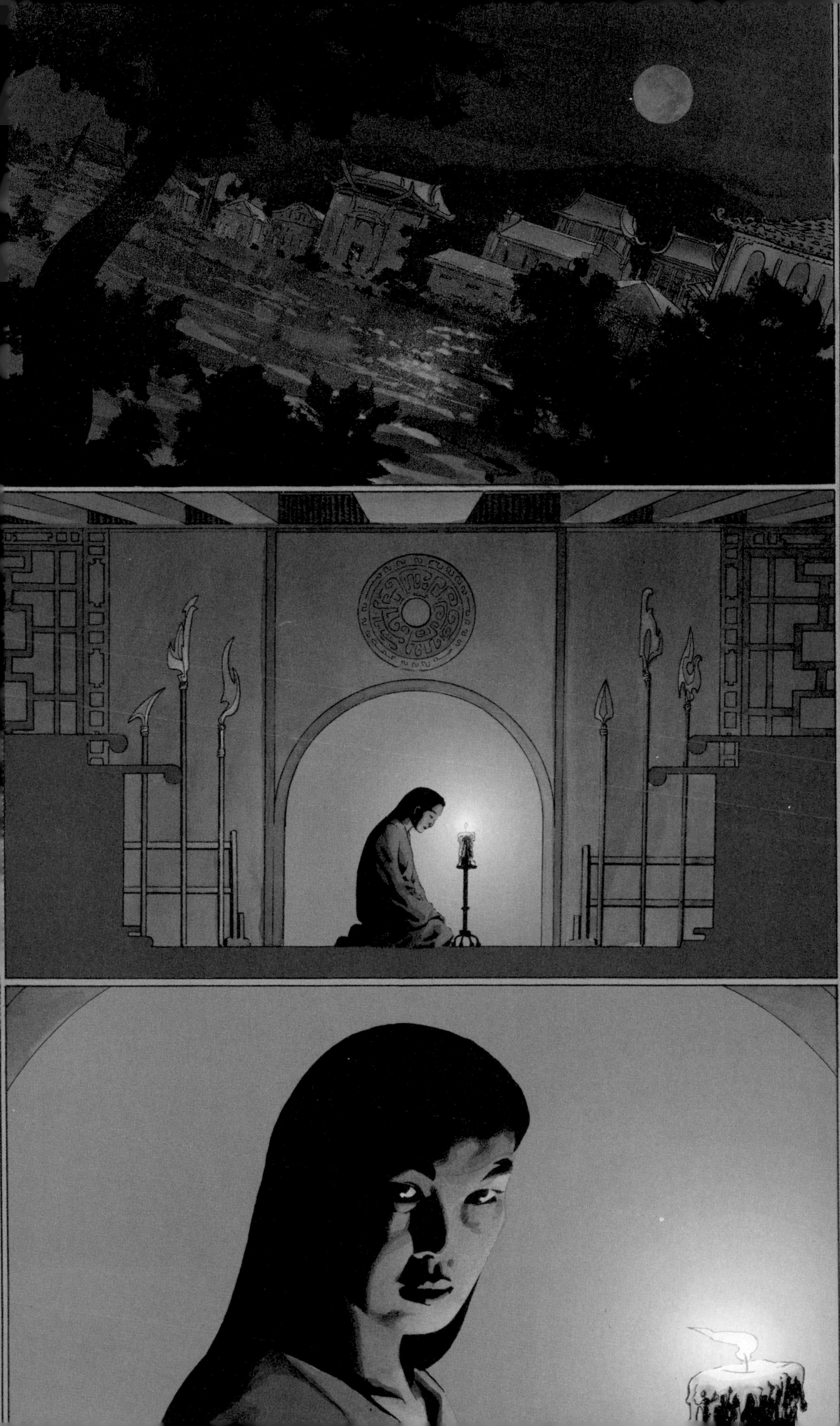

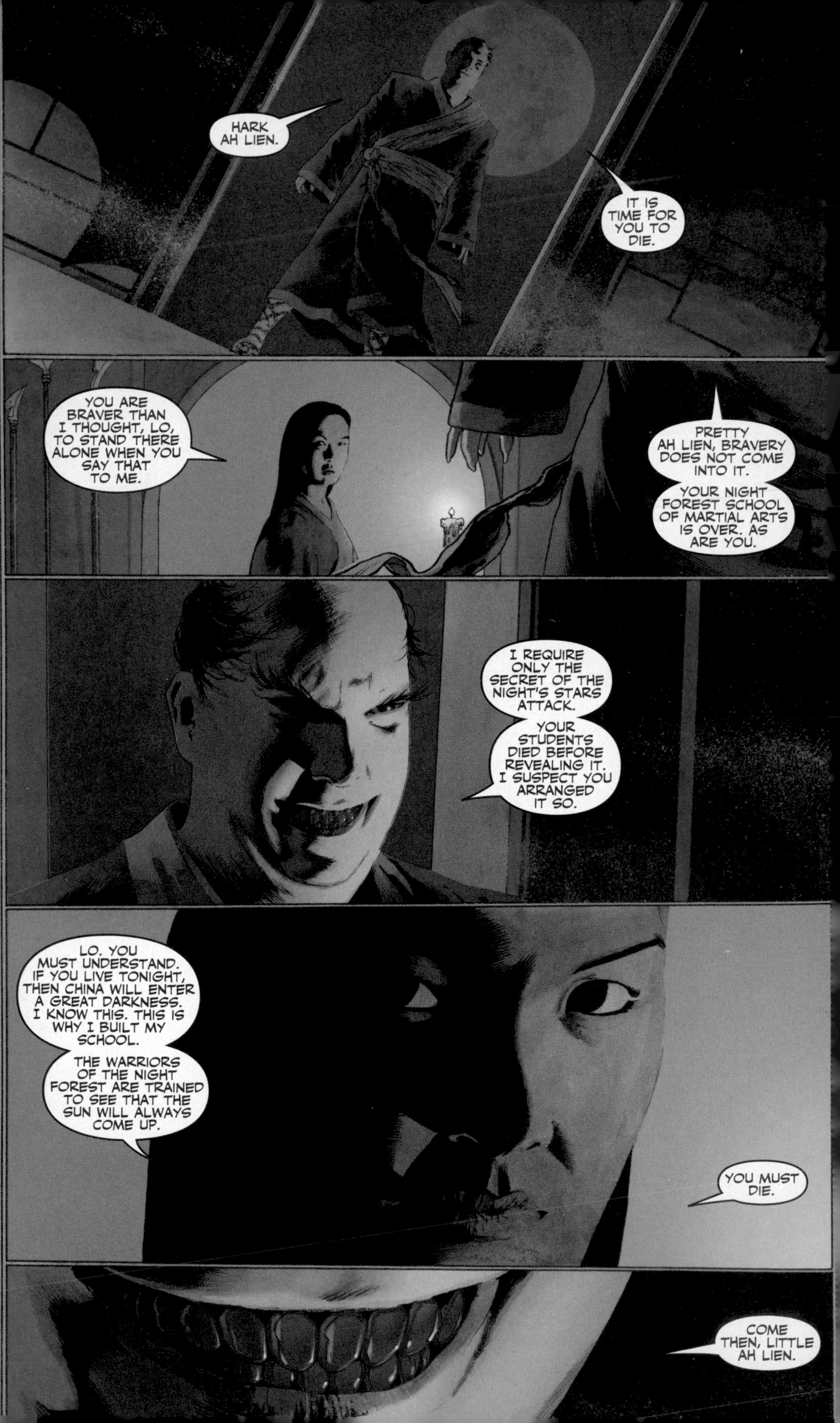
HARK AH LIEN.
IT IS TIME FOR YOU TO DIE.
YOU ARE BRAVER THAN I THOUGHT, LO, TO STAND THERE ALONE WHEN YOU SAY THAT TO ME.
PRETTY AH LIEN, BRAVERY DOES NOT COME INTO IT.
YOUR NIGHT FOREST SCHOOL OF MARTIAL ARTS IS OVER. AS ARE YOU.
I REQUIRE ONLY THE SECRET OF THE NIGHT'S STARS ATTACK.
YOUR STUDENTS DIED BEFORE REVEALING IT. I SUSPECT YOU ARRANGED IT SO.
LO. YOU MUST UNDERSTAND. IF YOU LIVE TONIGHT, THEN CHINA WILL ENTER A GREAT DARKNESS. I KNOW THIS. THIS IS WHY I BUILT MY SCHOOL.
THE WARRIORS OF THE NIGHT FOREST ARE TRAINED TO SEE THAT THE SUN WILL ALWAYS COME UP.
YOU MUST DIE.
COME THEN, LITTLE AH LIEN.

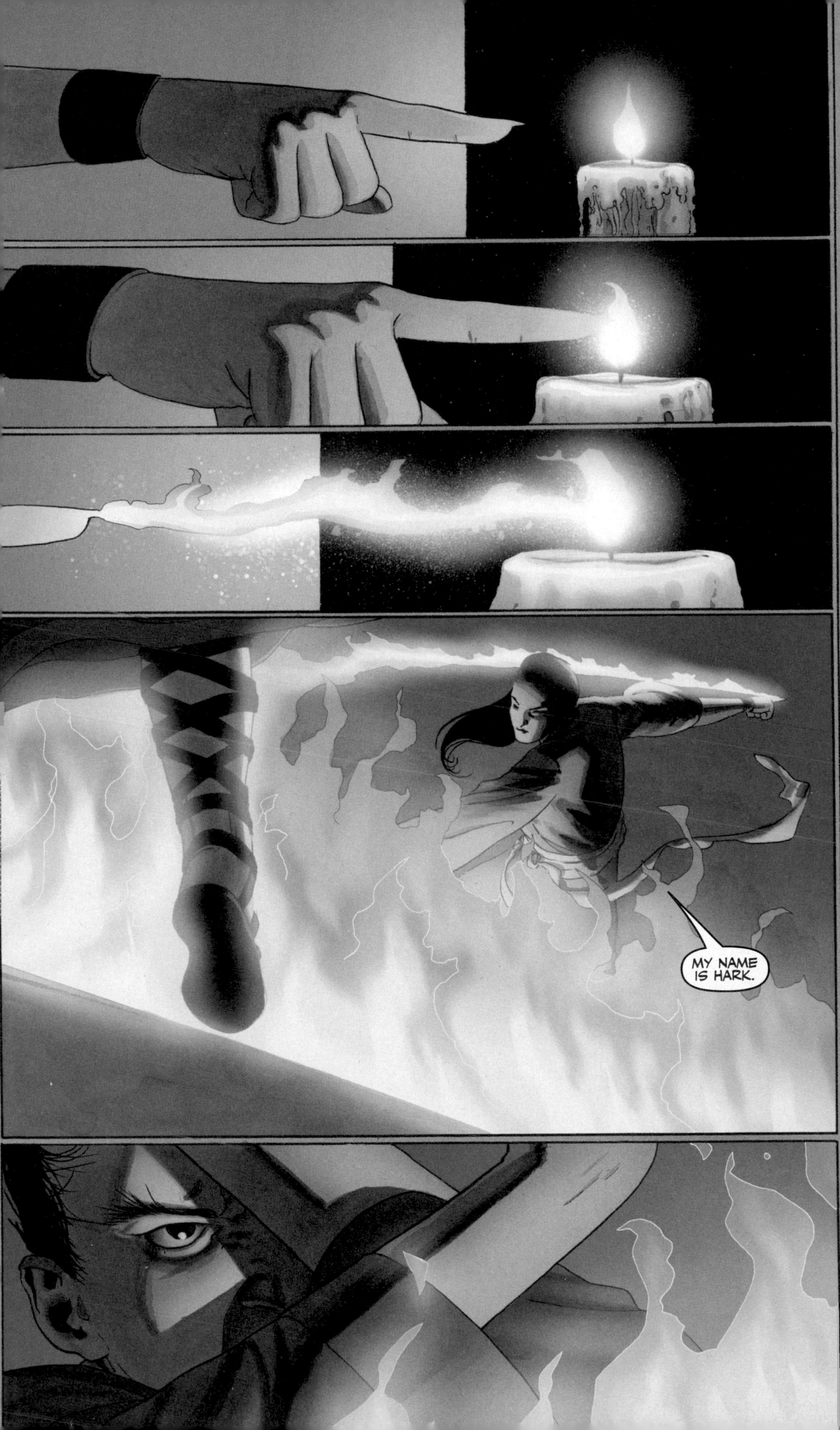
MY NAME IS HARK.

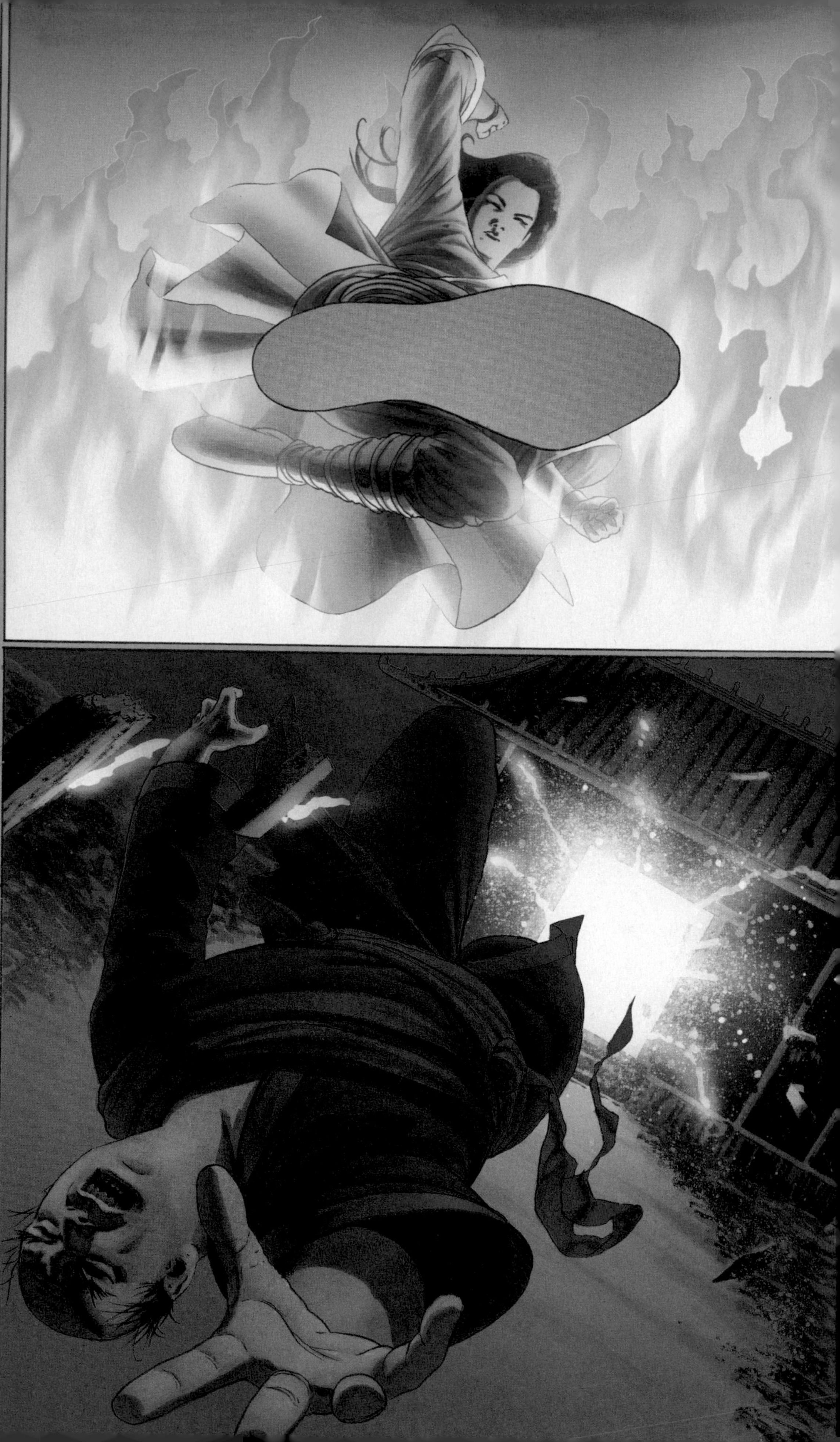

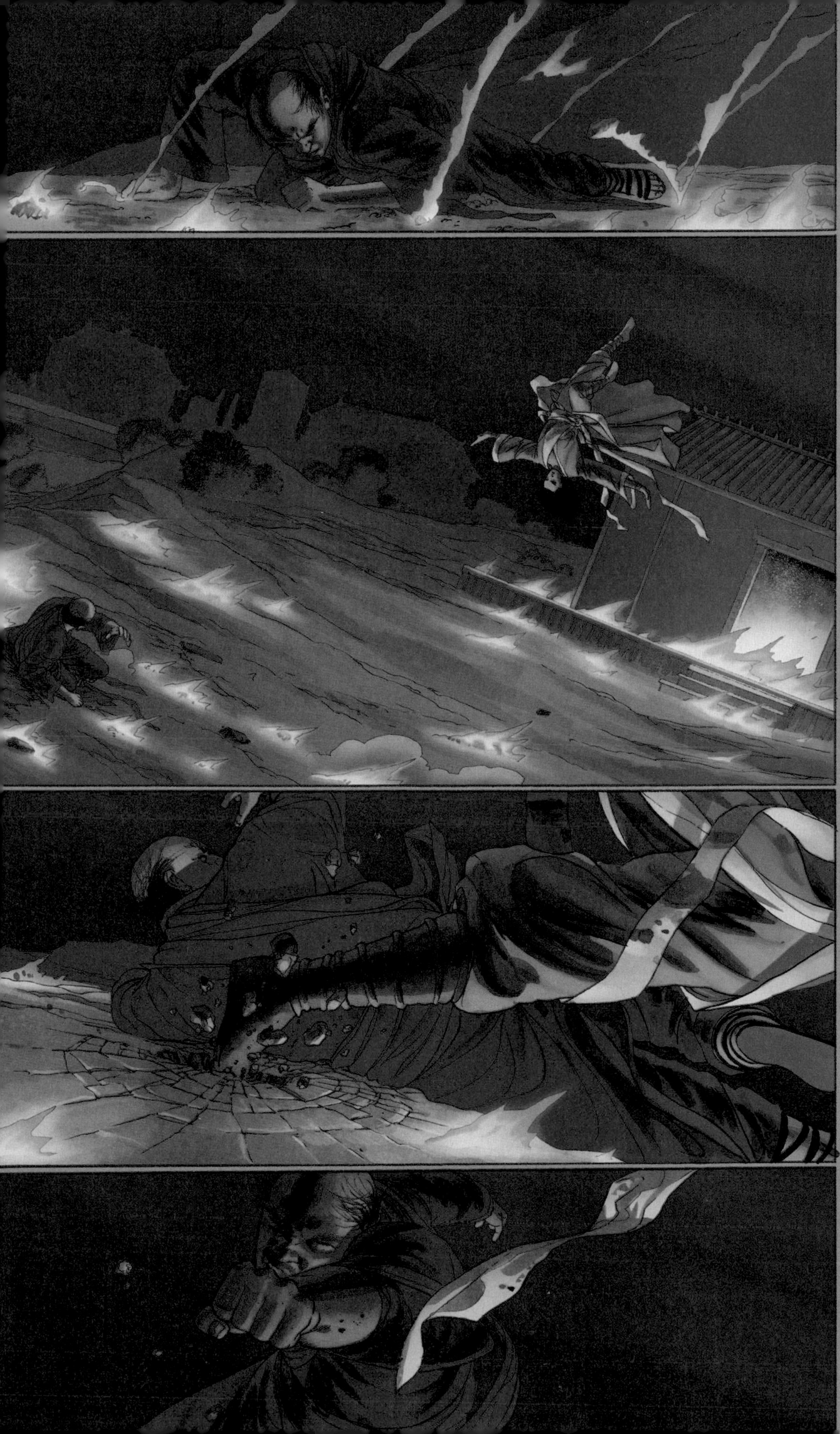

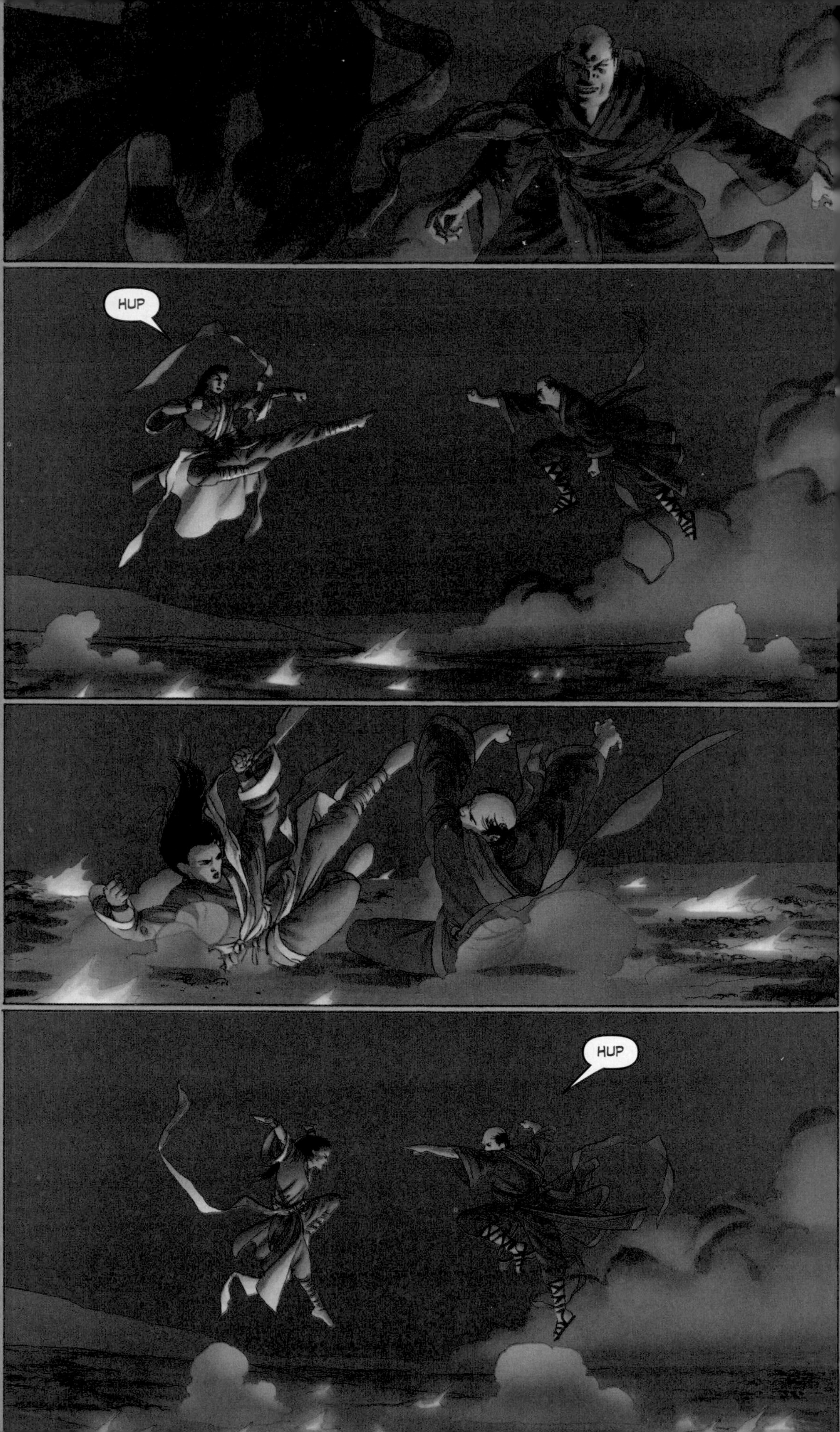
HUP
HUP

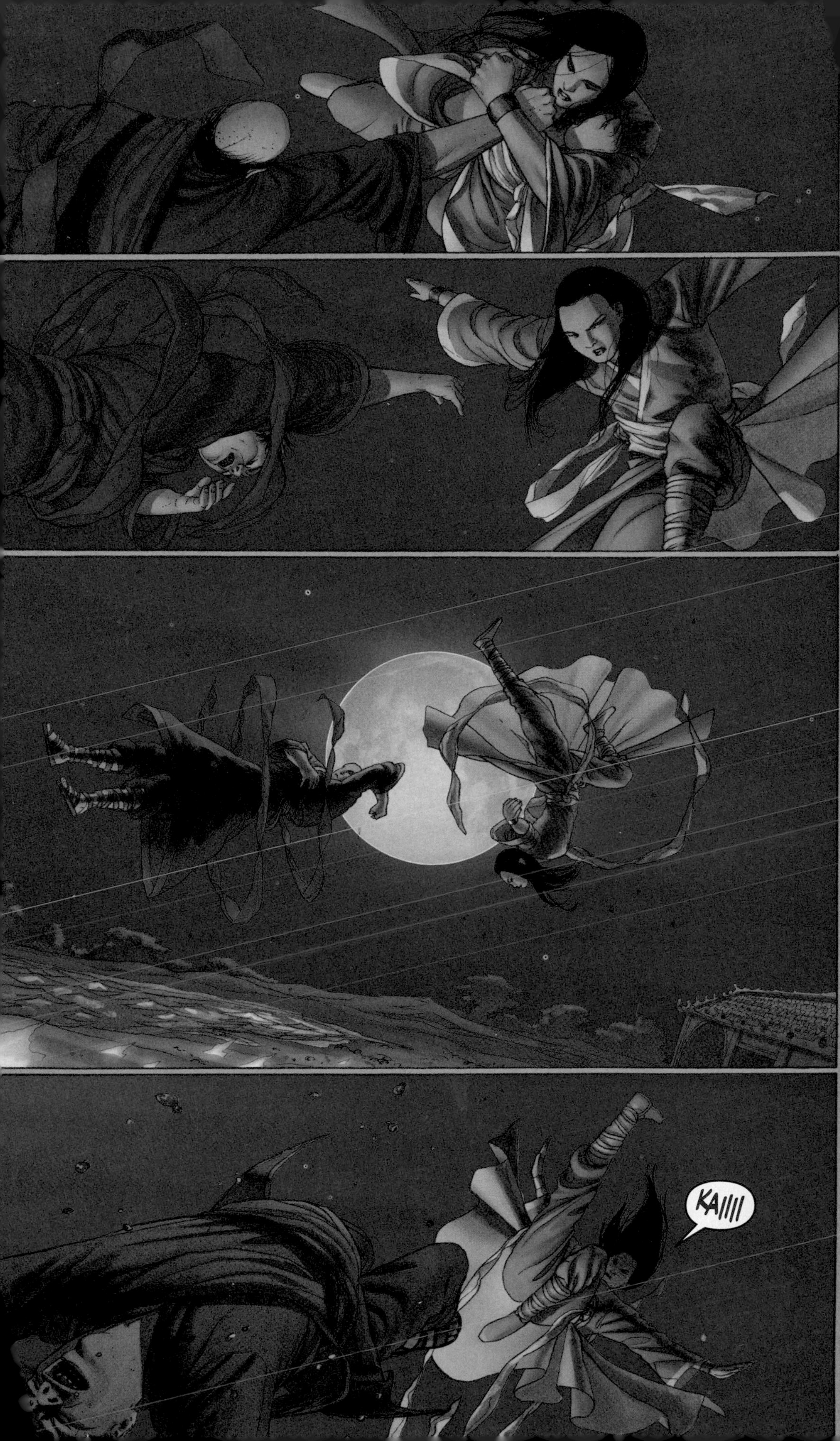
KAIIII

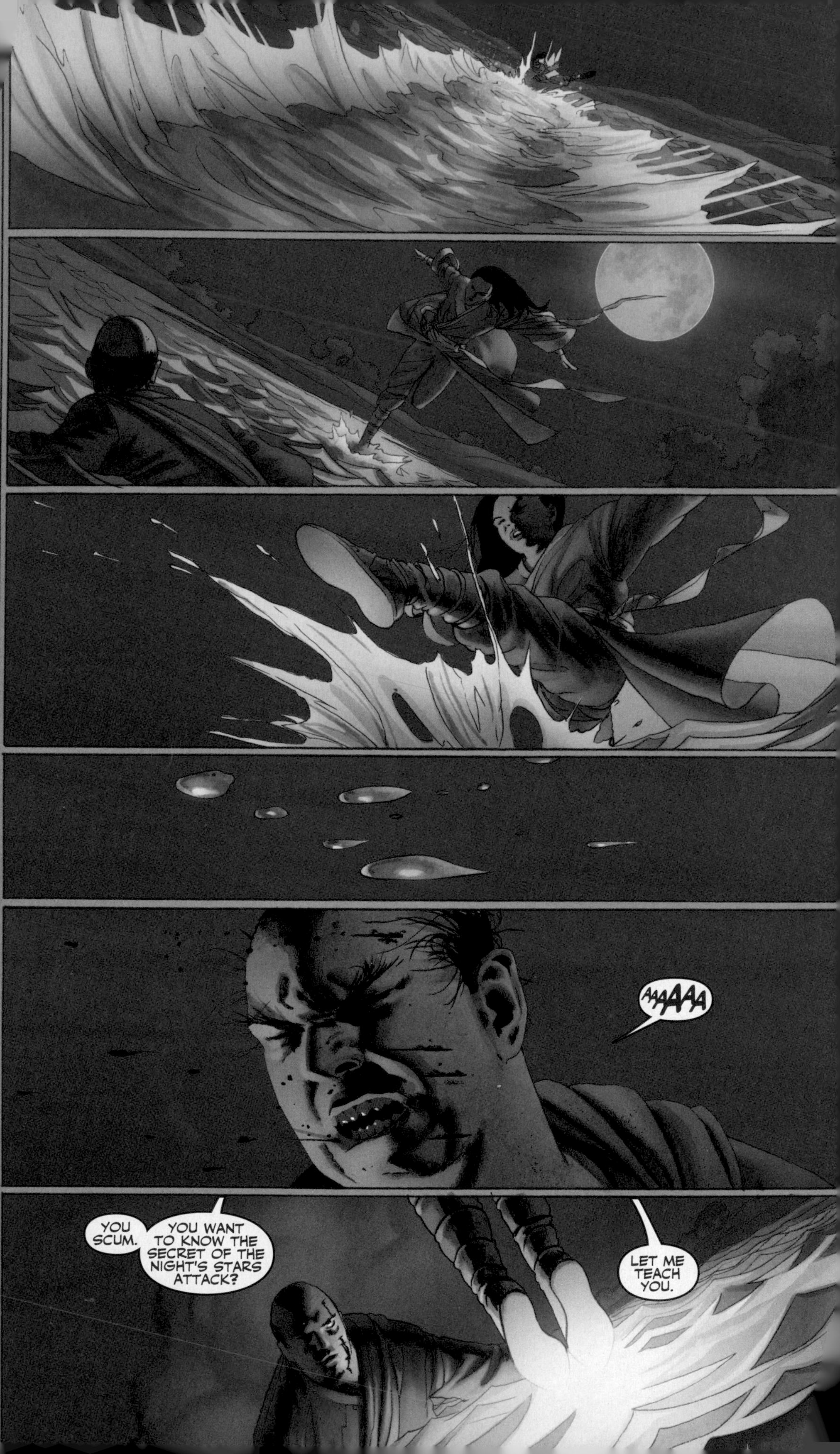
AAAAAA
YOU SCUM.
YOU WANT TO KNOW THE SECRET OF THE NIGHT'S STARS ATTACK?
LET ME TEACH YOU.

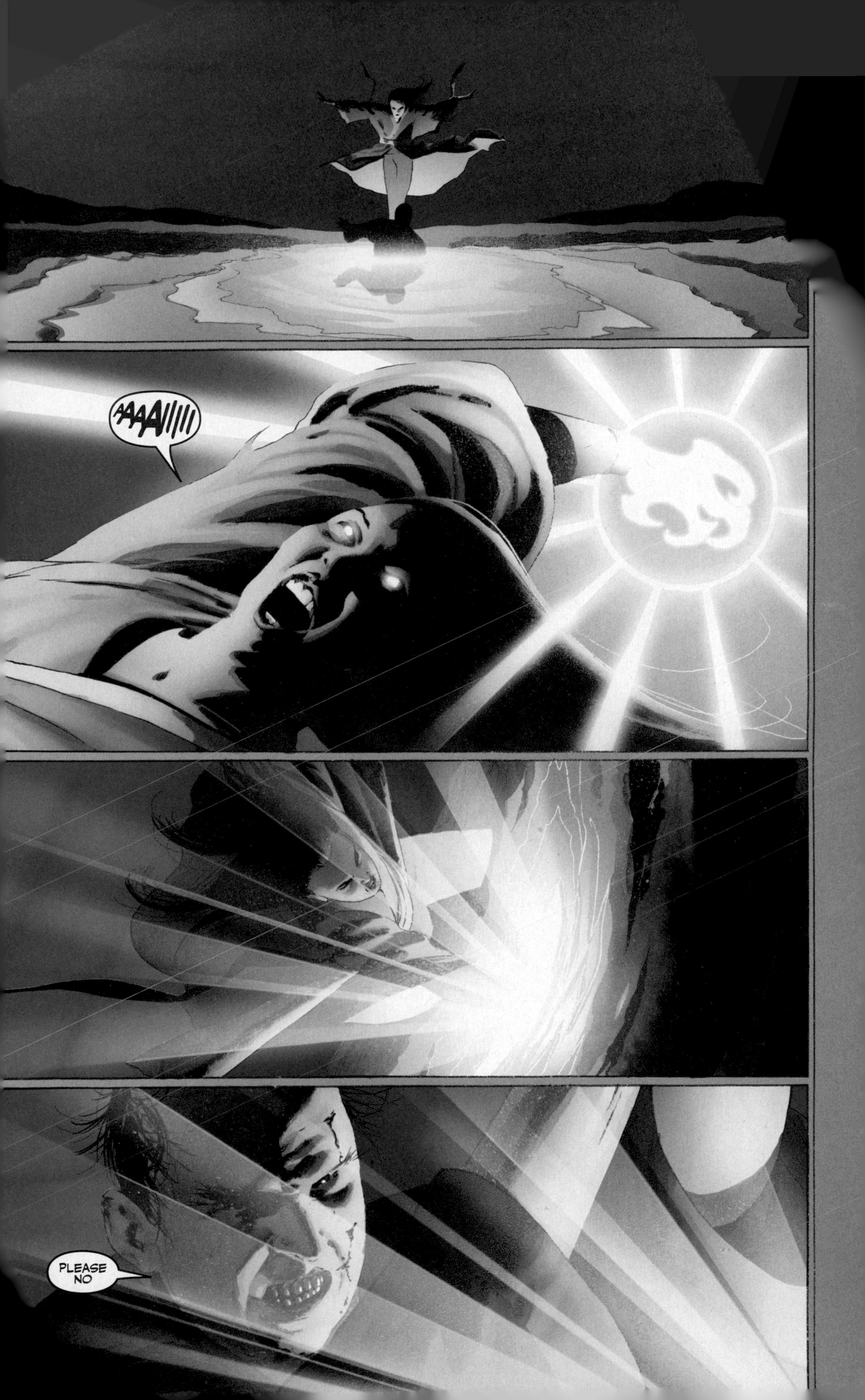
AAAAI!!!!!
PLEASE NO

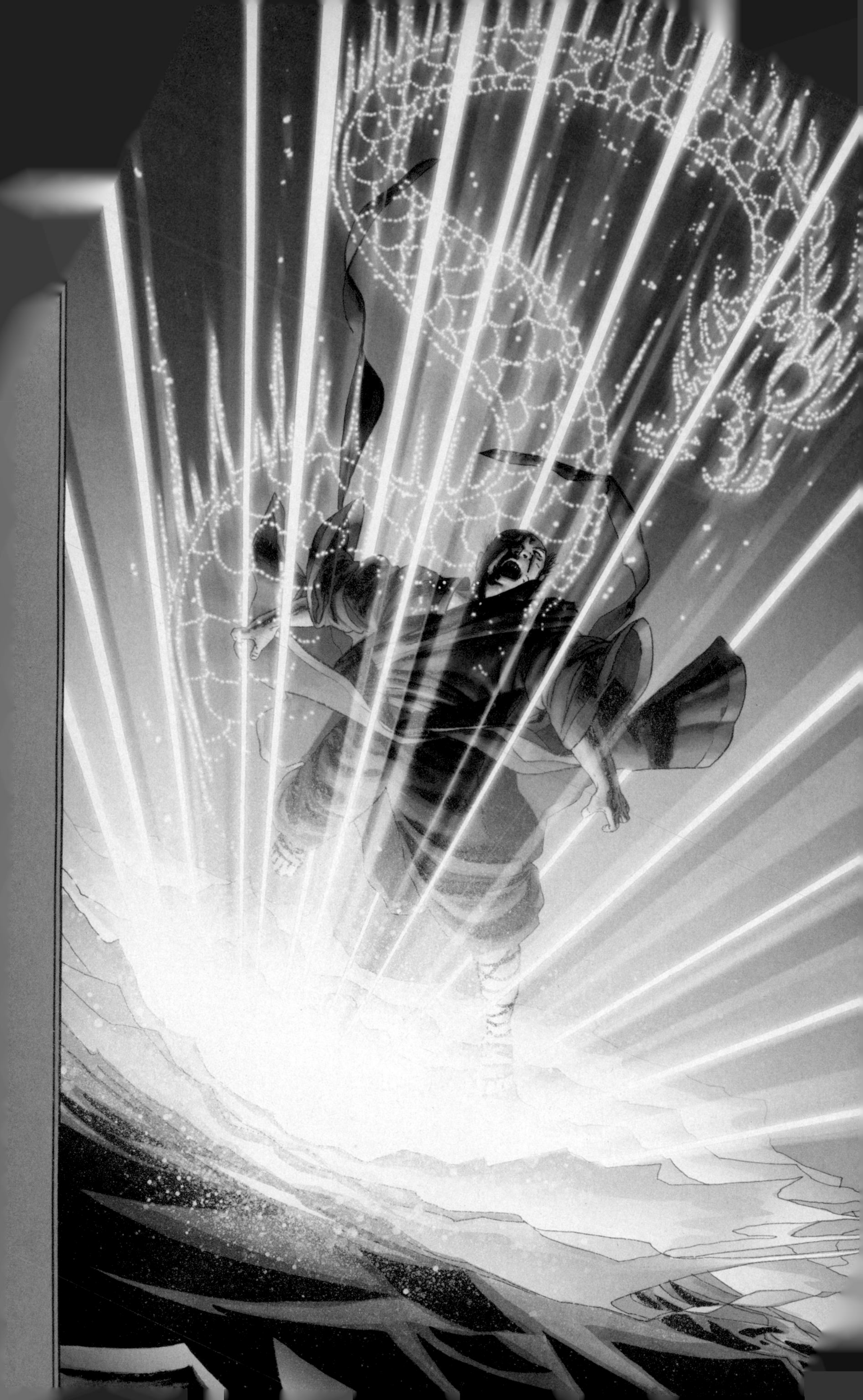

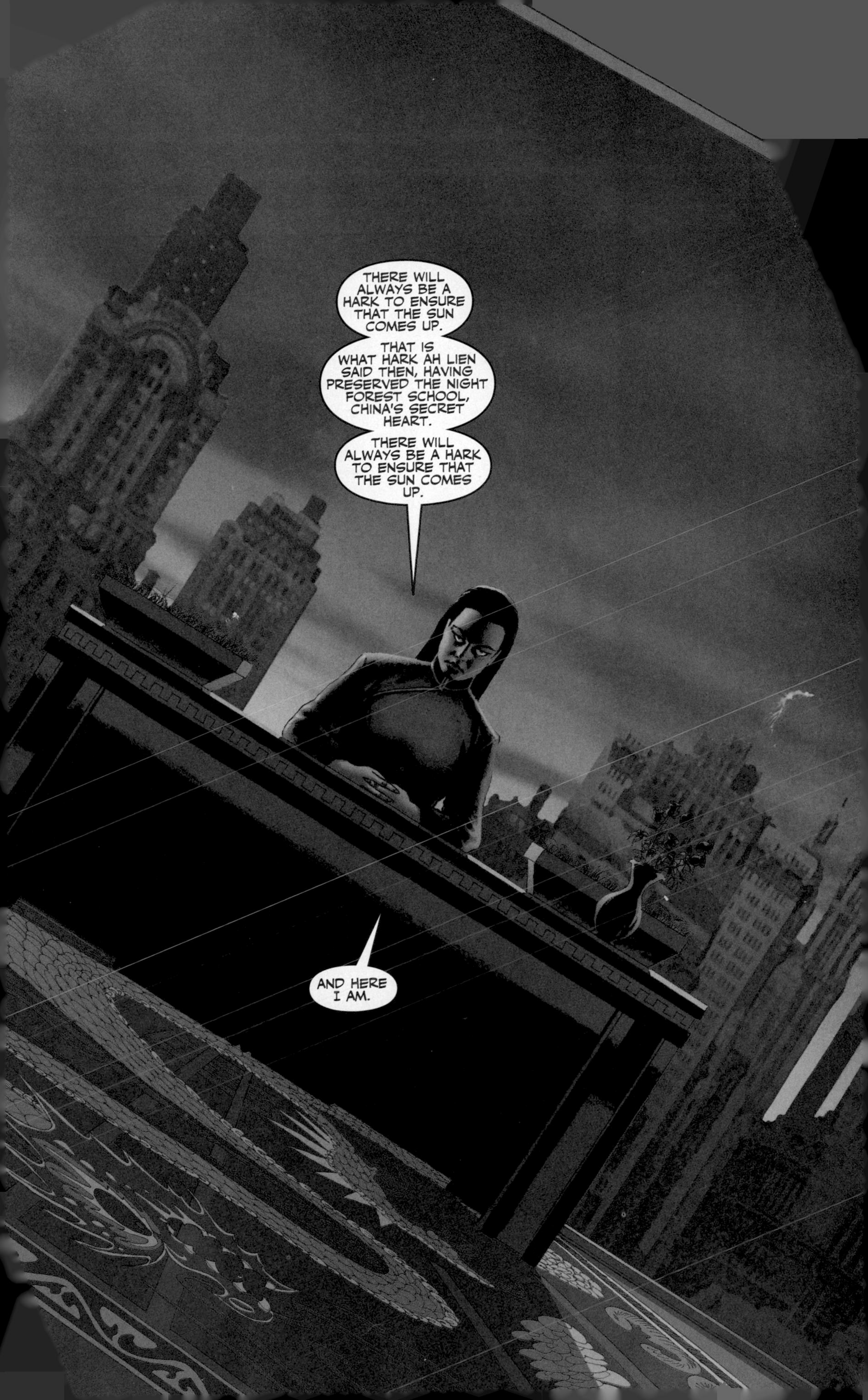
THERE WILL ALWAYS BE A HARK TO ENSURE THAT THE SUN COMES UP.
THAT IS WHAT HARK AH LIEN SAID THEN, HAVING PRESERVED THE NIGHT FOREST SCHOOL, CHINA'S SECRET HEART.
THERE WILL ALWAYS BE A HARK TO ENSURE THAT THE SUN COMES UP.
AND HERE I AM.

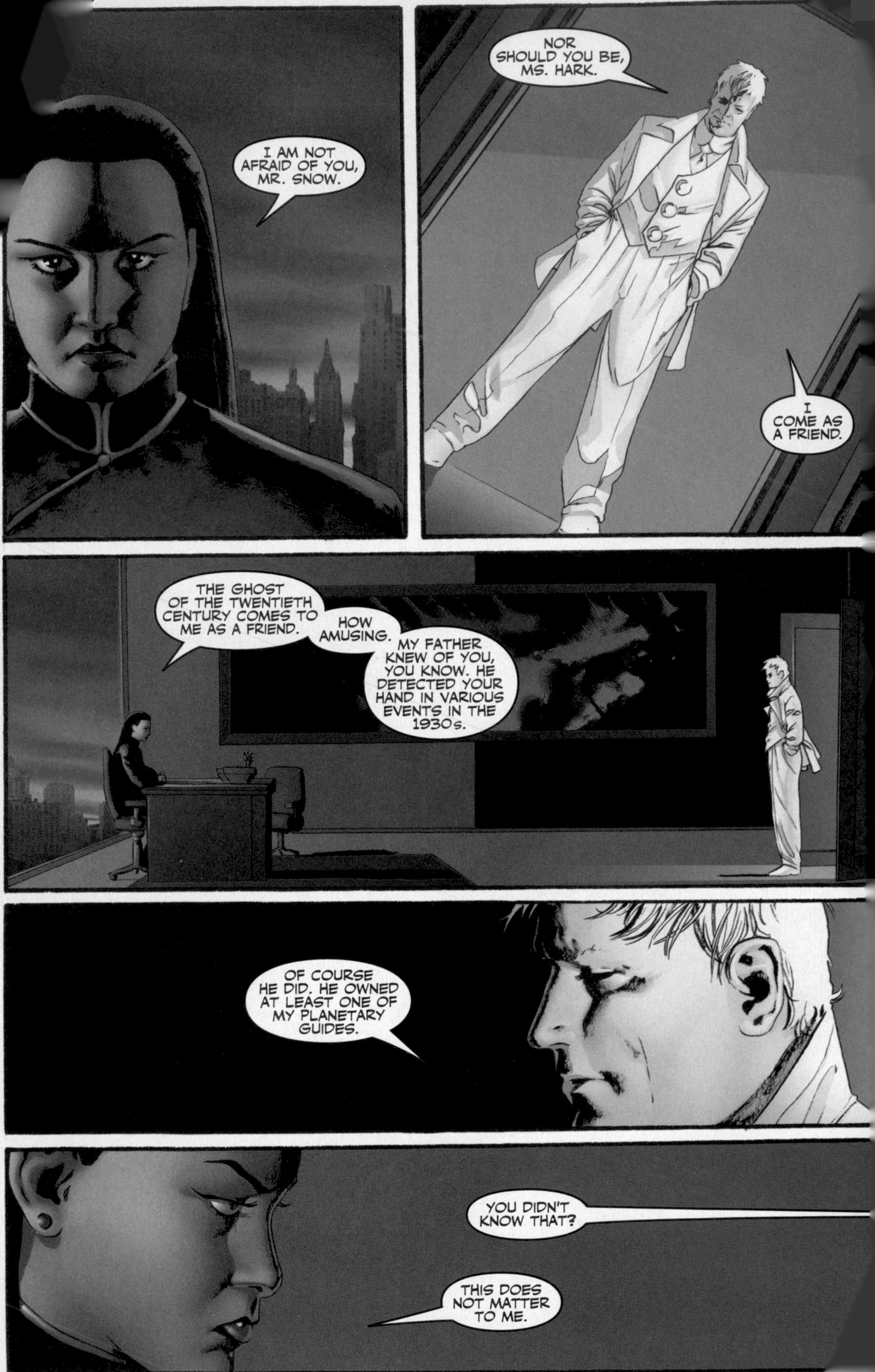
I AM NOT AFRAID OF YOU, MR. SNOW.
NOR SHOULD YOU BE, MS. HARK.
I COME AS A FRIEND.
THE GHOST OF THE TWENTIETH CENTURY COMES TO ME AS A FRIEND.
HOW AMUSING.
MY FATHER KNEW OF YOU, YOU KNOW. HE DETECTED YOUR HAND IN VARIOUS EVENTS IN THE 1930s.
OF COURSE HE DID. HE OWNED AT LEAST ONE OF MY PLANETARY GUIDES.
YOU DIDN'T KNOW THAT?
THIS DOES NOT MATTER TO ME.

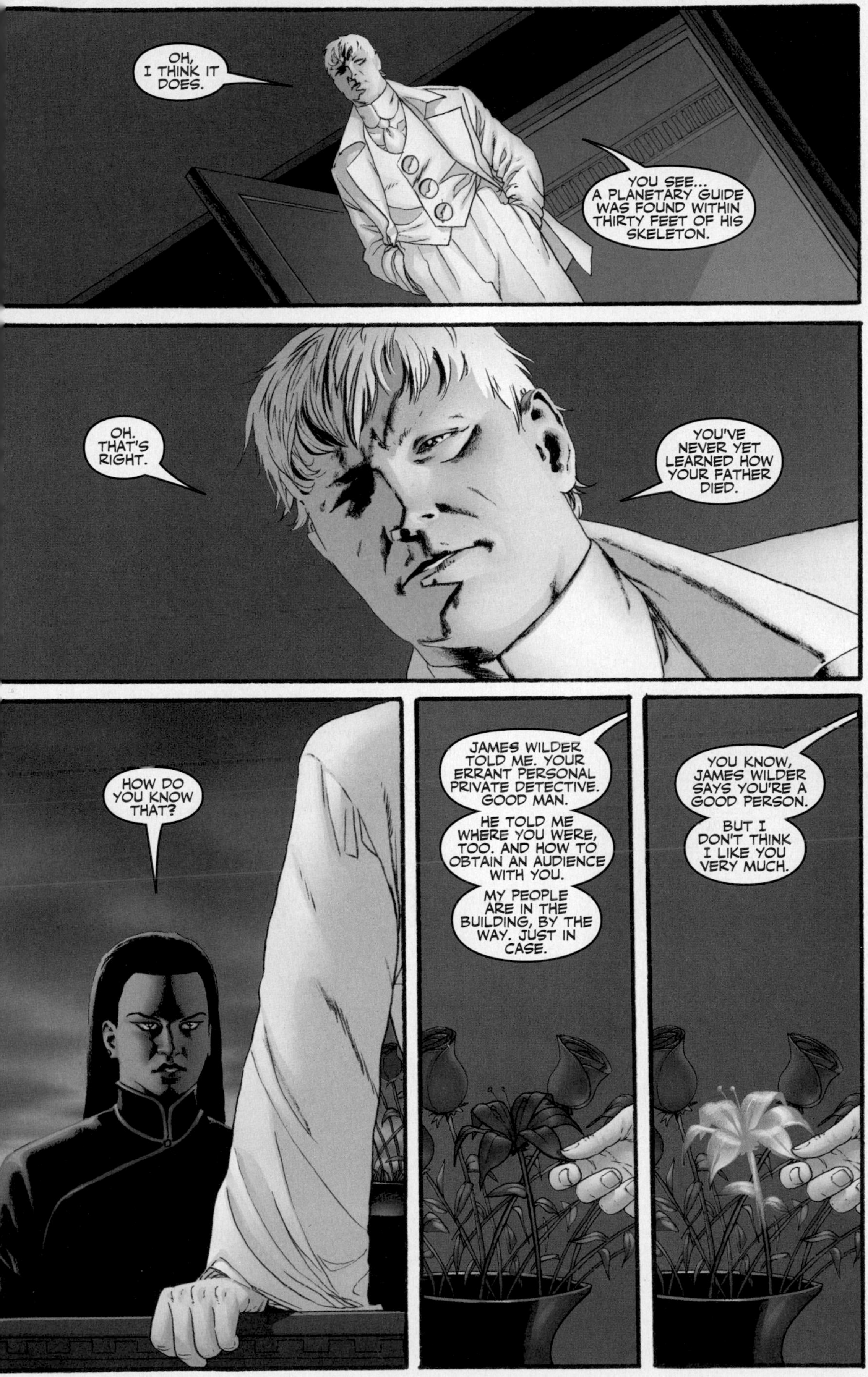
OH, I THINK IT DOES.
YOU SEE... A PLANETARY GUIDE WAS FOUND WITHIN THIRTY FEET OF HIS SKELETON.
OH. THAT'S RIGHT.
YOU'VE NEVER YET LEARNED HOW YOUR FATHER DIED.
HOW DO YOU KNOW THAT?
JAMES WILDER TOLD ME. YOUR ERRANT PERSONAL PRIVATE DETECTIVE. GOOD MAN.
HE TOLD ME WHERE YOU WERE, TOO. AND HOW TO OBTAIN AN AUDIENCE WITH YOU.
MY PEOPLE ARE IN THE BUILDING, BY THE WAY. JUST IN CASE.
YOU KNOW, JAMES WILDER SAYS YOU'RE A GOOD PERSON.
BUT I DON'T THINK I LIKE YOU VERY MUCH.

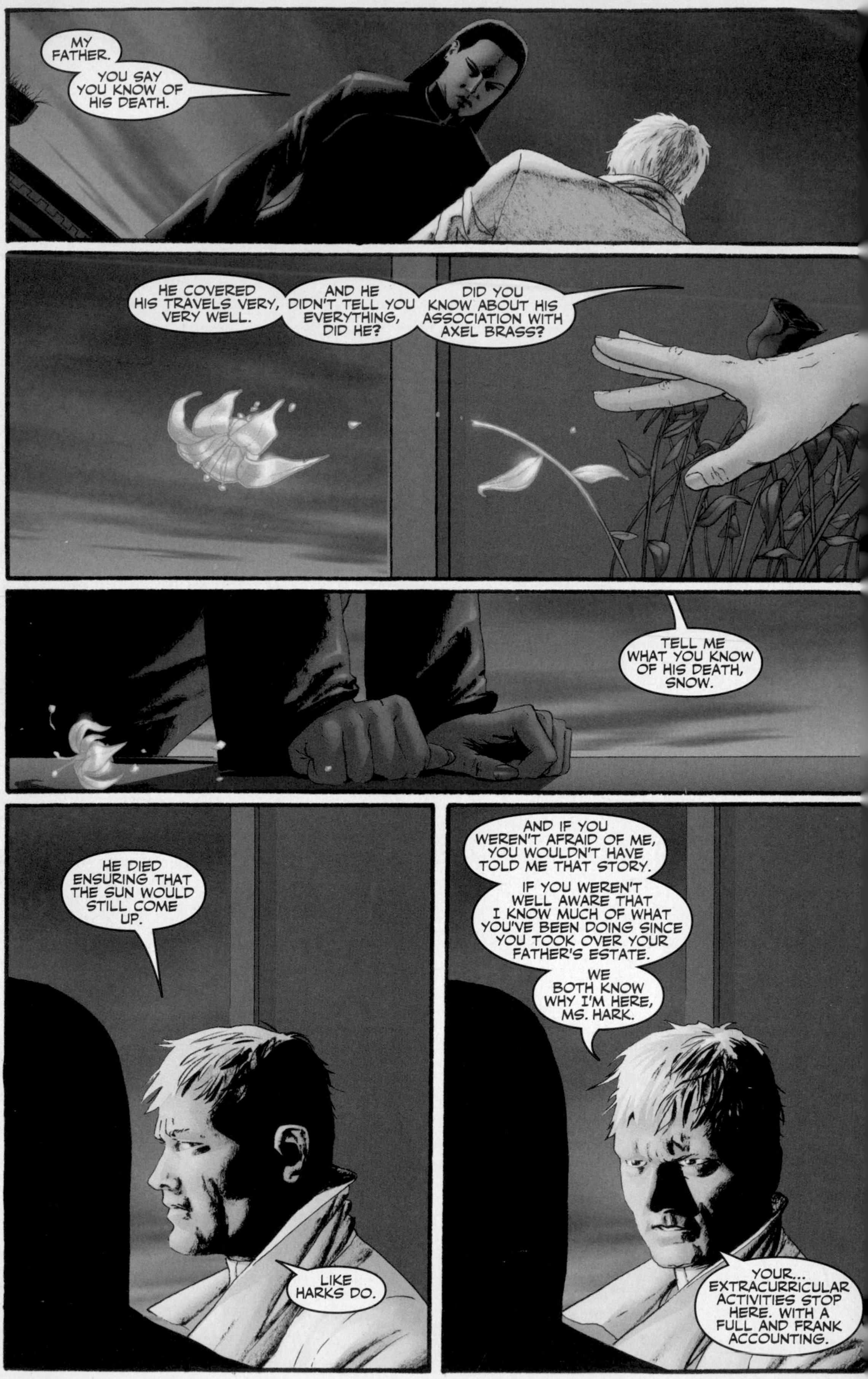
MY FATHER.
YOU SAY YOU KNOW OF HIS DEATH.
HE COVERED HIS TRAVELS VERY, VERY WELL.
AND HE DIDN'T TELL YOU EVERYTHING, DID HE?
DID YOU KNOW ABOUT HIS ASSOCIATION WITH AXEL BRASS?
TELL ME WHAT YOU KNOW OF HIS DEATH, SNOW.
HE DIED ENSURING THAT THE SUN WOULD STILL COME UP.
LIKE HARKS DO.
AND IF YOU WEREN'T AFRAID OF ME, YOU WOULDN'T HAVE TOLD ME THAT STORY.
IF YOU WEREN'T WELL AWARE THAT I KNOW MUCH OF WHAT YOU'VE BEEN DOING SINCE YOU TOOK OVER YOUR FATHER'S ESTATE.
WE BOTH KNOW WHY I'M HERE, MS. HARK.
YOUR... EXTRACURRICULAR ACTIVITIES STOP HERE. WITH A FULL AND FRANK ACCOUNTING.

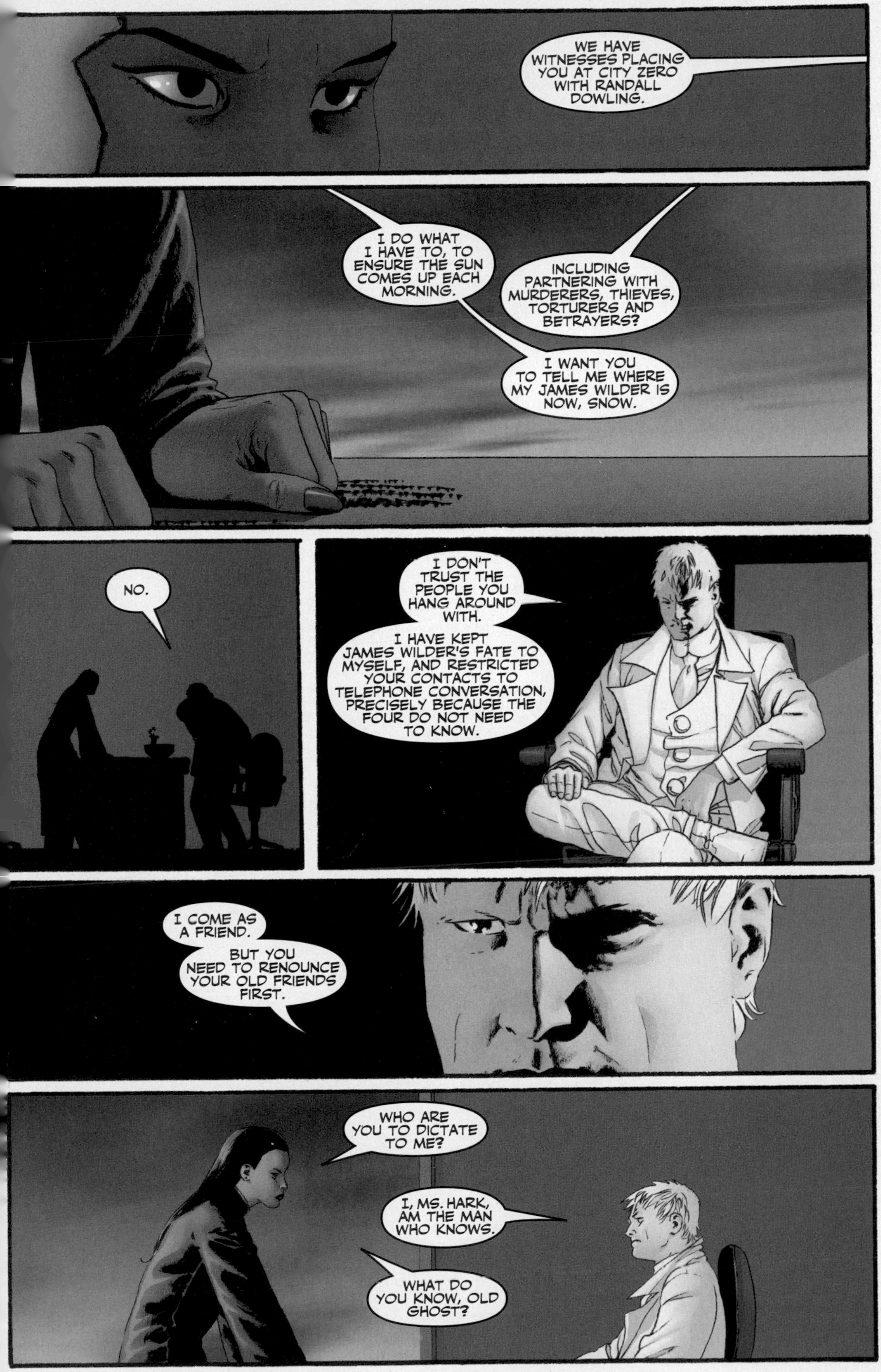
WE HAVE WITNESSES PLACING YOU AT CITY ZERO WITH RANDALL DOWLING.
I DO WHAT I HAVE TO, TO ENSURE THE SUN COMES UP EACH MORNING.
INCLUDING PARTNERING WITH MURDERERS, THIEVES, TORTURERS AND BETRAYERS?
I WANT YOU TO TELL ME WHERE MY JAMES WILDER IS NOW, SNOW.
NO.
I DON'T TRUST THE PEOPLE YOU HANG AROUND WITH.
I HAVE KEPT JAMES WILDER'S FATE TO MYSELF, AND RESTRICTED YOUR CONTACTS TO TELEPHONE CONVERSATION, PRECISELY BECAUSE THE FOUR DO NOT NEED TO KNOW.
I COME AS A FRIEND.
BUT YOU NEED TO RENOUNCE YOUR OLD FRIENDS FIRST.
WHO ARE YOU TO DICTATE TO ME?
I, MS. HARK, AM THE MAN WHO KNOWS.
WHAT DO YOU KNOW, OLD GHOST?

TWO THINGS.

I KNOW THAT I CAN AND WILL REMOVE THE FOUR FROM THIS PLANET, AND PUT THEIR KNOWLEDGE, AS WELL AS MY OWN, IN THE SERVICE OF THE PEOPLE OF THIS WORLD.

I'M ON THIS PLANET WITH YOU. IT IS IN MY BEST INTERESTS THAT THE SUN CONTINUE TO RISE EACH MORNING.

THIS PLACE IS A LAUNCHPAD FOR THE FOUR. ONE OF MANY. EARTH IS NO MORE THAN THAT TO THEM.

JOIN WITH ME, AND YOU CAN DO A HARK'S WORK WITH GREAT EFFECTIVENESS.

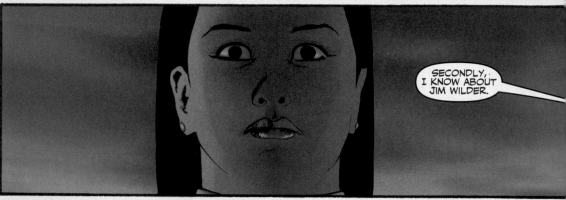

SECONDLY, I KNOW ABOUT JIM WILDER.

A HARK BUILDING BOMBED DOWN TO ITS FOUNDATIONS?

A STAGED MUGGING WHOSE PERPETRATOR LED WILDER RIGHT INTO THE BOMB SITE, AND LITERALLY RIGHT ACROSS THE TRAVELSTONE EXPOSED BY THE EXPLOSION?

YOUR FILES ARE VERY WELL DEFENDED. IT TOOK THE DRUMMER ALMOST A DAY TO HACK THE HARK CORPORATION SYSTEM.

YOU DIDN'T KNOW EXACTLY WHAT WAS DOWN THERE, BUT YOU HAD HEARD STORIES, AND MADE INTELLIGENT SUPPOSITIONS.

THIS WAS A CLEAR ATTEMPT TO CREATE A SUPERHUMAN.

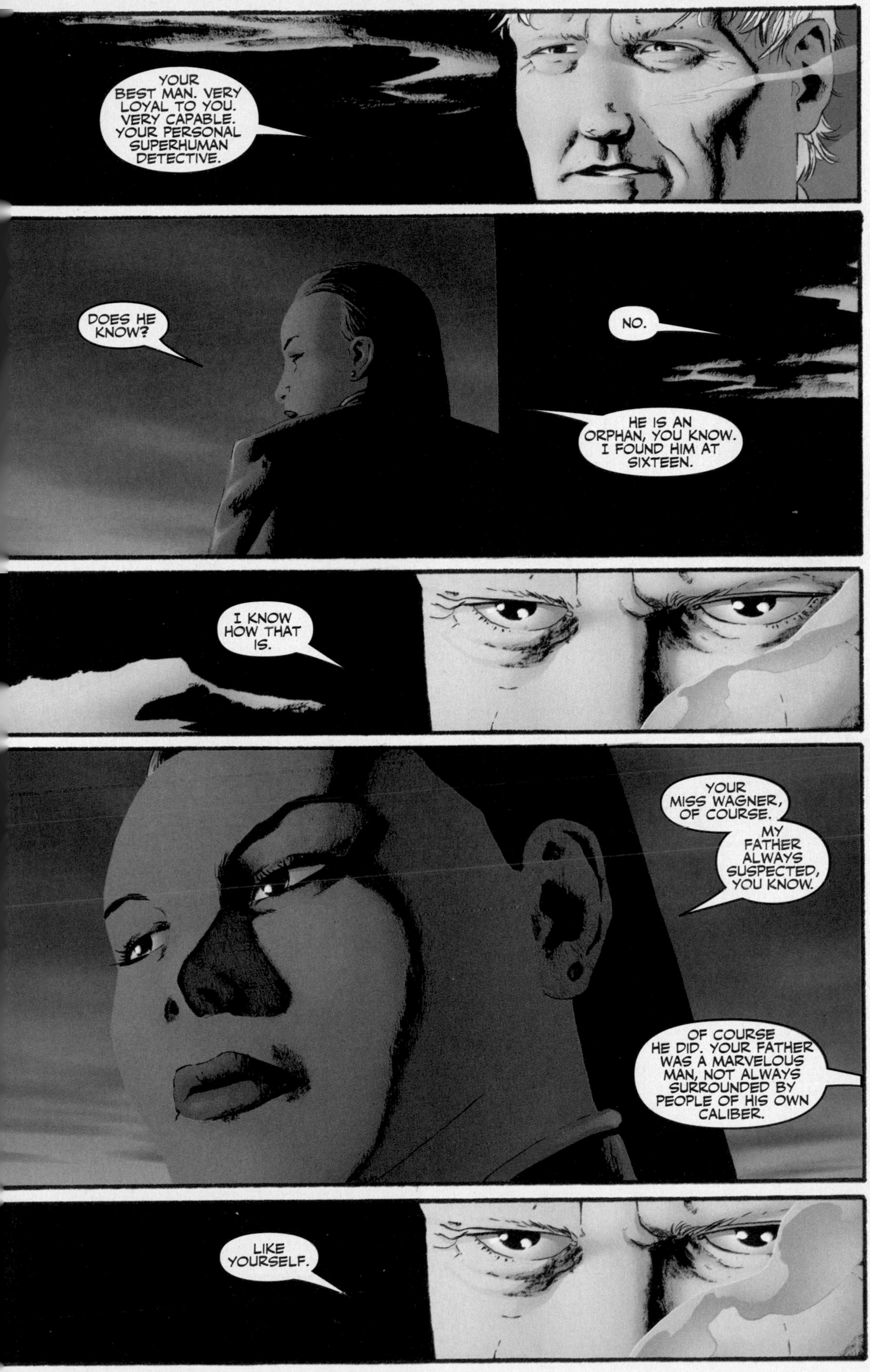
YOUR BEST MAN. VERY LOYAL TO YOU. VERY CAPABLE. YOUR PERSONAL SUPERHUMAN DETECTIVE.
DOES HE KNOW?
NO.
HE IS AN ORPHAN, YOU KNOW. I FOUND HIM AT SIXTEEN.
I KNOW HOW THAT IS.
YOUR MISS WAGNER, OF COURSE.
MY FATHER ALWAYS SUSPECTED, YOU KNOW.
OF COURSE HE DID. YOUR FATHER WAS A MARVELOUS MAN, NOT ALWAYS SURROUNDED BY PEOPLE OF HIS OWN CALIBER.
LIKE YOURSELF.

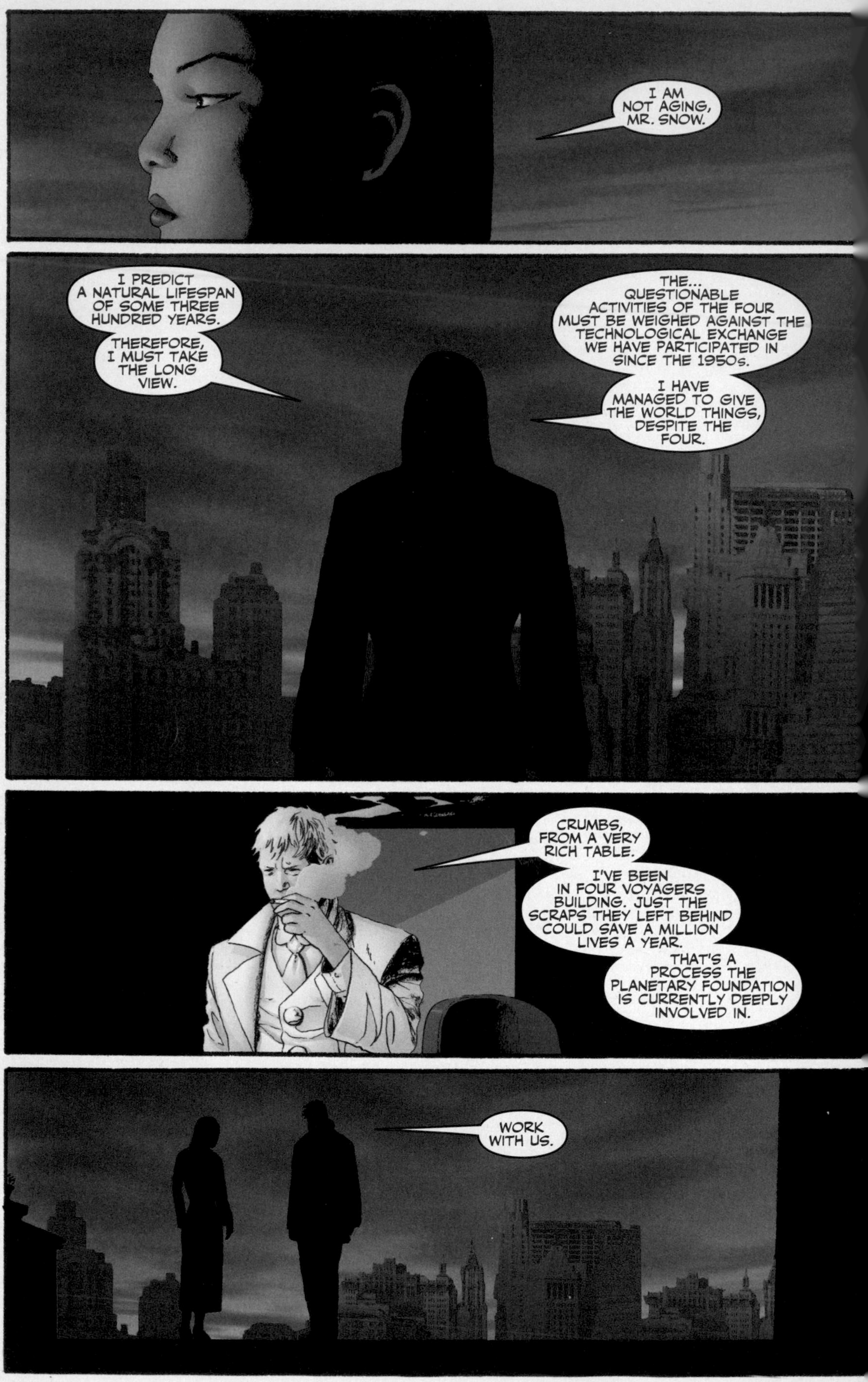
I AM NOT AGING, MR. SNOW.
I PREDICT A NATURAL LIFESPAN OF SOME THREE HUNDRED YEARS.
THEREFORE, I MUST TAKE THE LONG VIEW.
THE... QUESTIONABLE ACTIVITIES OF THE FOUR MUST BE WEIGHED AGAINST THE TECHNOLOGICAL EXCHANGE WE HAVE PARTICIPATED IN SINCE THE 1950s.
I HAVE MANAGED TO GIVE THE WORLD THINGS, DESPITE THE FOUR.
CRUMBS, FROM A VERY RICH TABLE.
I'VE BEEN IN FOUR VOYAGERS BUILDING. JUST THE SCRAPS THEY LEFT BEHIND COULD SAVE A MILLION LIVES A YEAR.
THAT'S A PROCESS THE PLANETARY FOUNDATION IS CURRENTLY DEEPLY INVOLVED IN.
WORK WITH US.

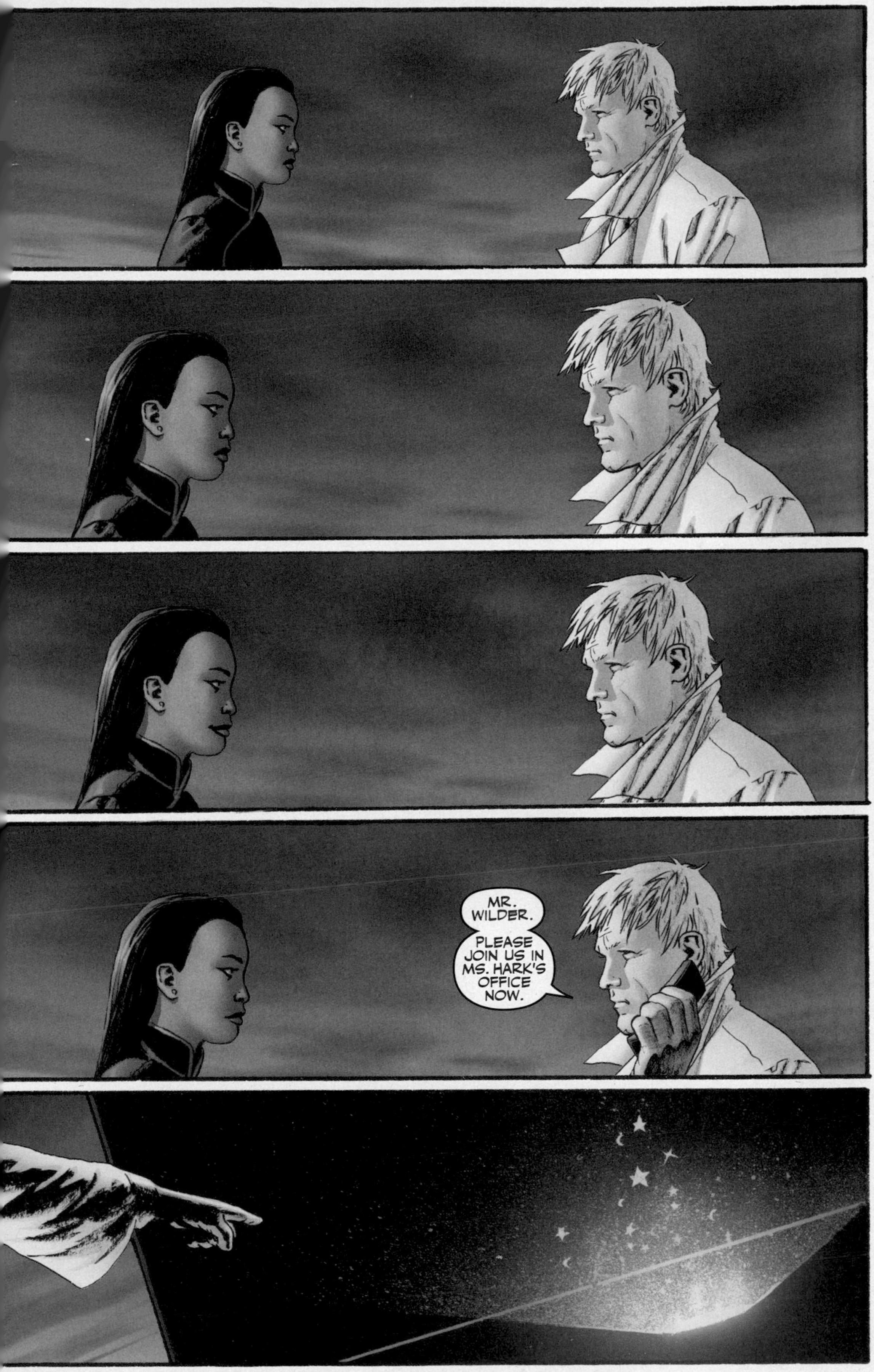
MR. WILDER.
PLEASE JOIN US IN MS. HARK'S OFFICE NOW.

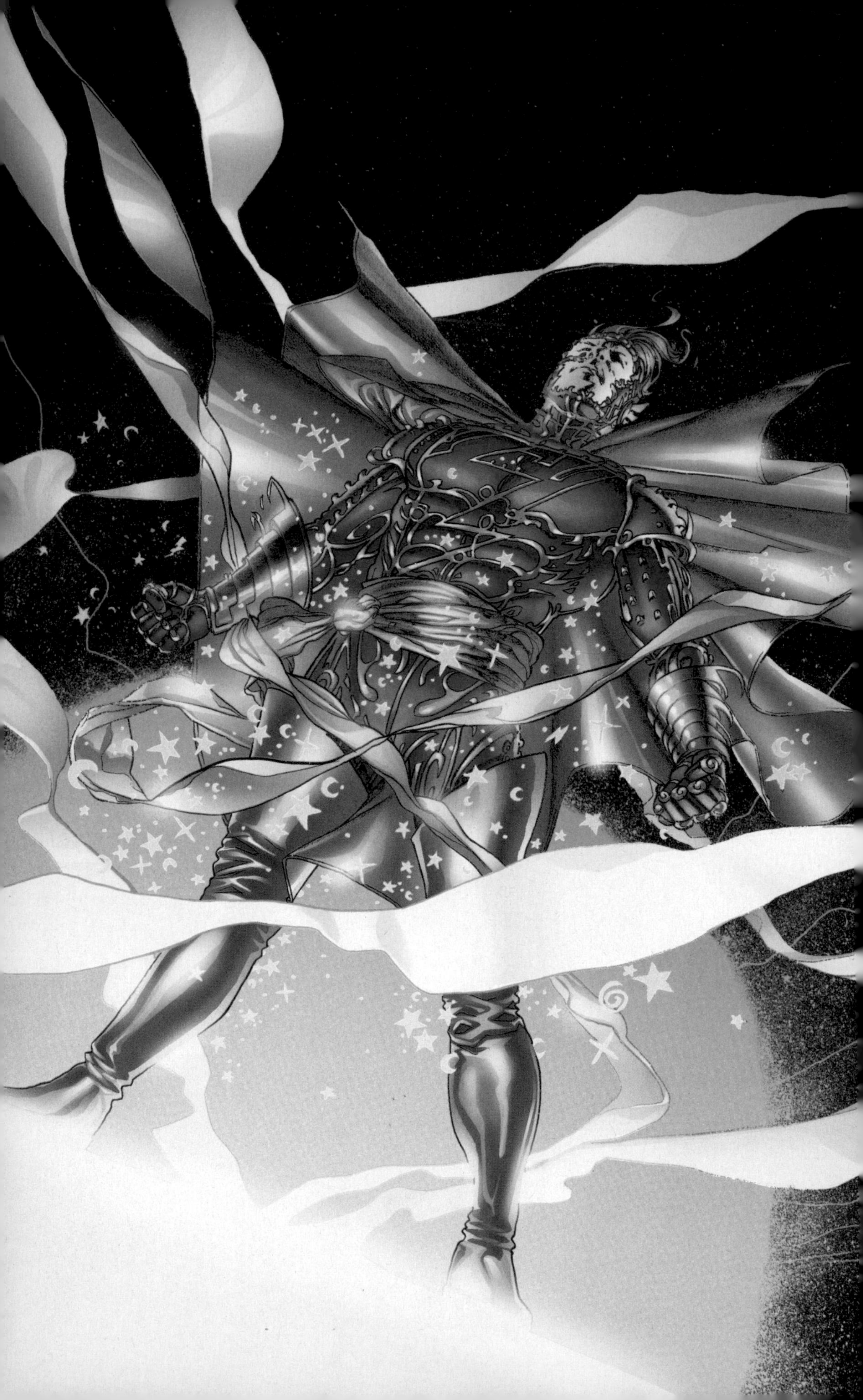

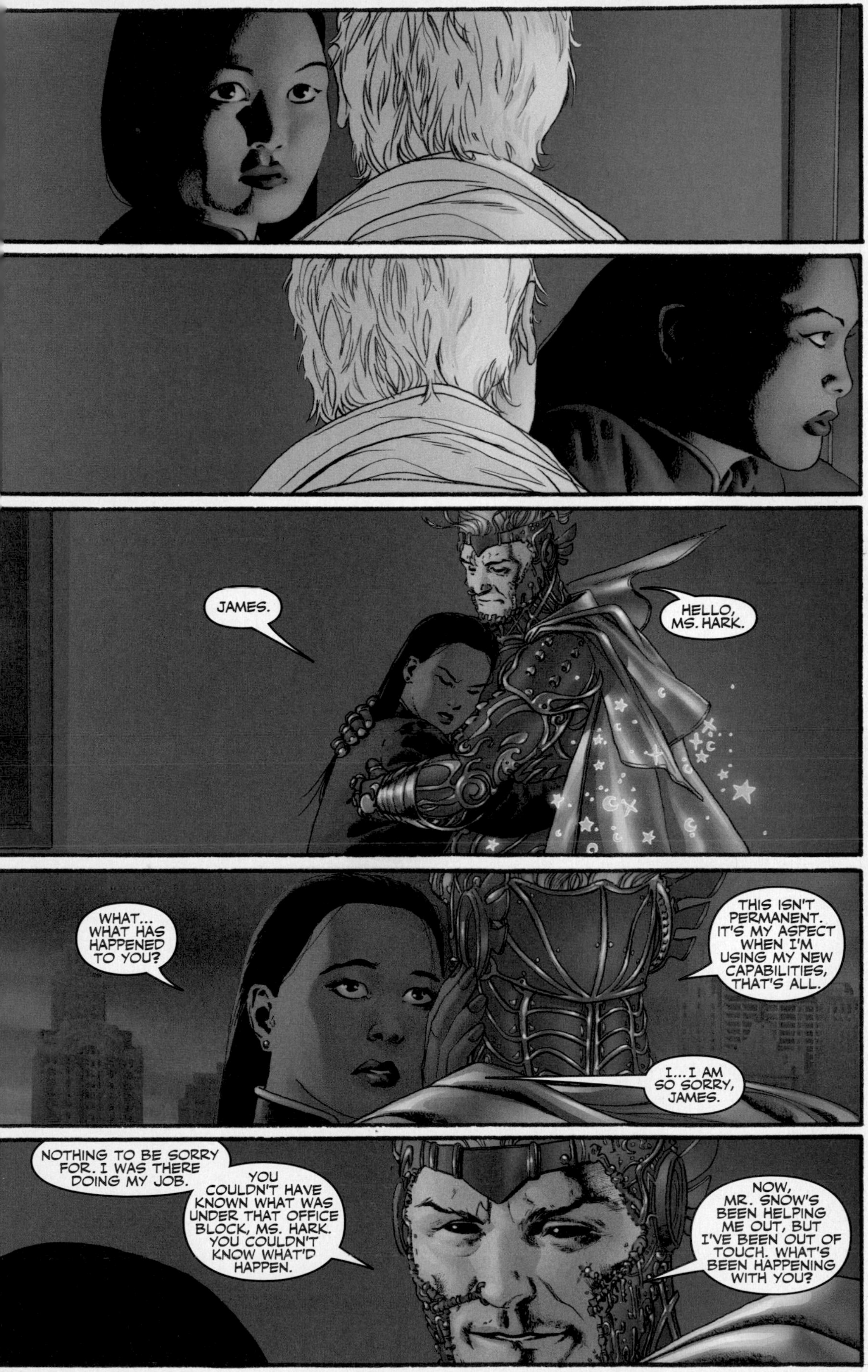

JAMES.
HELLO, MS. HARK.
WHAT... WHAT HAS HAPPENED TO YOU?
THIS ISN'T PERMANENT. IT'S MY ASPECT WHEN I'M USING MY NEW CAPABILITIES, THAT'S ALL.
I...I AM SO SORRY, JAMES.
NOTHING TO BE SORRY FOR. I WAS THERE DOING MY JOB.
YOU COULDN'T HAVE KNOWN WHAT WAS UNDER THAT OFFICE BLOCK, MS. HARK. YOU COULDN'T KNOW WHAT'D HAPPEN.
NOW, MR. SNOW'S BEEN HELPING ME OUT, BUT I'VE BEEN OUT OF TOUCH. WHAT'S BEEN HAPPENING WITH YOU?

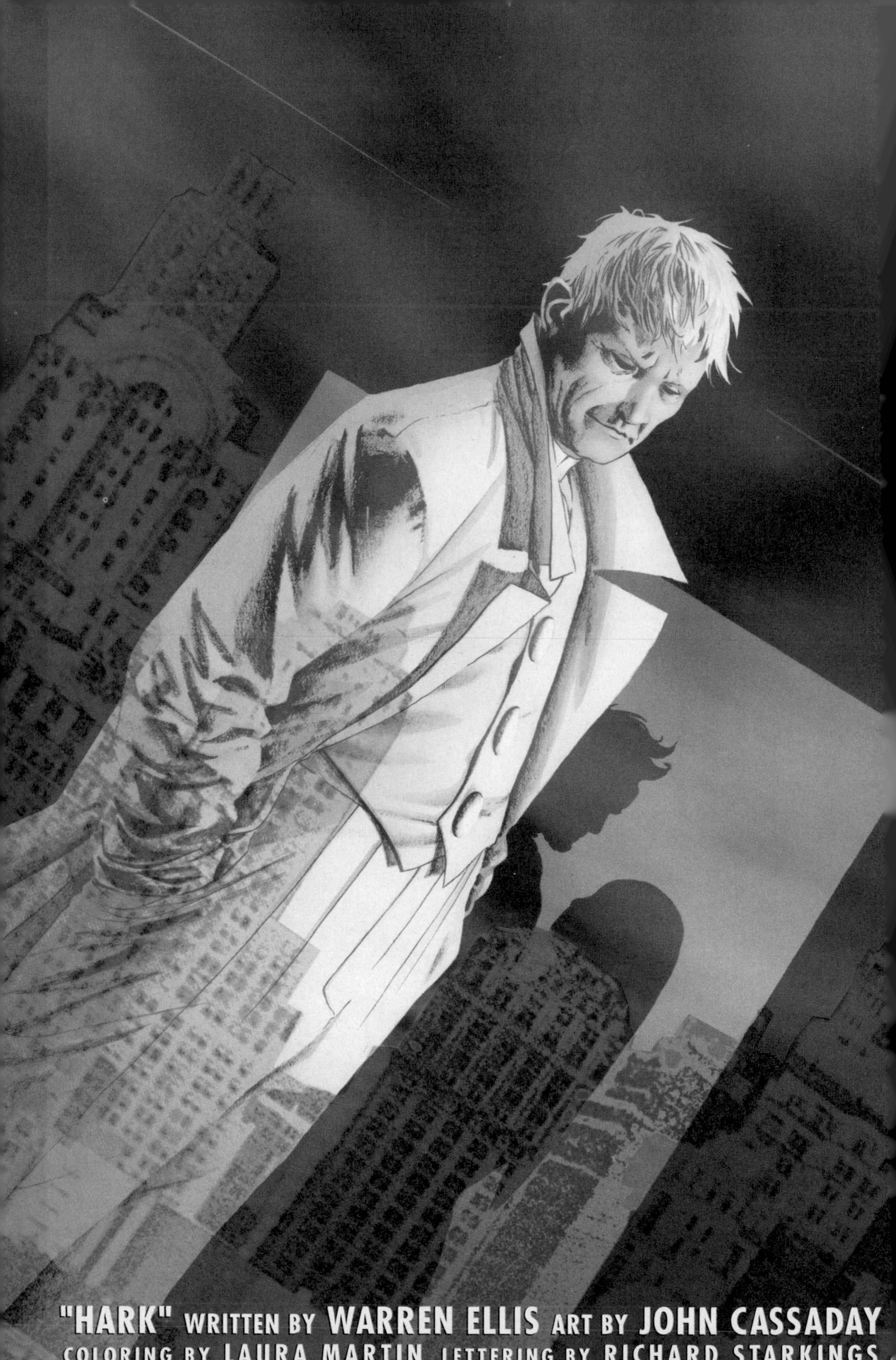

"HARK" WRITTEN BY WARREN ELLIS ART BY JOHN CASSADAY
COLORING BY LAURA MARTIN LETTERING BY RICHARD STARKINGS
ASSISTANT EDITOR KRISTY QUINN EDITOR SCOTT DUNBIER

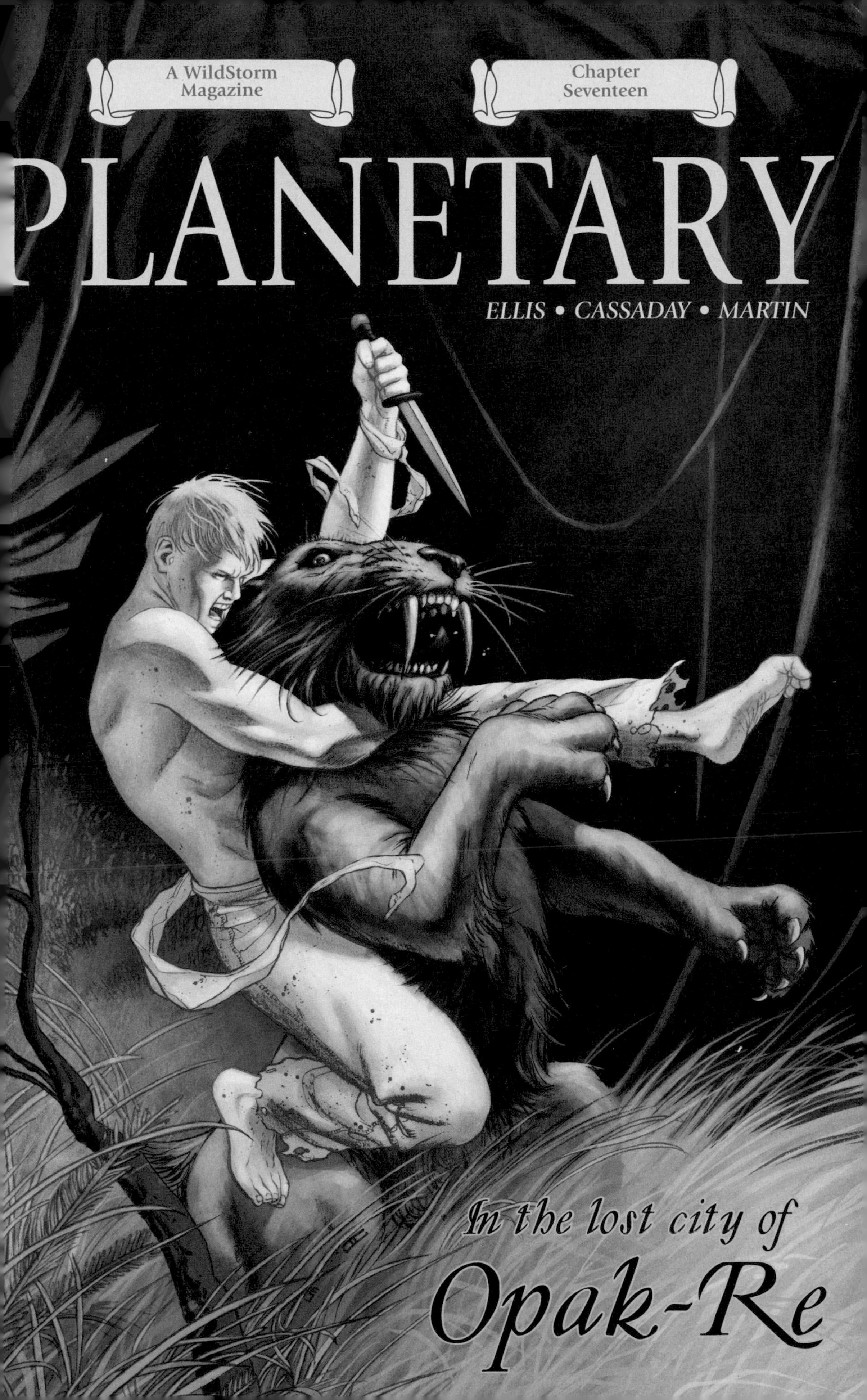

A WildStorm Magazine
Chapter Seventeen
PLANETARY
ELLIS • CASSADAY • MARTIN
In the lost city of
Opak-Re

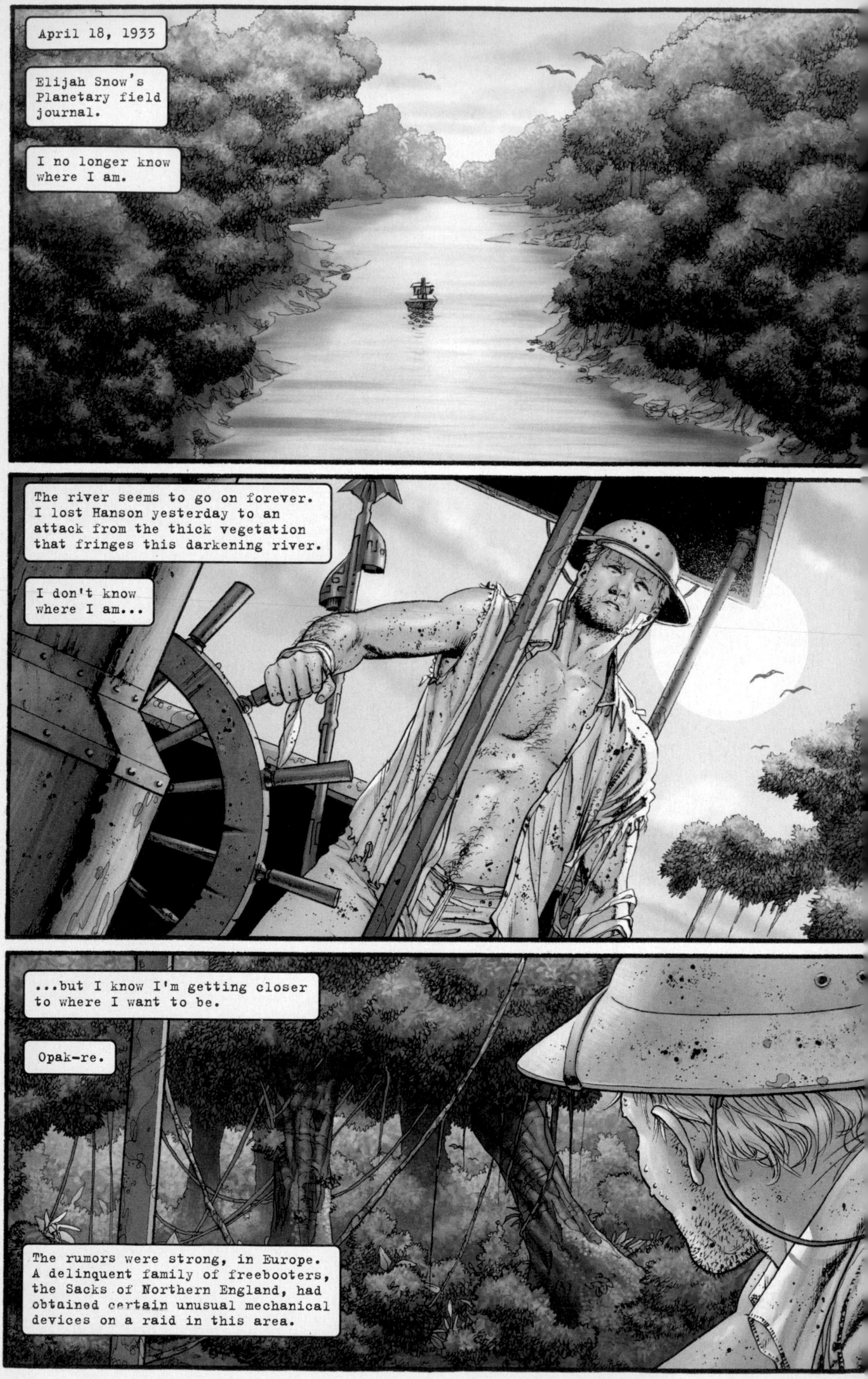
April 18, 1933
Elijah Snow's Planetary field journal.
I no longer know where I am.
The river seems to go on forever. I lost Hanson yesterday to an attack from the thick vegetation that fringes this darkening river.
I don't know where I am...
...but I know I'm getting closer to where I want to be.
Opak-re.
The rumors were strong, in Europe. A delinquent family of freebooters, the Sacks of Northern England, had obtained certain unusual mechanical devices on a raid in this area.

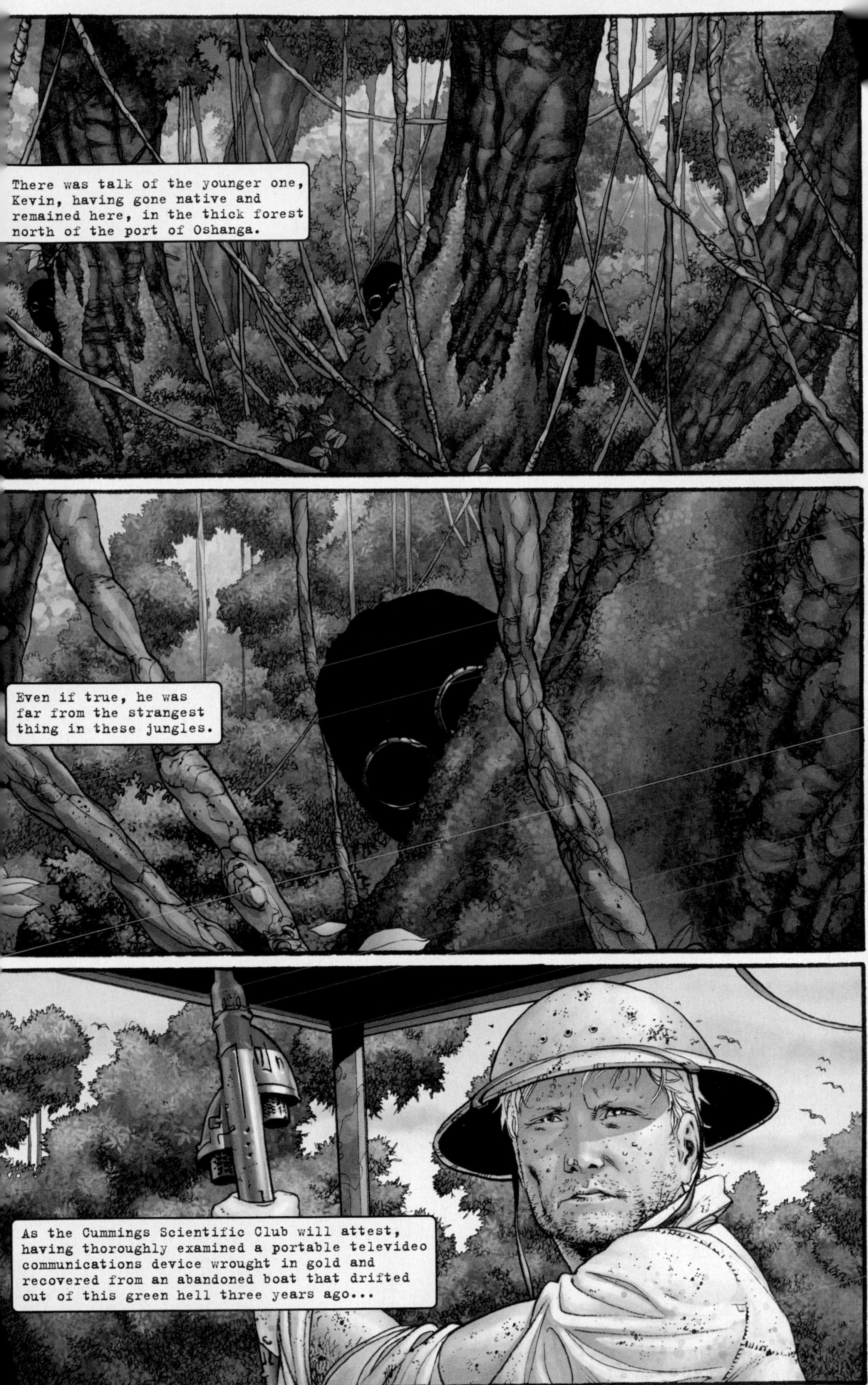
There was talk of the younger one, Kevin, having gone native and remained here, in the thick forest north of the port of Oshanga.
Even if true, he was far from the strangest thing in these jungles.
As the Cummings Scientific Club will attest, having thoroughly examined a portable televideo communications device wrought in gold and recovered from an abandoned boat that drifted out of this green hell three years ago...

...from Opak-re.

"OPAK-RE"

WRITTEN BY **WARREN ELLIS** ART BY **JOHN CASSADAY**
COLORING BY **LAURA MARTIN** LETTERING BY **RICHARD STARKING**
ASSISTANT EDITOR **KRISTY QUINN** EDITOR **SCOTT DUNBIE**

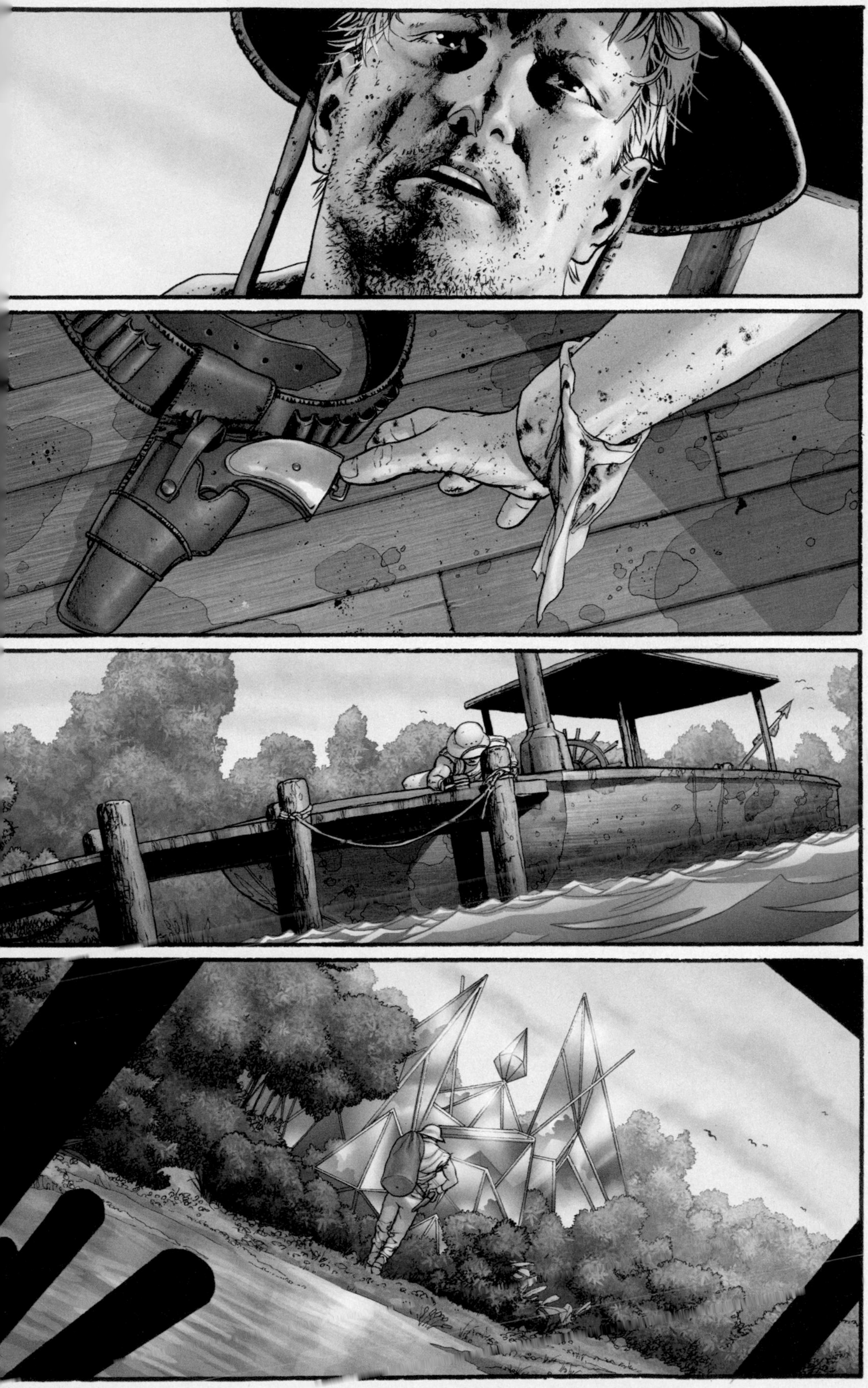

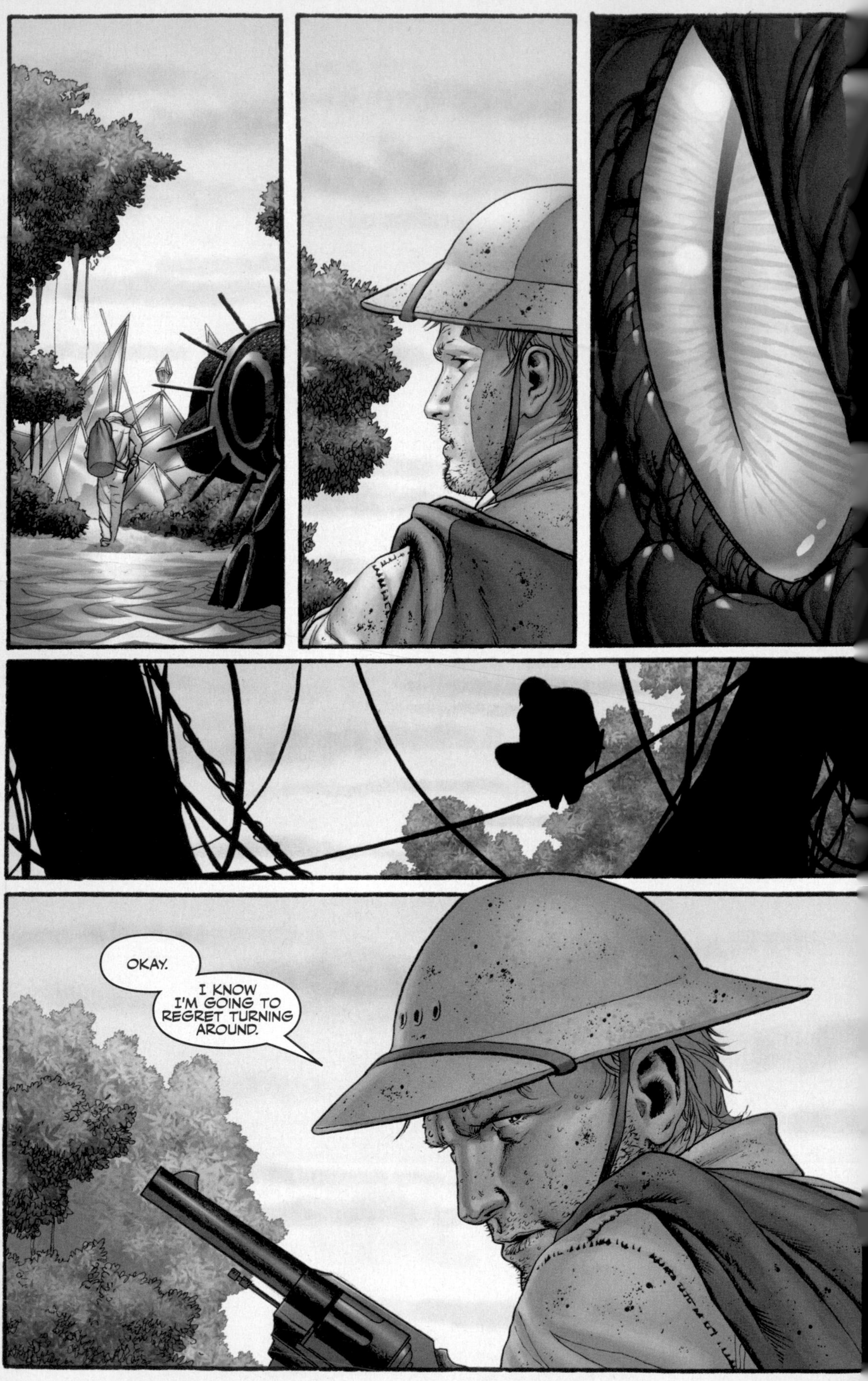
OKAY.
I KNOW I'M GOING TO REGRET TURNING AROUND.

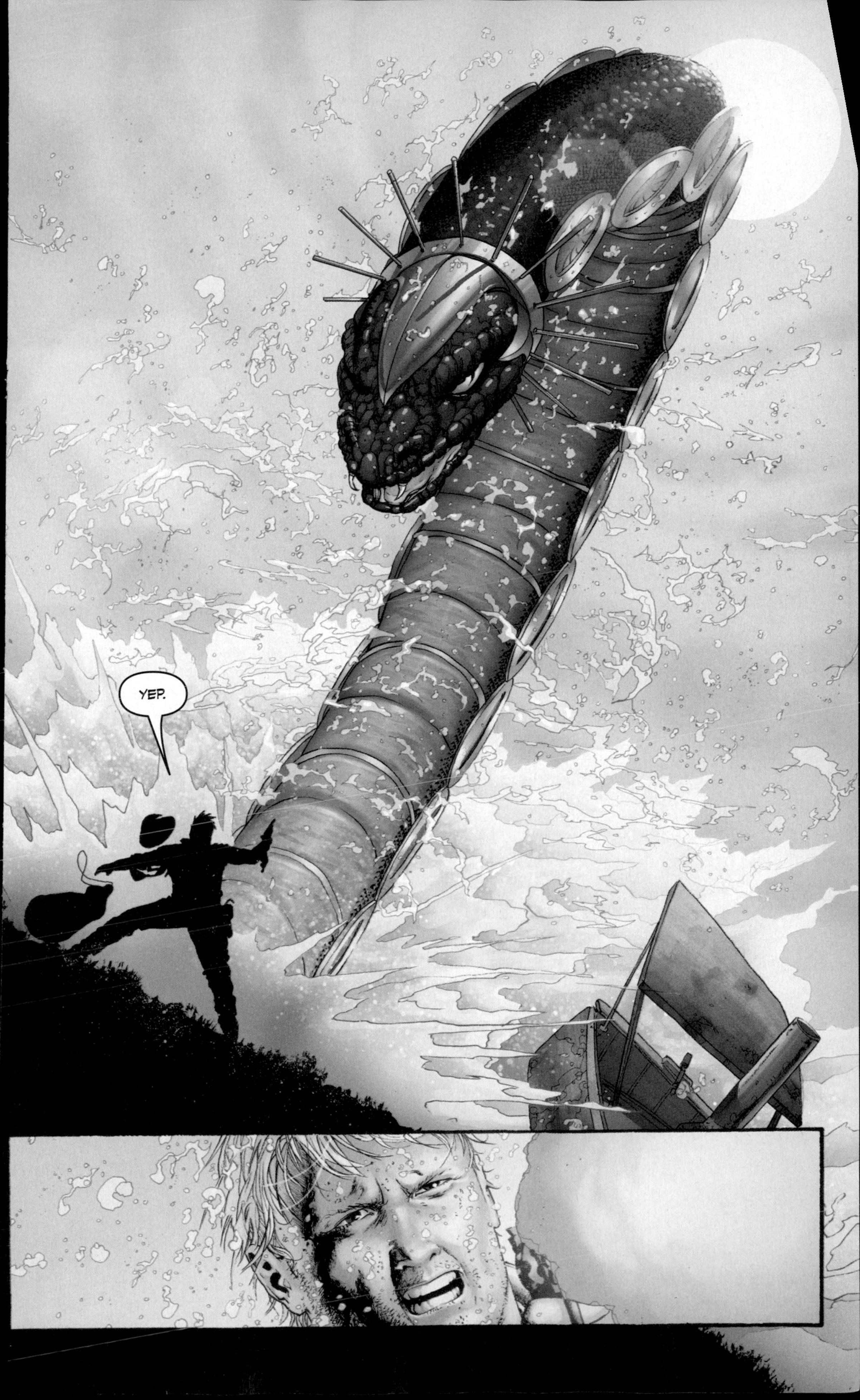
YEP.

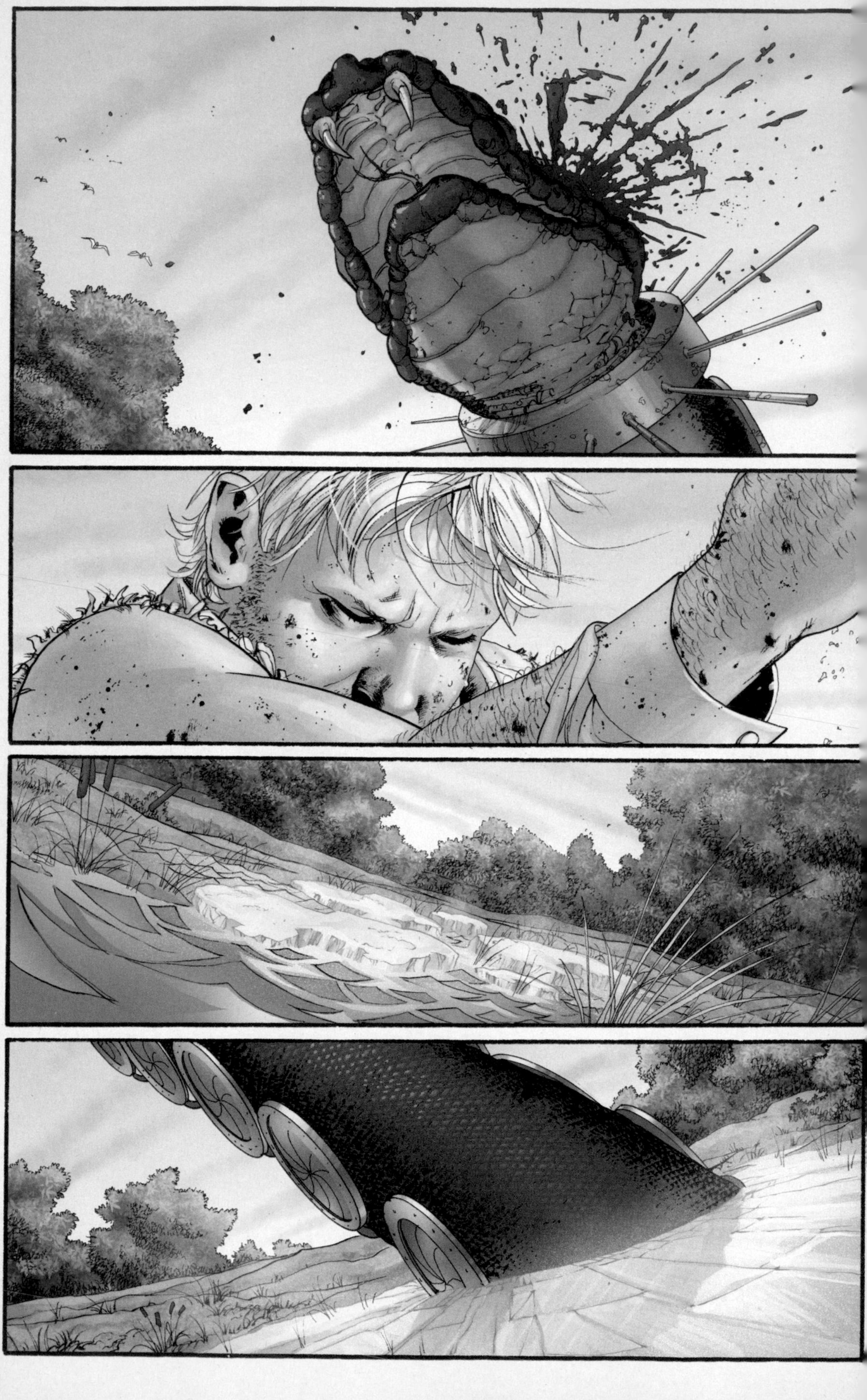

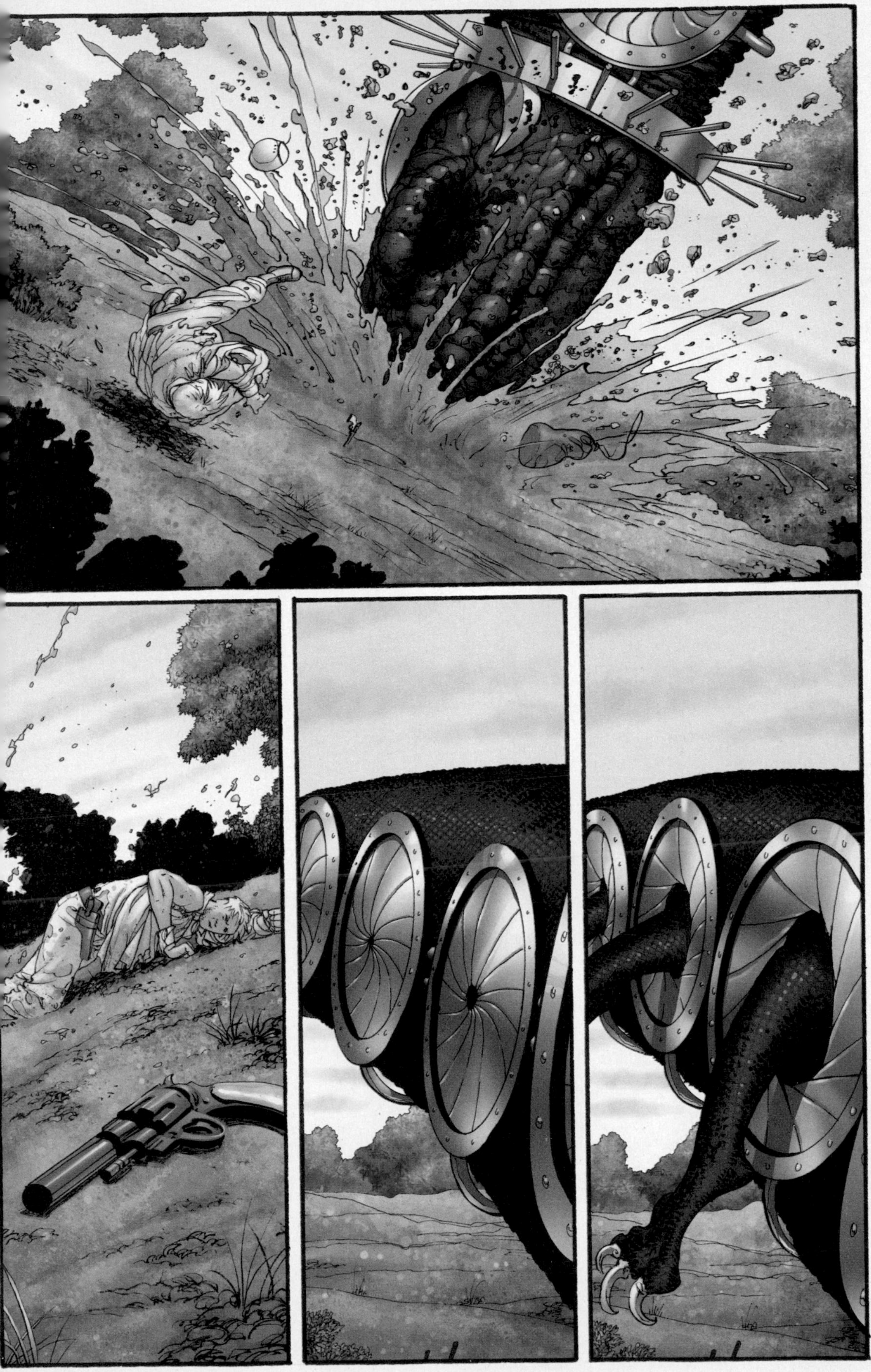

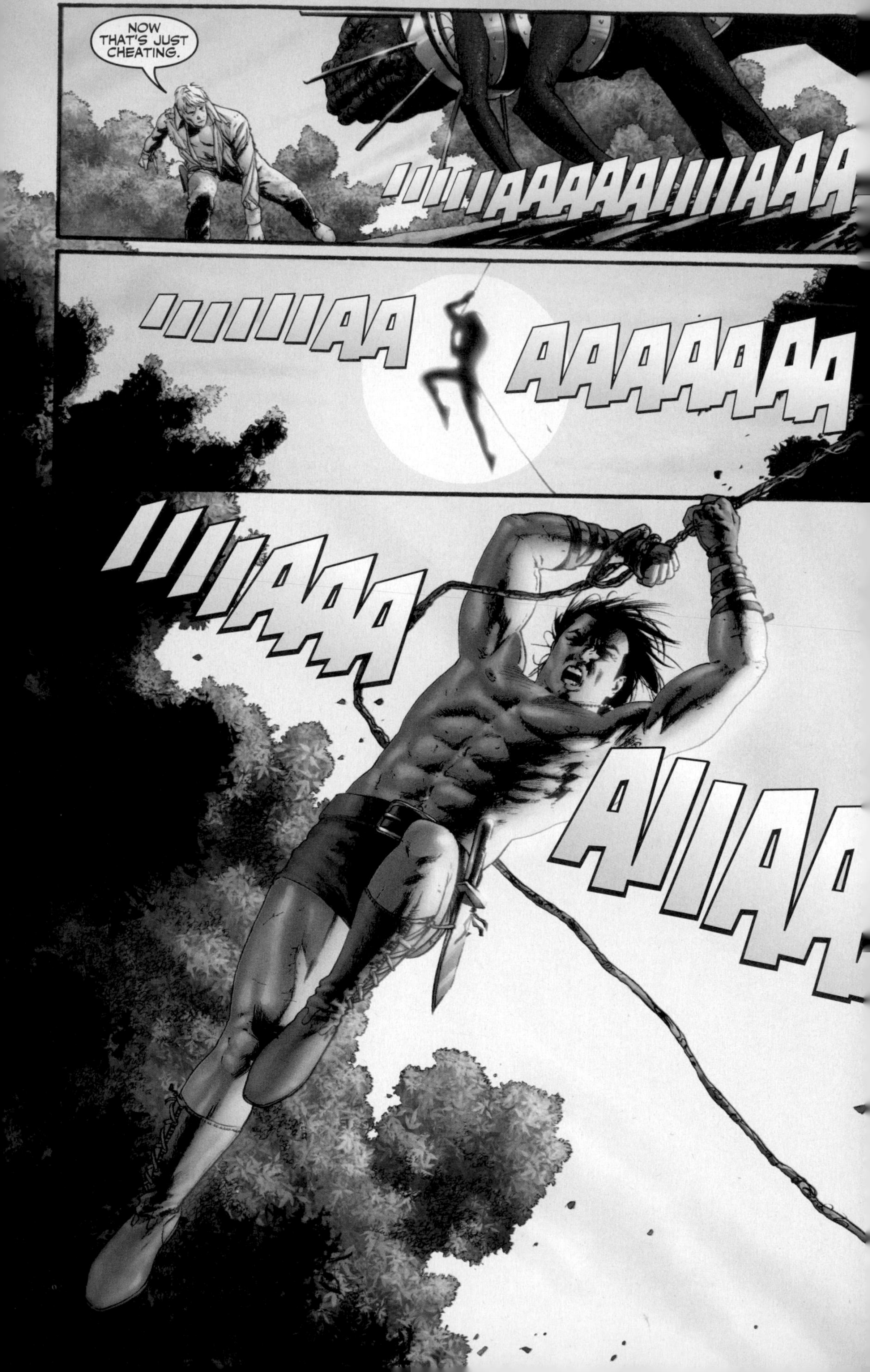
NOW THAT'S JUST CHEATING.
IIIIIAAAAAIIIIAAA
IIIIIIIAA
AAAAAAA
IIIIAAA
AIIAA

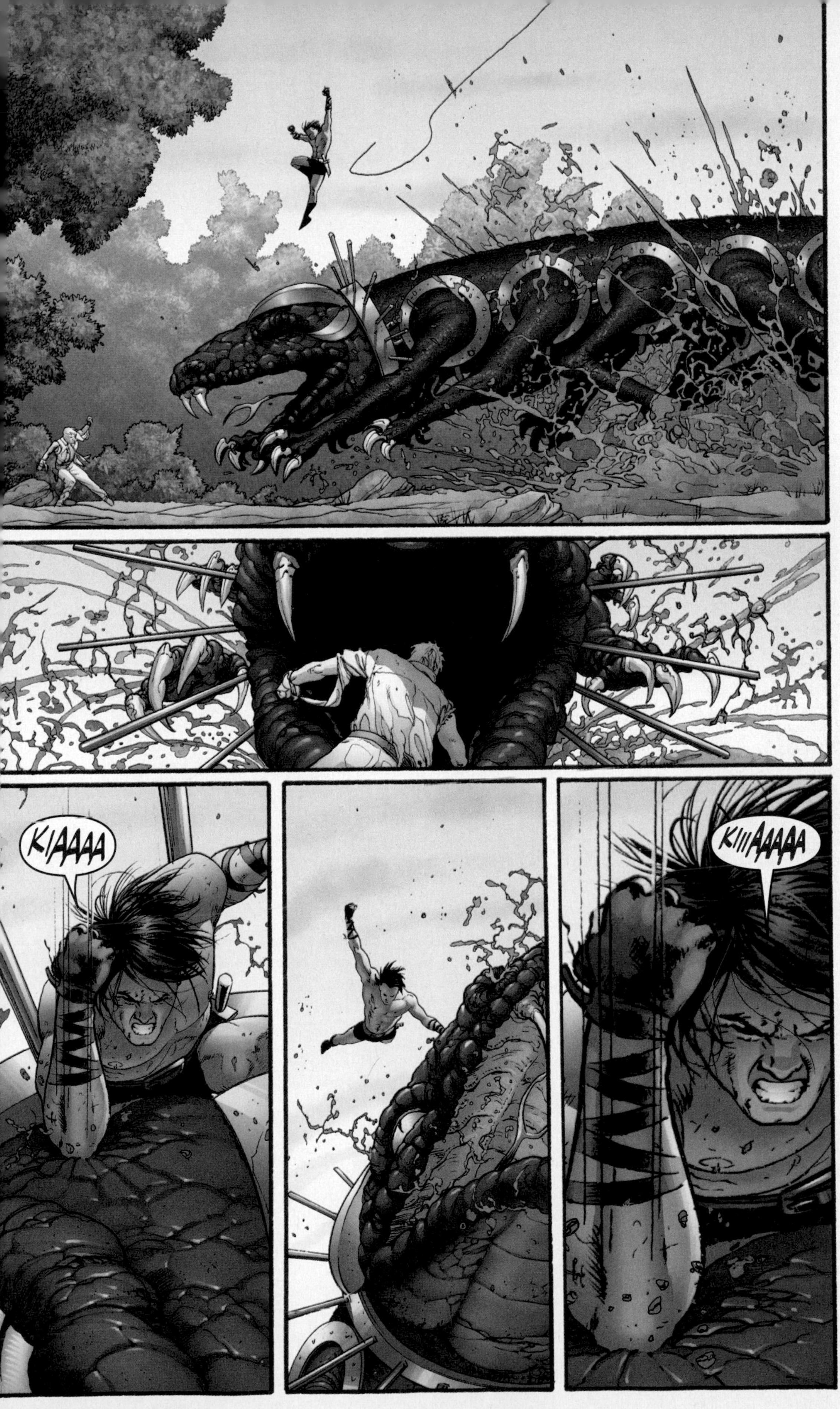
KIAAAA
KIIIAAAAA

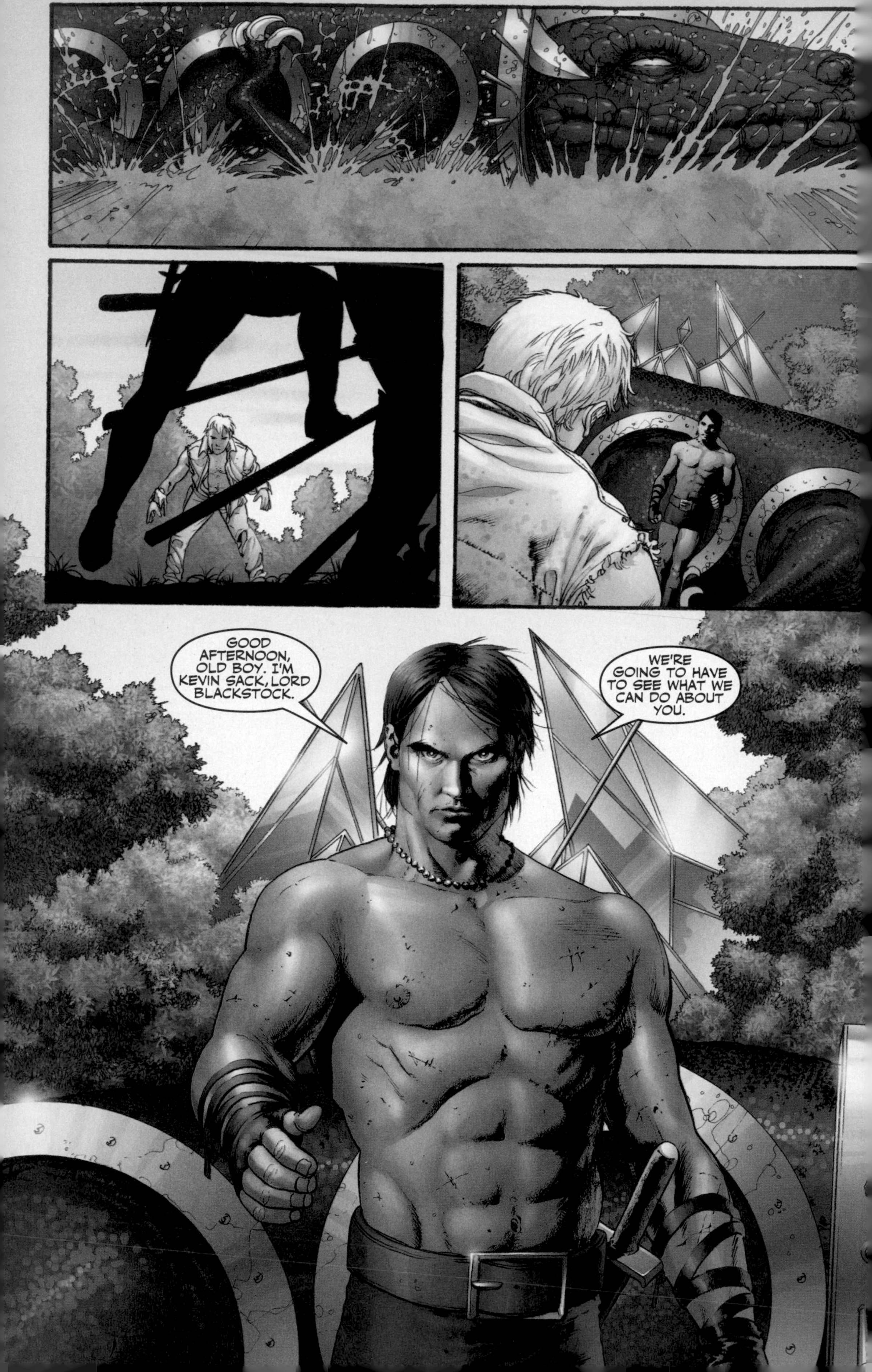
GOOD AFTERNOON, OLD BOY. I'M KEVIN SACK, LORD BLACKSTOCK.
WE'RE GOING TO HAVE TO SEE WHAT WE CAN DO ABOUT YOU.

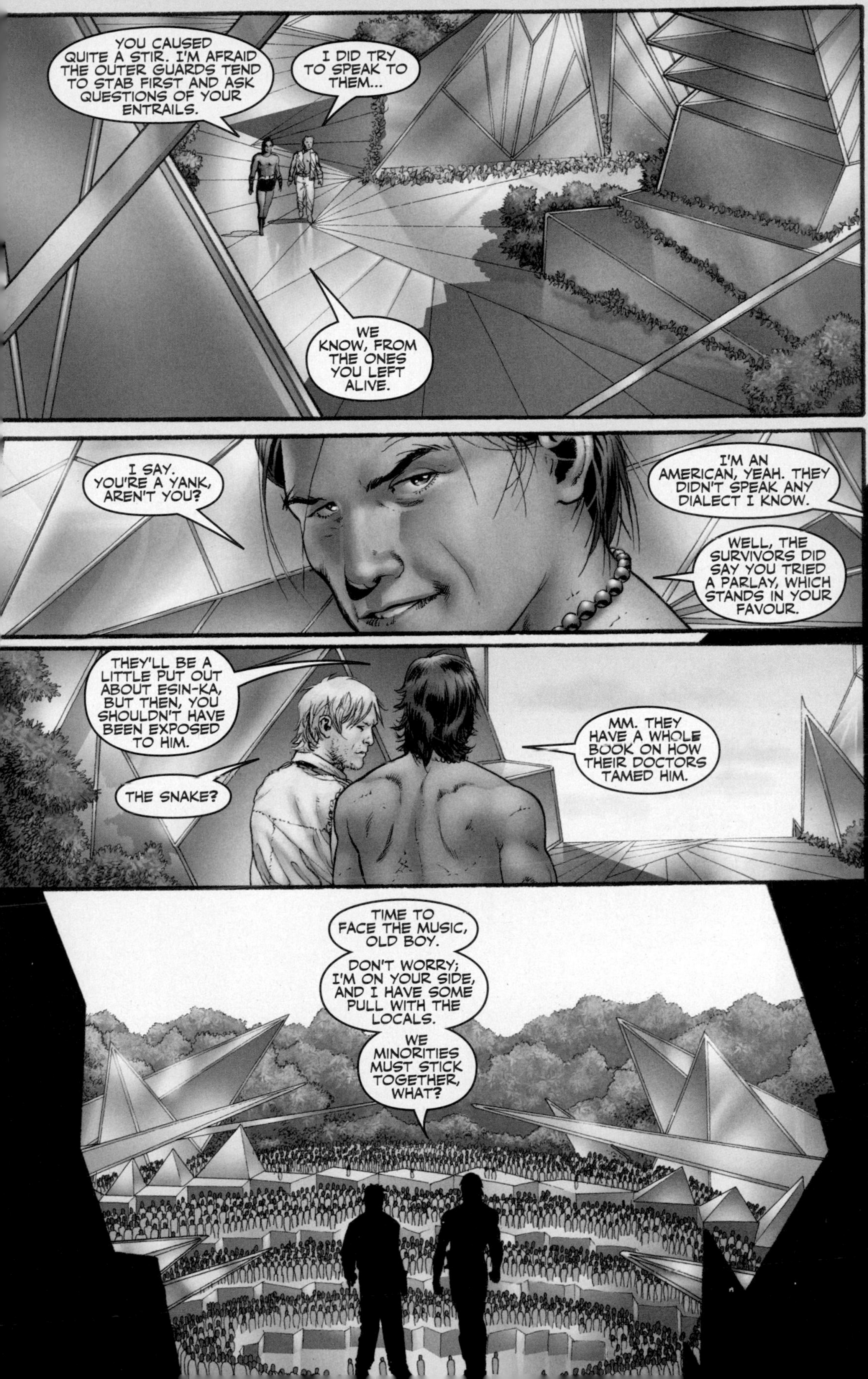
YOU CAUSED QUITE A STIR. I'M AFRAID THE OUTER GUARDS TEND TO STAB FIRST AND ASK QUESTIONS OF YOUR ENTRAILS.
I DID TRY TO SPEAK TO THEM...
WE KNOW, FROM THE ONES YOU LEFT ALIVE.
I SAY. YOU'RE A YANK, AREN'T YOU?
I'M AN AMERICAN, YEAH. THEY DIDN'T SPEAK ANY DIALECT I KNOW.
WELL, THE SURVIVORS DID SAY YOU TRIED A PARLAY, WHICH STANDS IN YOUR FAVOUR.
THEY'LL BE A LITTLE PUT OUT ABOUT ESIN-KA, BUT THEN, YOU SHOULDN'T HAVE BEEN EXPOSED TO HIM.
THE SNAKE?
MM. THEY HAVE A WHOLE BOOK ON HOW THEIR DOCTORS TAMED HIM.
TIME TO FACE THE MUSIC, OLD BOY.
DON'T WORRY; I'M ON YOUR SIDE, AND I HAVE SOME PULL WITH THE LOCALS.
WE MINORITIES MUST STICK TOGETHER, WHAT?

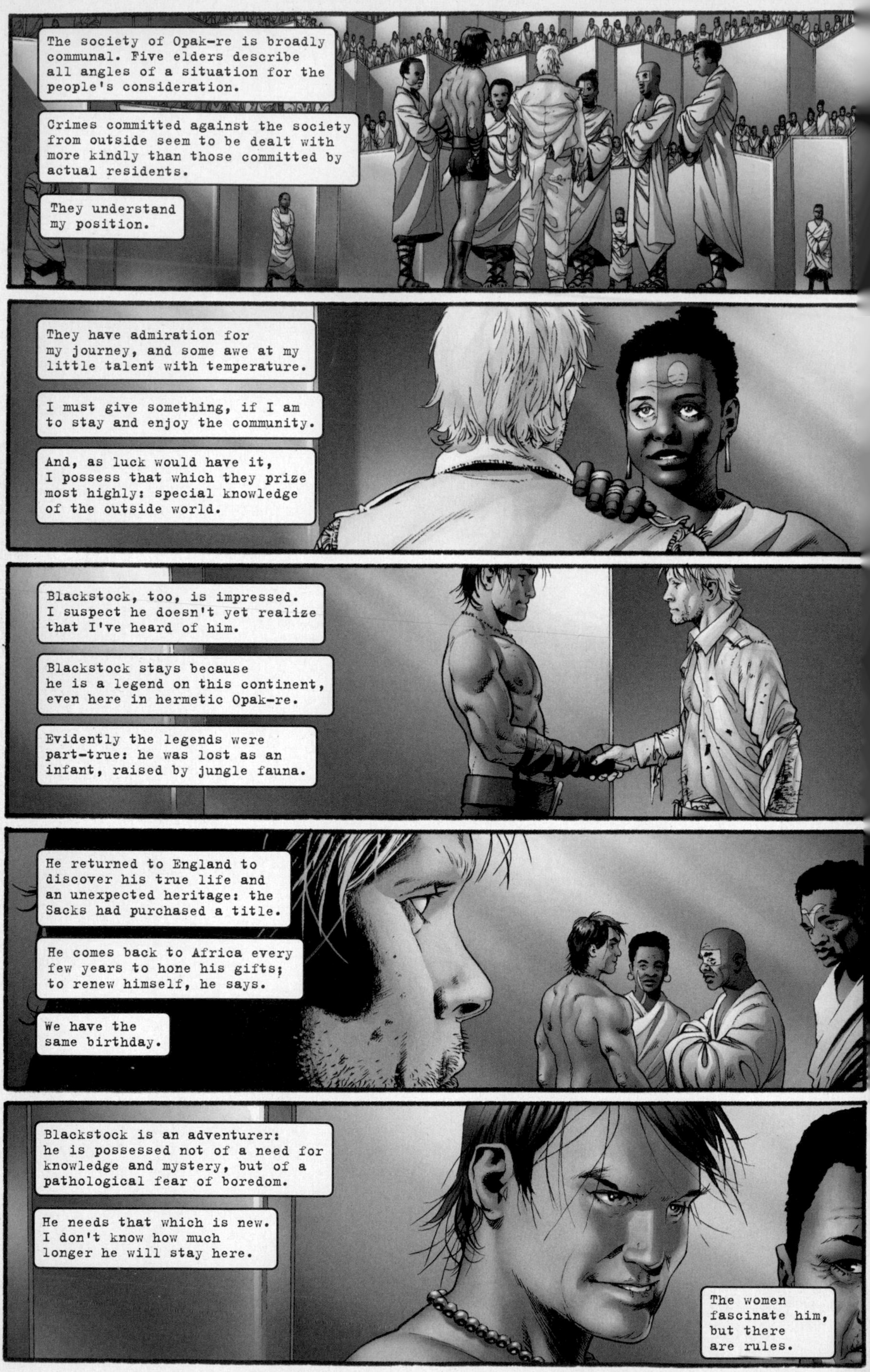
The society of Opak-re is broadly communal. Five elders describe all angles of a situation for the people's consideration.
Crimes committed against the society from outside seem to be dealt with more kindly than those committed by actual residents.
They understand my position.
They have admiration for my journey, and some awe at my little talent with temperature.
I must give something, if I am to stay and enjoy the community.
And, as luck would have it, I possess that which they prize most highly: special knowledge of the outside world.
Blackstock, too, is impressed. I suspect he doesn't yet realize that I've heard of him.
Blackstock stays because he is a legend on this continent, even here in hermetic Opak-re.
Evidently the legends were part-true: he was lost as an infant, raised by jungle fauna.
He returned to England to discover his true life and an unexpected heritage: the Sacks had purchased a title.
He comes back to Africa every few years to hone his gifts; to renew himself, he says.
We have the same birthday.
Blackstock is an adventurer: he is possessed not of a need for knowledge and mystery, but of a pathological fear of boredom.
He needs that which is new. I don't know how much longer he will stay here.
The women fascinate him, but there are rules.

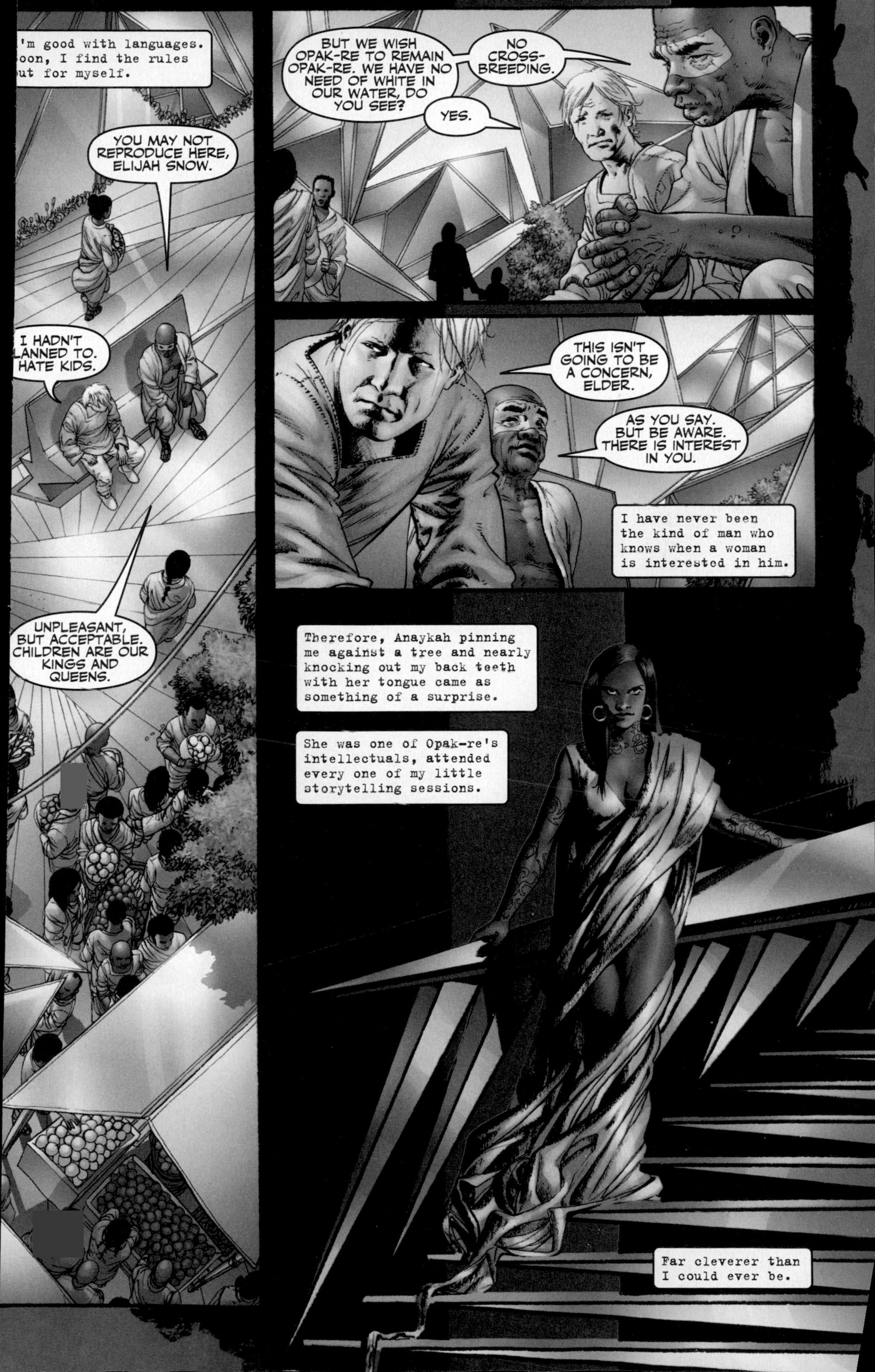
'm good with languages. oon, I find the rules ut for myself.
YOU MAY NOT REPRODUCE HERE, ELIJAH SNOW.
I HADN'T LANNED TO. HATE KIDS.
UNPLEASANT, BUT ACCEPTABLE. CHILDREN ARE OUR KINGS AND QUEENS.
BUT WE WISH OPAK-RE TO REMAIN OPAK-RE. WE HAVE NO NEED OF WHITE IN OUR WATER, DO YOU SEE?
NO CROSS-BREEDING.
YES.
THIS ISN'T GOING TO BE A CONCERN, ELDER.
AS YOU SAY. BUT BE AWARE. THERE IS INTEREST IN YOU.
I have never been the kind of man who knows when a woman is interested in him.
Therefore, Anaykah pinning me against a tree and nearly knocking out my back teeth with her tongue came as something of a surprise.
She was one of Opak-re's intellectuals, attended every one of my little storytelling sessions.
Far cleverer than I could ever be.

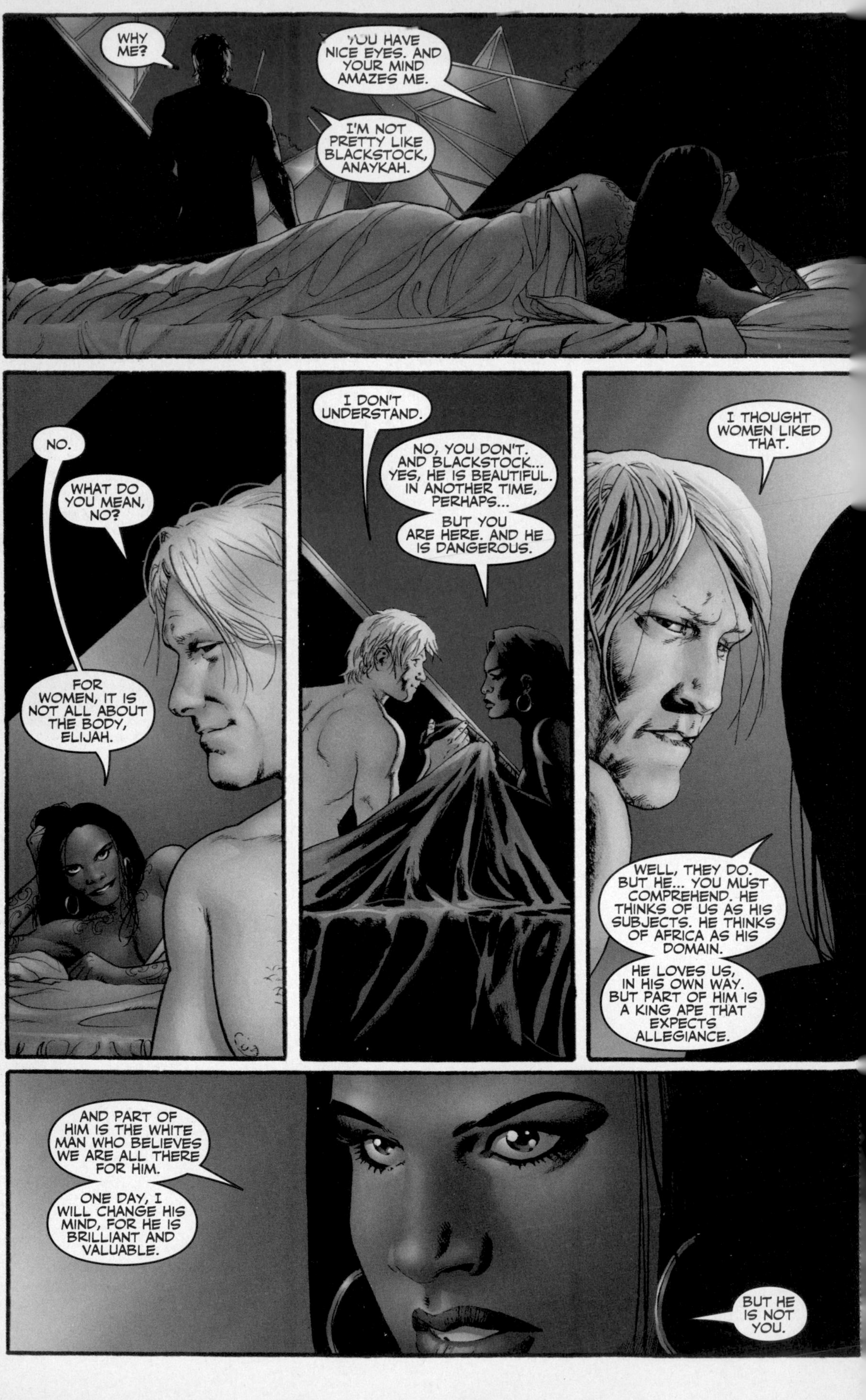
WHY ME?
YOU HAVE NICE EYES. AND YOUR MIND AMAZES ME.
I'M NOT PRETTY LIKE BLACKSTOCK, ANAYKAH.
NO.
WHAT DO YOU MEAN, NO?
FOR WOMEN, IT IS NOT ALL ABOUT THE BODY, ELIJAH.
I DON'T UNDERSTAND.
NO, YOU DON'T. AND BLACKSTOCK... YES, HE IS BEAUTIFUL. IN ANOTHER TIME, PERHAPS...
BUT YOU ARE HERE. AND HE IS DANGEROUS.
I THOUGHT WOMEN LIKED THAT.
WELL, THEY DO. BUT HE... YOU MUST COMPREHEND. HE THINKS OF US AS HIS SUBJECTS. HE THINKS OF AFRICA AS HIS DOMAIN.
HE LOVES US, IN HIS OWN WAY. BUT PART OF HIM IS A KING APE THAT EXPECTS ALLEGIANCE.
AND PART OF HIM IS THE WHITE MAN WHO BELIEVES WE ARE ALL THERE FOR HIM.
ONE DAY, I WILL CHANGE HIS MIND, FOR HE IS BRILLIANT AND VALUABLE.
BUT HE IS NOT YOU.

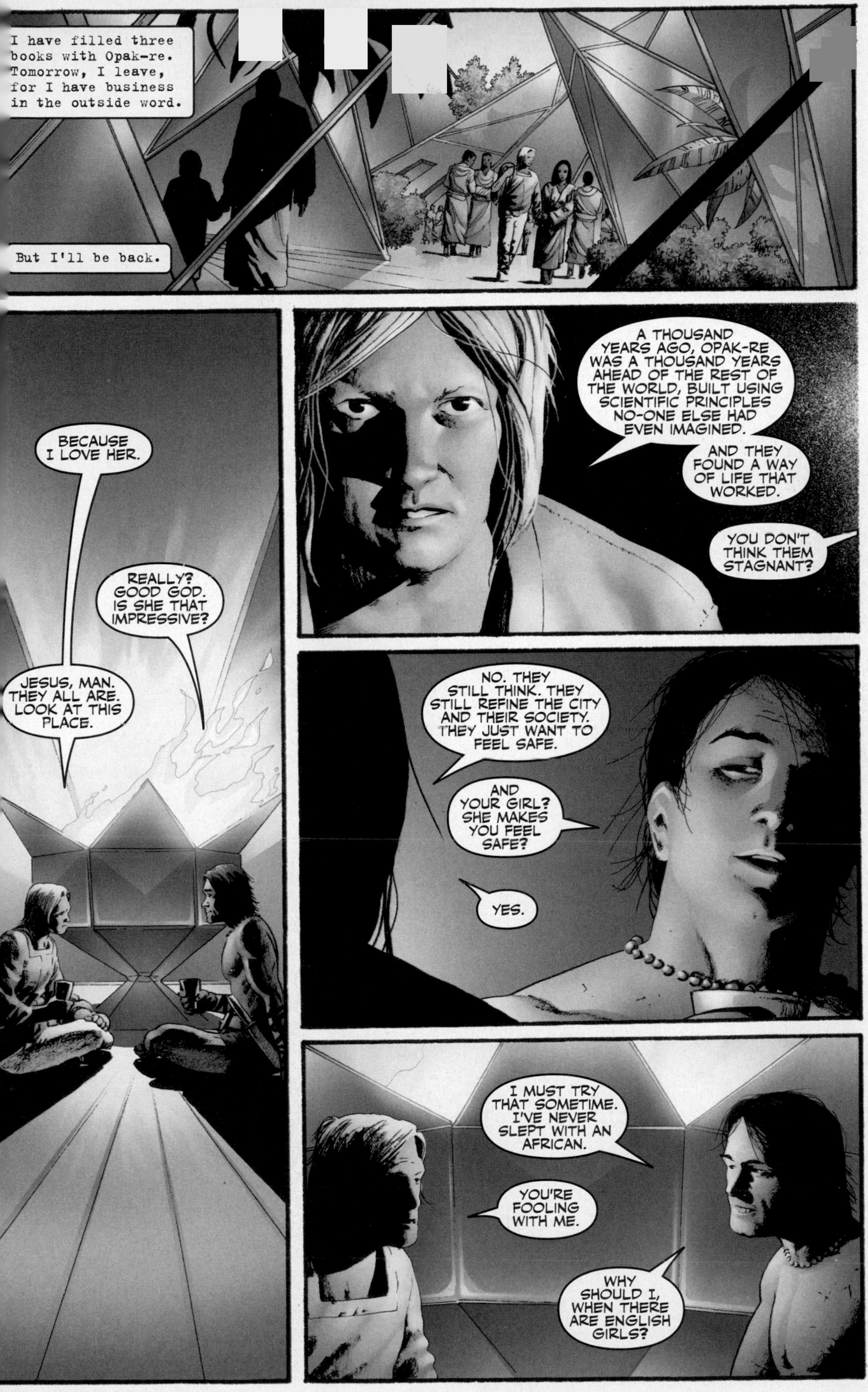

I have filled three books with Opak-re. Tomorrow, I leave, for I have business in the outside word.
But I'll be back.
A THOUSAND YEARS AGO, OPAK-RE WAS A THOUSAND YEARS AHEAD OF THE REST OF THE WORLD, BUILT USING SCIENTIFIC PRINCIPLES NO-ONE ELSE HAD EVEN IMAGINED.
AND THEY FOUND A WAY OF LIFE THAT WORKED.
YOU DON'T THINK THEM STAGNANT?
NO. THEY STILL THINK. THEY STILL REFINE THE CITY AND THEIR SOCIETY. THEY JUST WANT TO FEEL SAFE.
AND YOUR GIRL? SHE MAKES YOU FEEL SAFE?
YES.
BECAUSE I LOVE HER.
REALLY? GOOD GOD. IS SHE THAT IMPRESSIVE?
JESUS, MAN. THEY ALL ARE. LOOK AT THIS PLACE.
I MUST TRY THAT SOMETIME. I'VE NEVER SLEPT WITH AN AFRICAN.
YOU'RE FOOLING WITH ME.
WHY SHOULD I, WHEN THERE ARE ENGLISH GIRLS?

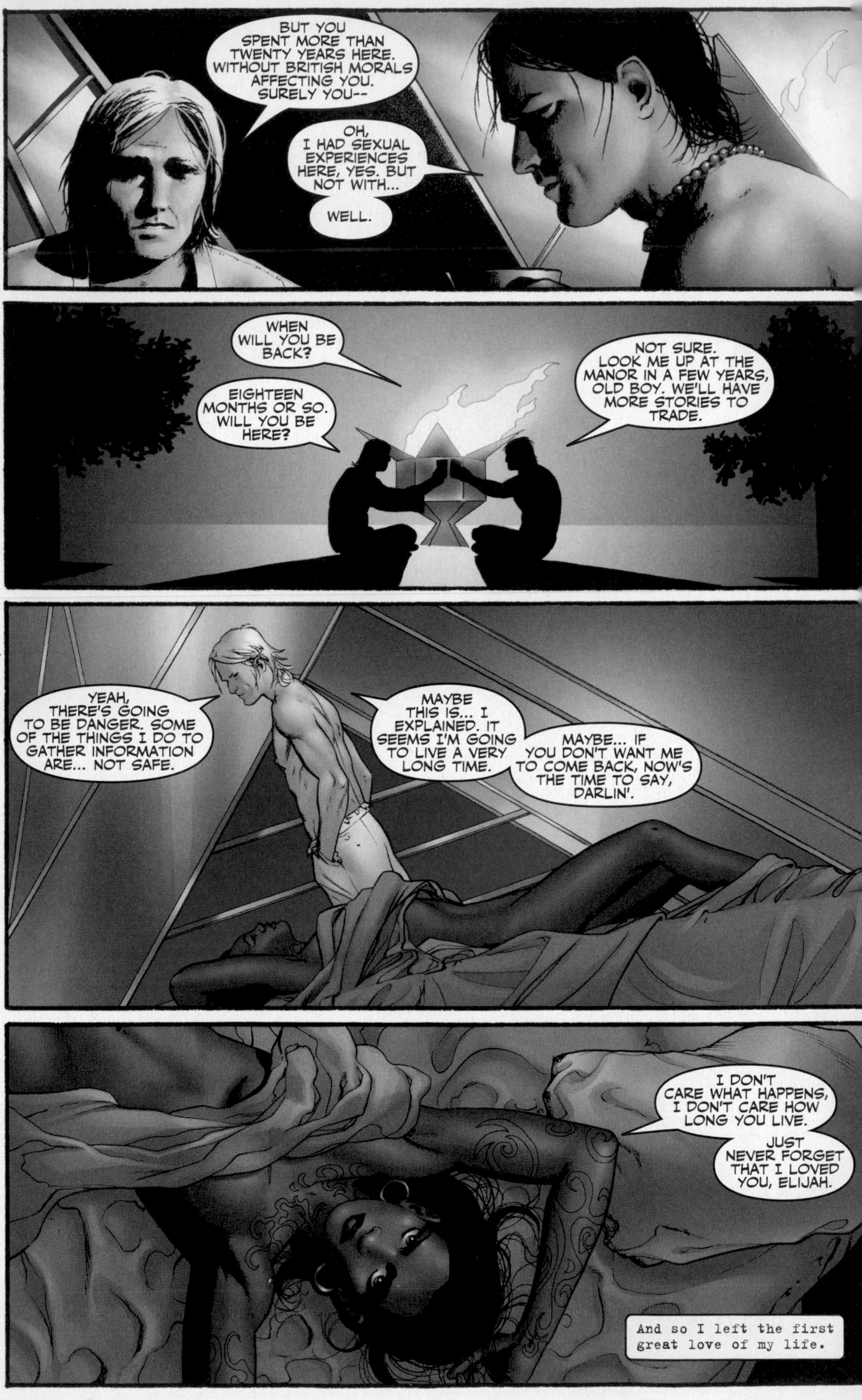
BUT YOU SPENT MORE THAN TWENTY YEARS HERE. WITHOUT BRITISH MORALS AFFECTING YOU. SURELY YOU--
OH, I HAD SEXUAL EXPERIENCES HERE, YES. BUT NOT WITH...
WELL.
WHEN WILL YOU BE BACK?
EIGHTEEN MONTHS OR SO. WILL YOU BE HERE?
NOT SURE. LOOK ME UP AT THE MANOR IN A FEW YEARS, OLD BOY. WE'LL HAVE MORE STORIES TO TRADE.
YEAH, THERE'S GOING TO BE DANGER. SOME OF THE THINGS I DO TO GATHER INFORMATION ARE... NOT SAFE.
MAYBE THIS IS... I EXPLAINED. IT SEEMS I'M GOING TO LIVE A VERY LONG TIME.
MAYBE... IF YOU DON'T WANT ME TO COME BACK, NOW'S THE TIME TO SAY, DARLIN'.
I DON'T CARE WHAT HAPPENS, I DON'T CARE HOW LONG YOU LIVE.
JUST NEVER FORGET THAT I LOVED YOU, ELIJAH.
And so I left the first great love of my life.

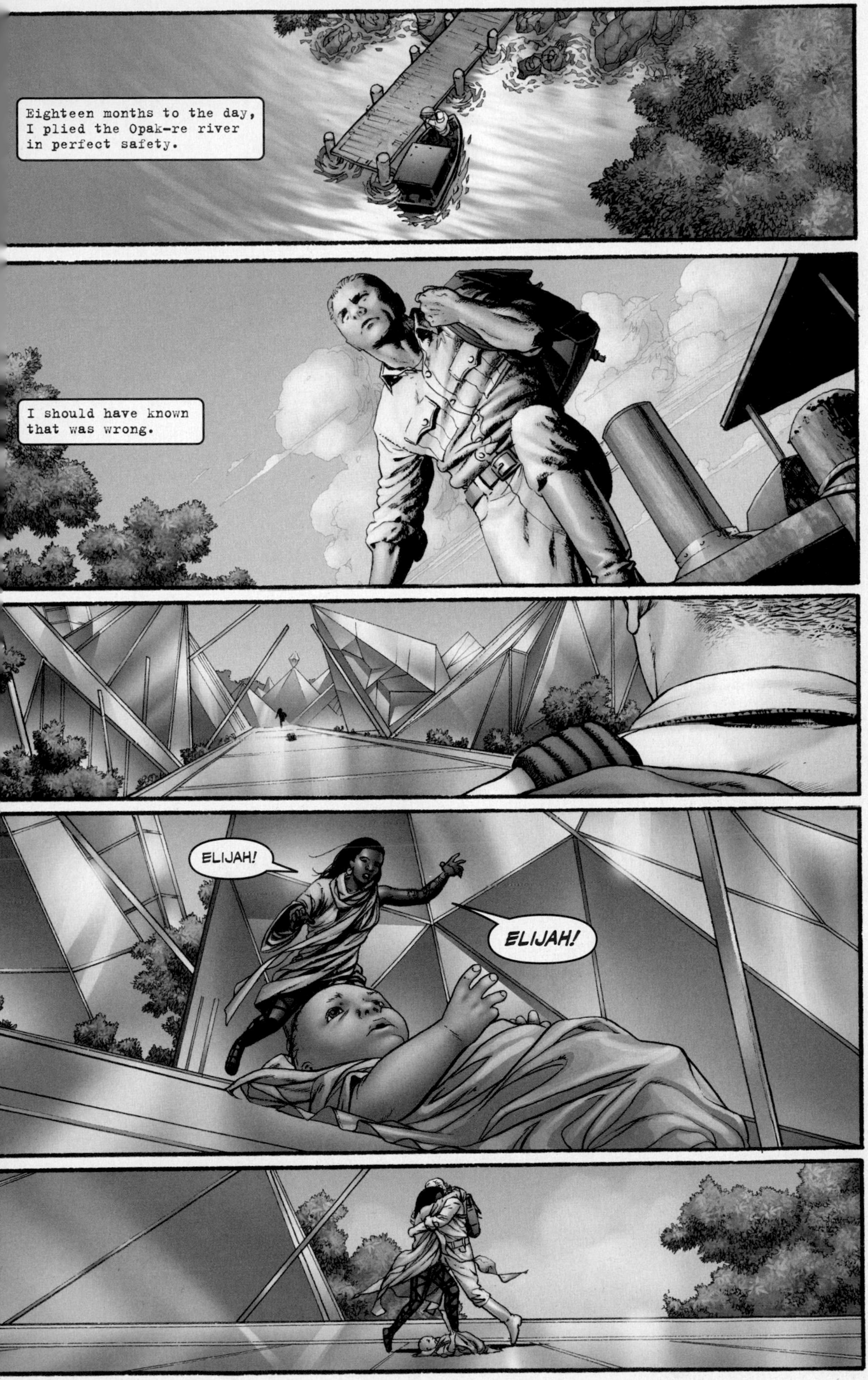
Eighteen months to the day, I plied the Opak-re river in perfect safety.
I should have known that was wrong.
ELIJAH!
ELIJAH!

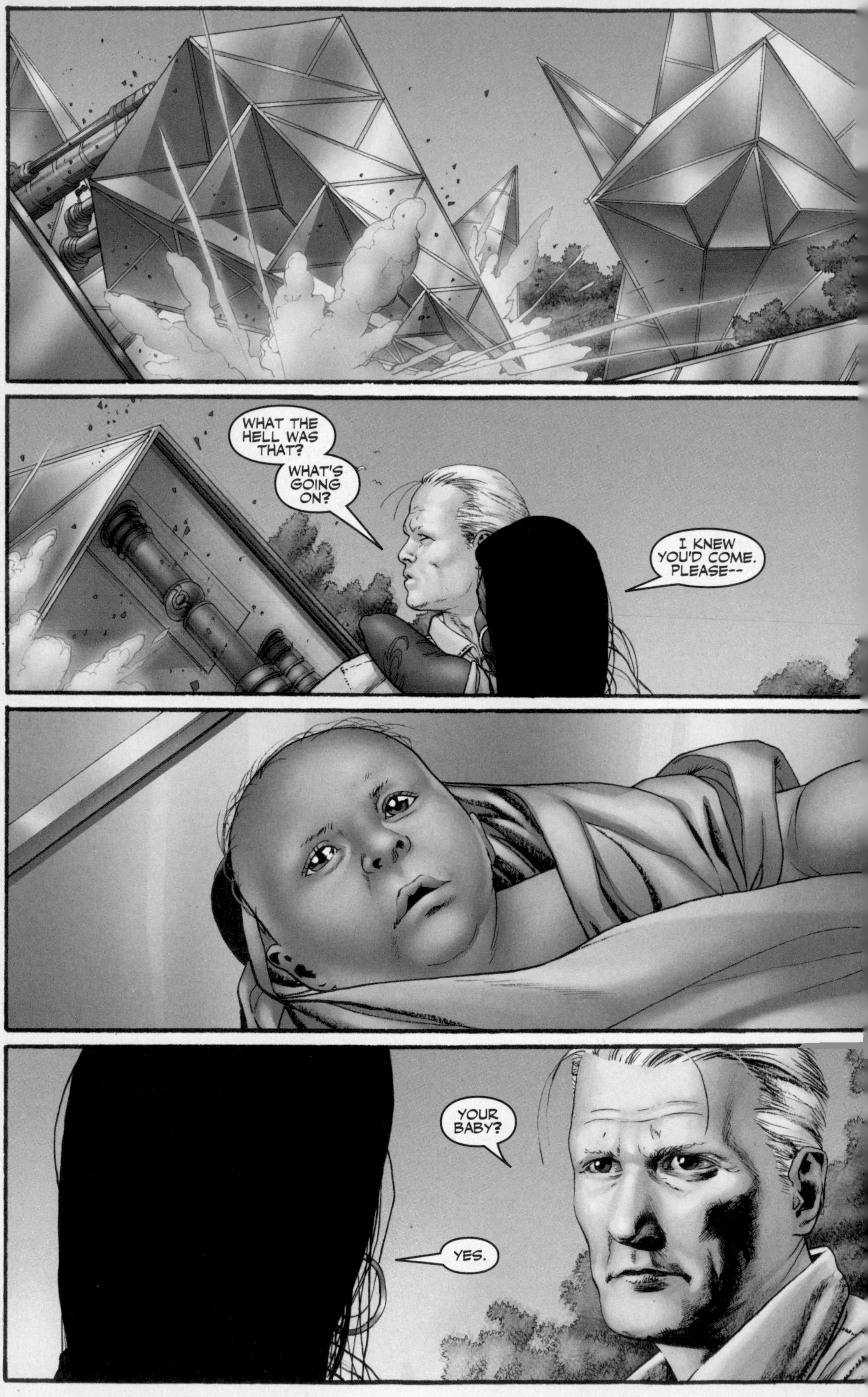
WHAT THE HELL WAS THAT?
WHAT'S GOING ON?
I KNEW YOU'D COME. PLEASE--
YOUR BABY?
YES.

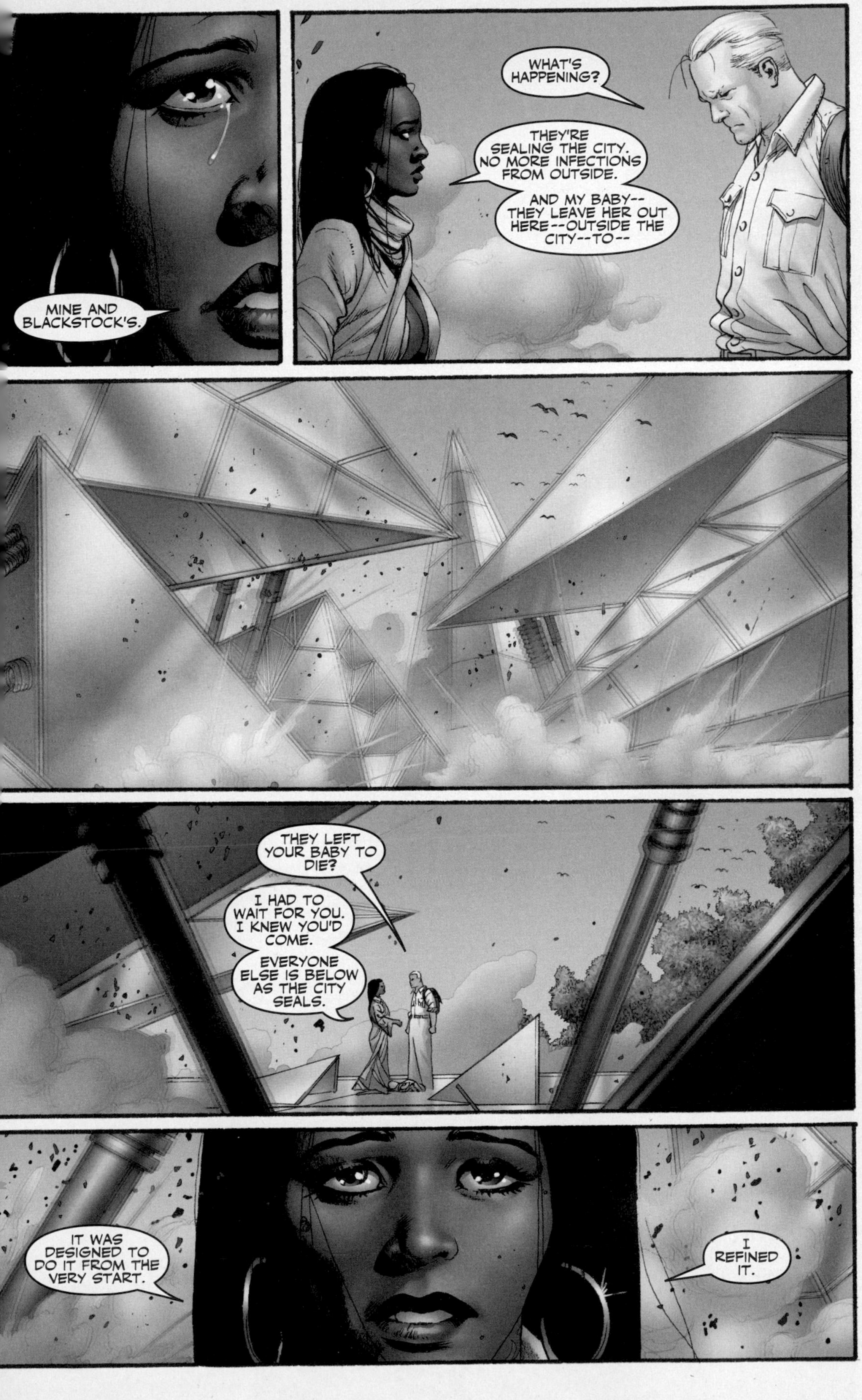
MINE AND BLACKSTOCK'S.
WHAT'S HAPPENING?
THEY'RE SEALING THE CITY. NO MORE INFECTIONS FROM OUTSIDE.
AND MY BABY-- THEY LEAVE HER OUT HERE--OUTSIDE THE CITY--TO--
THEY LEFT YOUR BABY TO DIE?
I HAD TO WAIT FOR YOU. I KNEW YOU'D COME.
EVERYONE ELSE IS BELOW AS THE CITY SEALS.
IT WAS DESIGNED TO DO IT FROM THE VERY START.
I REFINED IT.

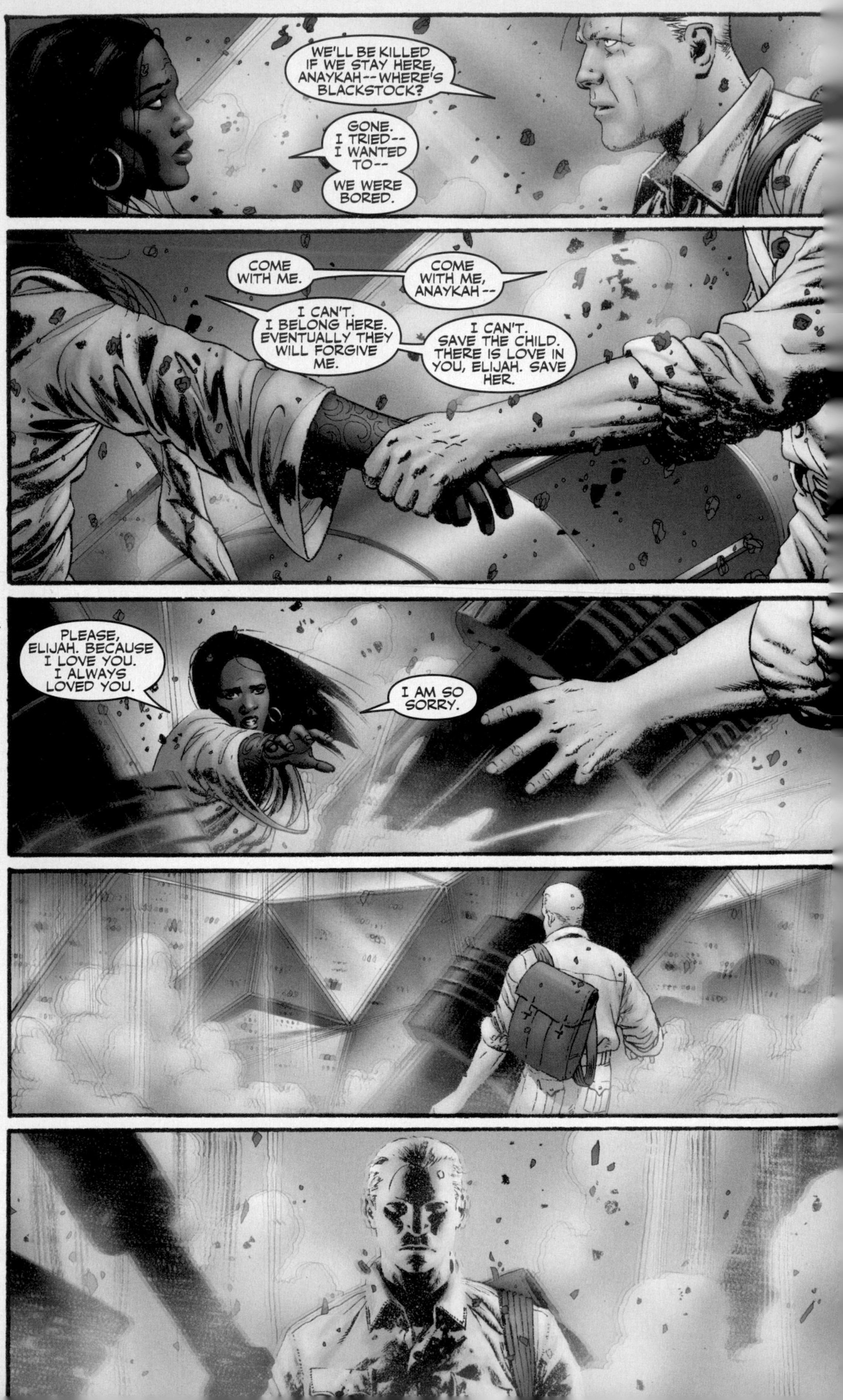
WE'LL BE KILLED IF WE STAY HERE, ANAYKAH--WHERE'S BLACKSTOCK?
GONE. I TRIED-- I WANTED TO--
WE WERE BORED.
COME WITH ME.
COME WITH ME, ANAYKAH--
I CAN'T. I BELONG HERE. EVENTUALLY THEY WILL FORGIVE ME.
I CAN'T. SAVE THE CHILD. THERE IS LOVE IN YOU, ELIJAH. SAVE HER.
PLEASE, ELIJAH. BECAUSE I LOVE YOU. I ALWAYS LOVED YOU.
I AM SO SORRY.

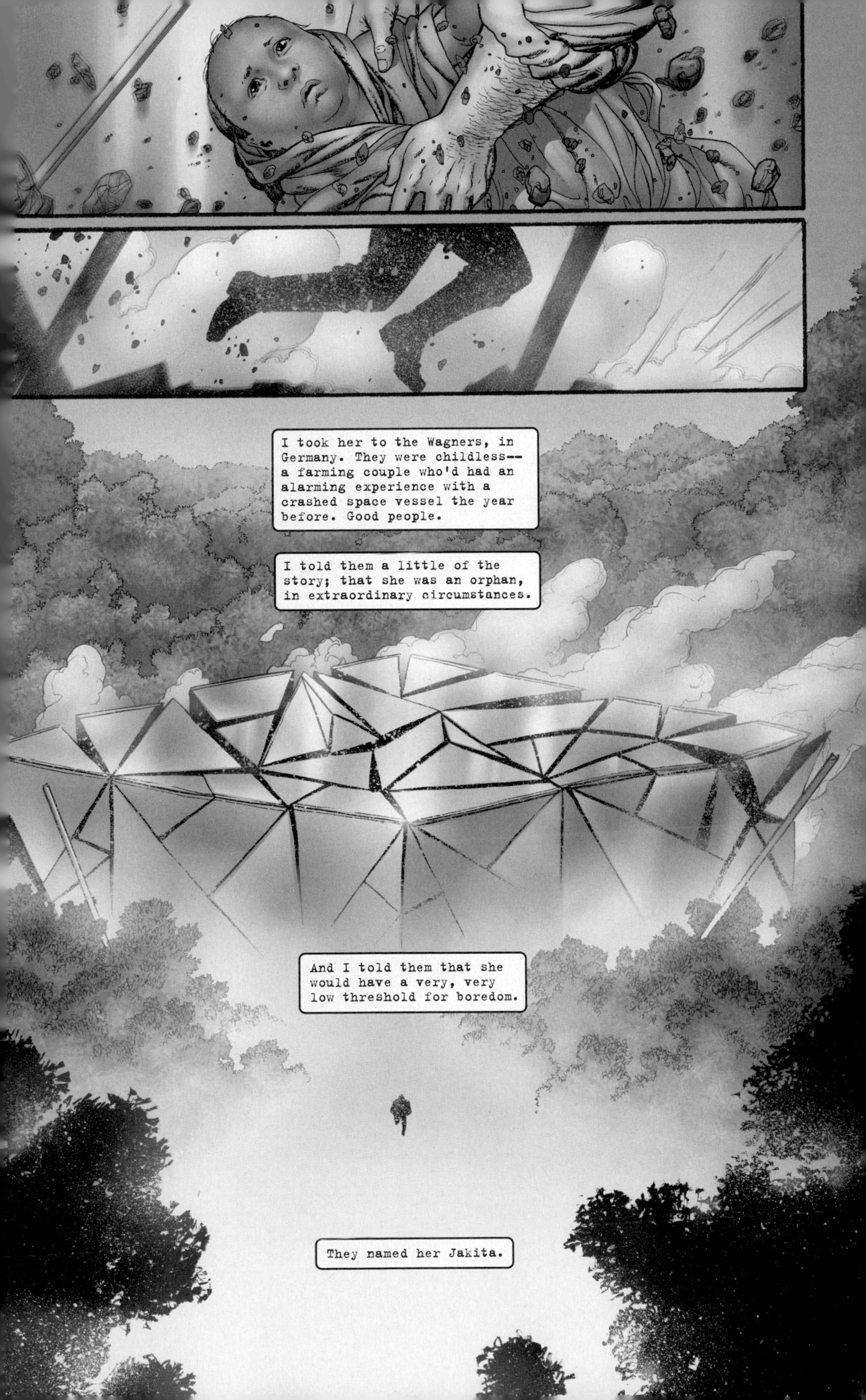
I took her to the Wagners, in Germany. They were childless-- a farming couple who'd had an alarming experience with a crashed space vessel the year before. Good people.
I told them a little of the story; that she was an orphan, in extraordinary circumstances.
And I told them that she would have a very, very low threshold for boredom.
They named her Jakita.

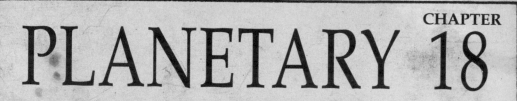

CHAPTER

PLANETARY 18

THE GUN CLUB

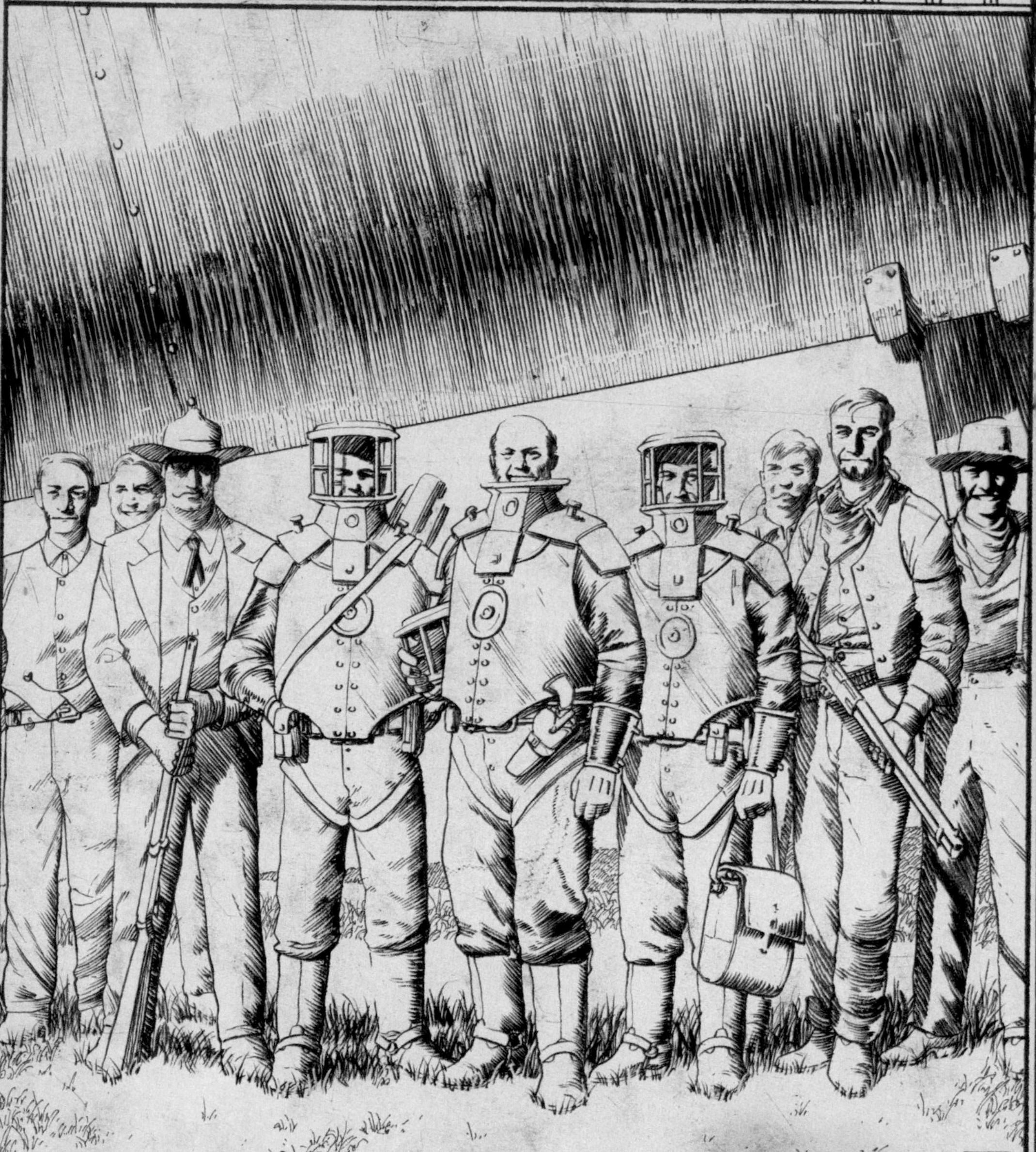

By W.G. Ellis and Johnny Mac Cassaday with Miss Laura J Martin

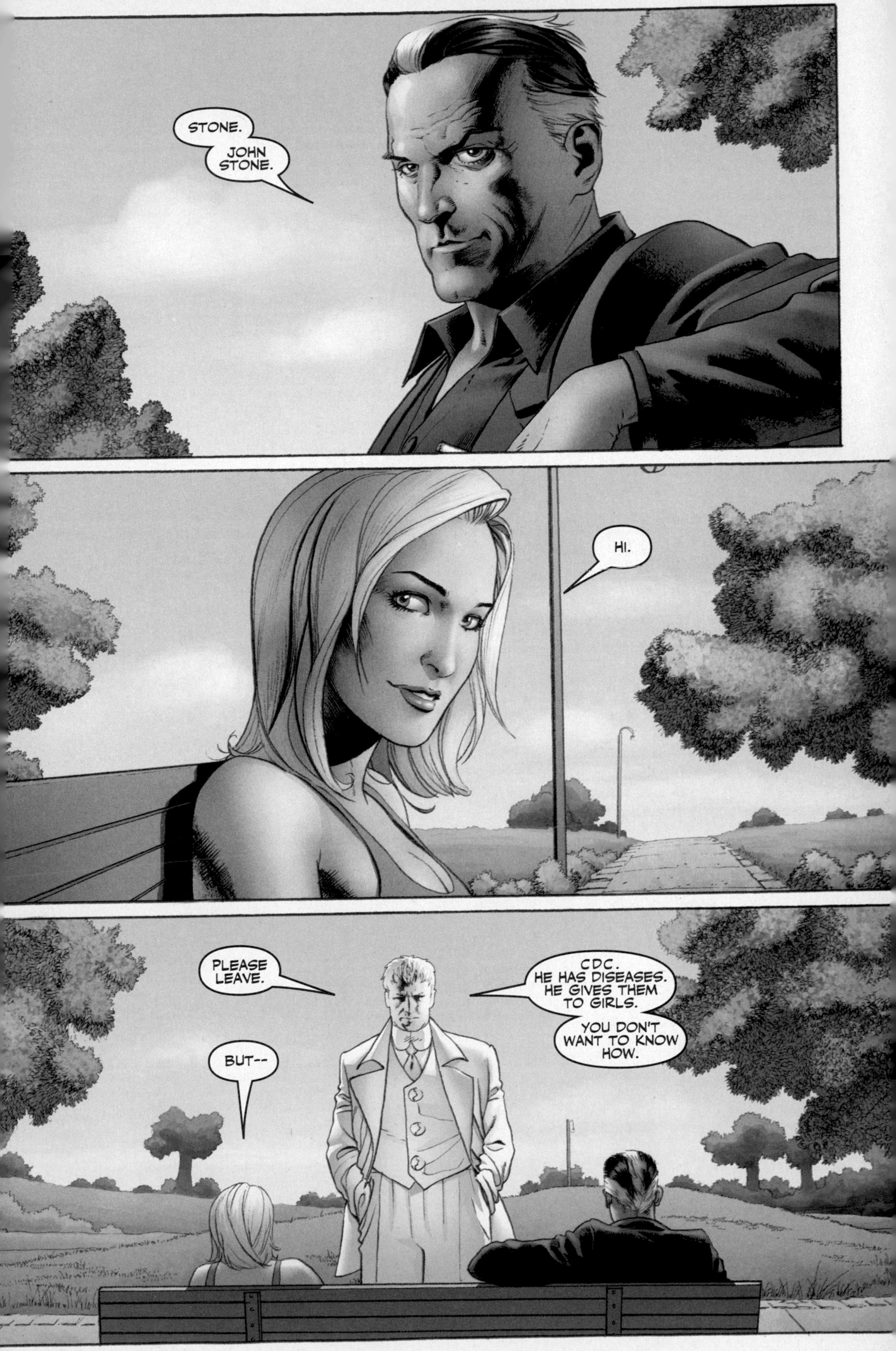
STONE.
JOHN STONE.
HI.
PLEASE LEAVE.
BUT--
CDC. HE HAS DISEASES. HE GIVES THEM TO GIRLS.
YOU DON'T WANT TO KNOW HOW.

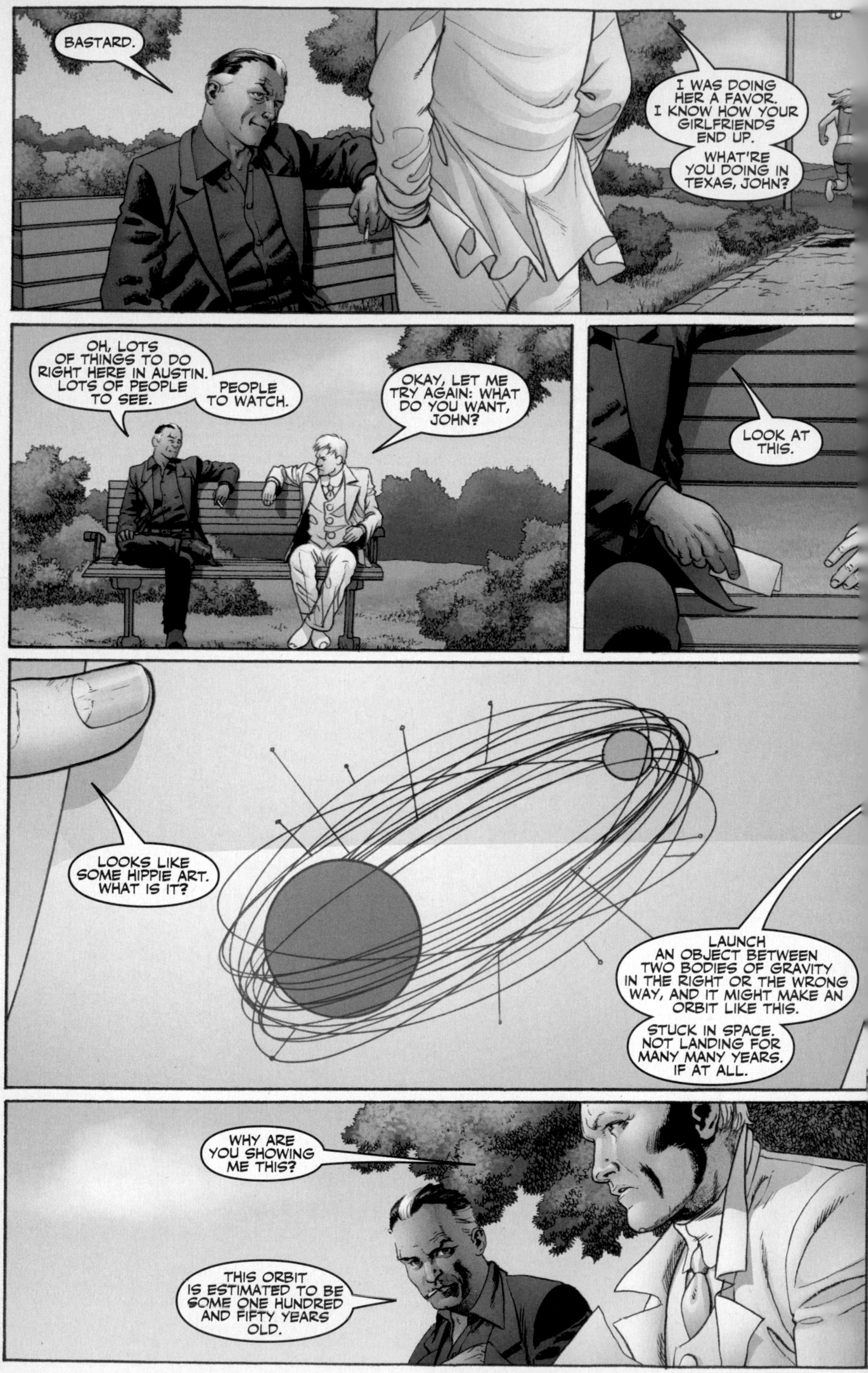
BASTARD.
I WAS DOING HER A FAVOR. I KNOW HOW YOUR GIRLFRIENDS END UP.
WHAT'RE YOU DOING IN TEXAS, JOHN?
OH, LOTS OF THINGS TO DO RIGHT HERE IN AUSTIN. LOTS OF PEOPLE TO SEE.
PEOPLE TO WATCH.
OKAY, LET ME TRY AGAIN: WHAT DO YOU WANT, JOHN?
LOOK AT THIS.
LOOKS LIKE SOME HIPPIE ART. WHAT IS IT?
LAUNCH AN OBJECT BETWEEN TWO BODIES OF GRAVITY IN THE RIGHT OR THE WRONG WAY, AND IT MIGHT MAKE AN ORBIT LIKE THIS.
STUCK IN SPACE. NOT LANDING FOR MANY MANY YEARS. IF AT ALL.
WHY ARE YOU SHOWING ME THIS?
THIS ORBIT IS ESTIMATED TO BE SOME ONE HUNDRED AND FIFTY YEARS OLD.

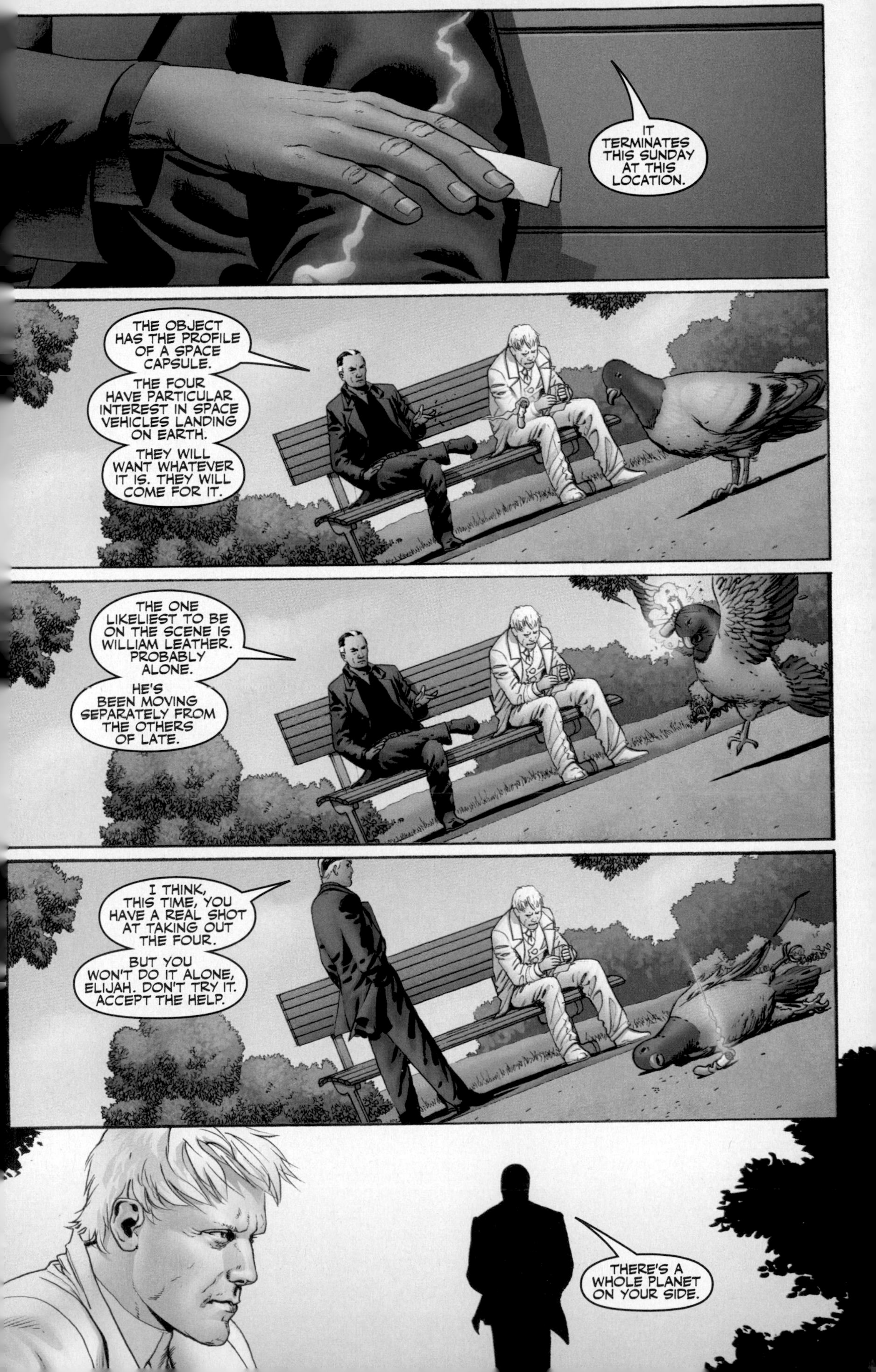
IT TERMINATES THIS SUNDAY AT THIS LOCATION.
THE OBJECT HAS THE PROFILE OF A SPACE CAPSULE.
THE FOUR HAVE PARTICULAR INTEREST IN SPACE VEHICLES LANDING ON EARTH.
THEY WILL WANT WHATEVER IT IS. THEY WILL COME FOR IT.
THE ONE LIKELIEST TO BE ON THE SCENE IS WILLIAM LEATHER. PROBABLY ALONE.
HE'S BEEN MOVING SEPARATELY FROM THE OTHERS OF LATE.
I THINK, THIS TIME, YOU HAVE A REAL SHOT AT TAKING OUT THE FOUR.
BUT YOU WON'T DO IT ALONE, ELIJAH. DON'T TRY IT. ACCEPT THE HELP.
THERE'S A WHOLE PLANET ON YOUR SIDE.

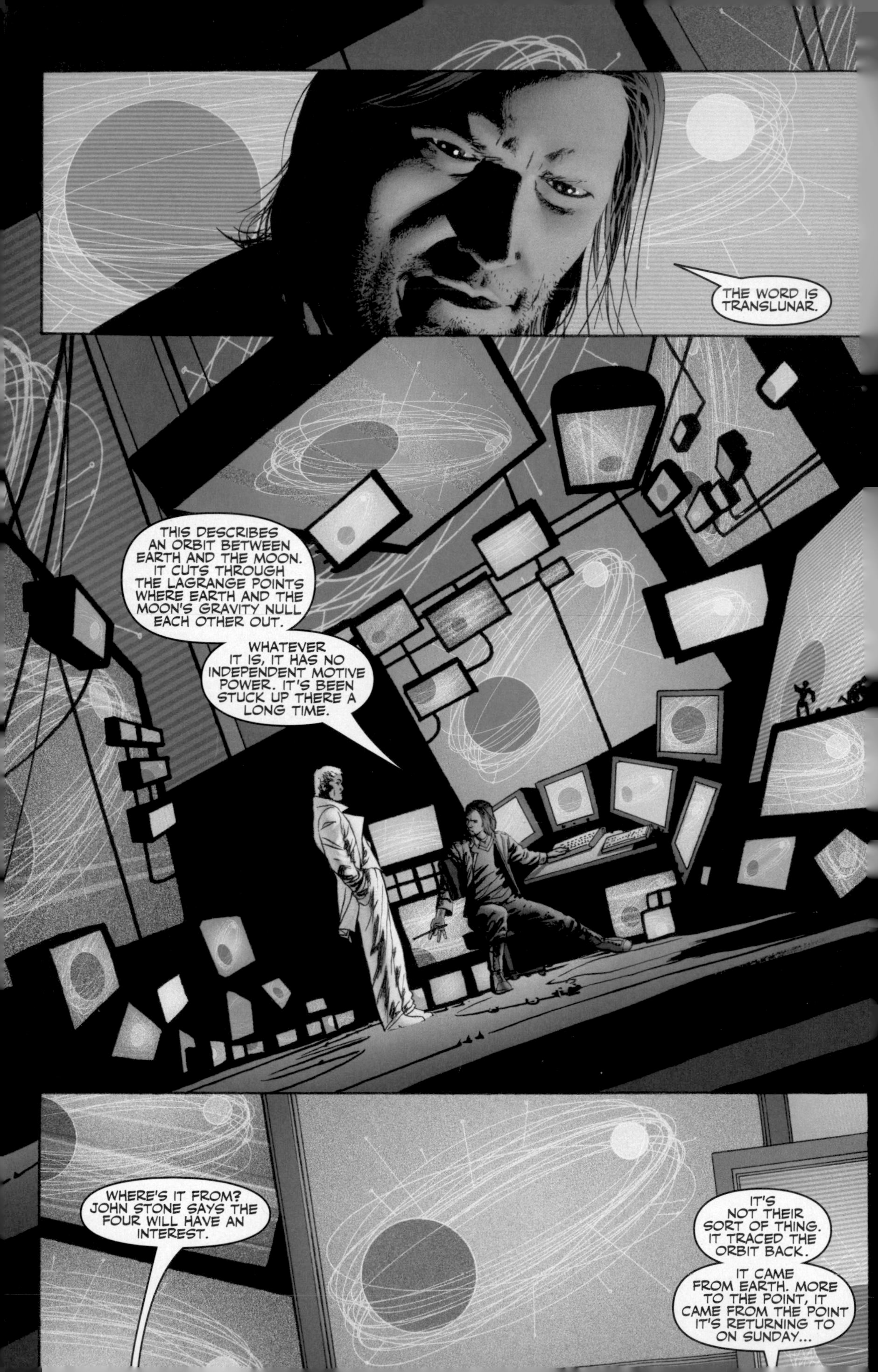
THE WORD IS TRANSLUNAR.
THIS DESCRIBES AN ORBIT BETWEEN EARTH AND THE MOON. IT CUTS THROUGH THE LAGRANGE POINTS WHERE EARTH AND THE MOON'S GRAVITY NULL EACH OTHER OUT.
WHATEVER IT IS, IT HAS NO INDEPENDENT MOTIVE POWER. IT'S BEEN STUCK UP THERE A LONG TIME.
WHERE'S IT FROM? JOHN STONE SAYS THE FOUR WILL HAVE AN INTEREST.
IT'S NOT THEIR SORT OF THING. IT TRACED THE ORBIT BACK.
IT CAME FROM EARTH. MORE TO THE POINT, IT CAME FROM THE POINT IT'S RETURNING TO ON SUNDAY...

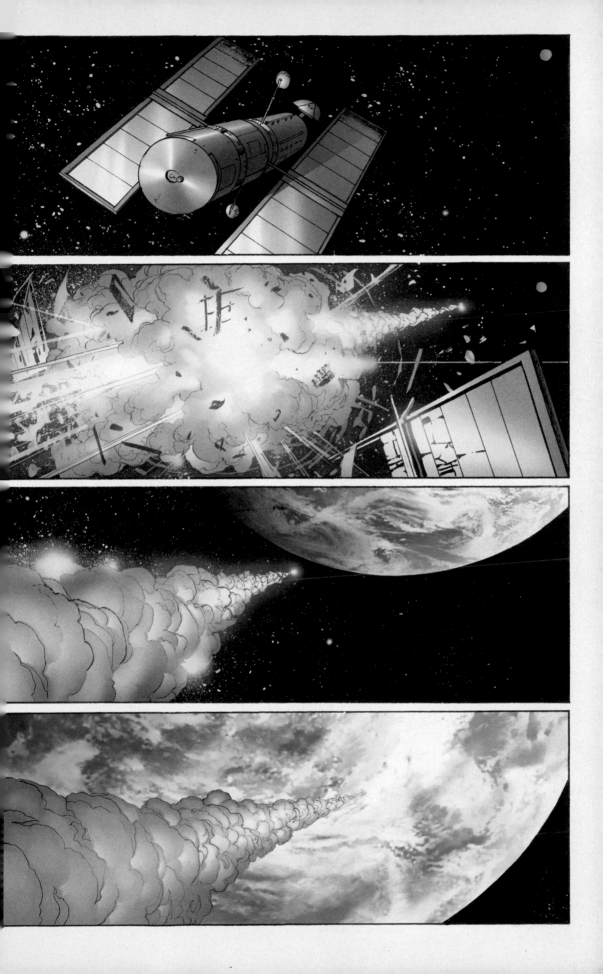

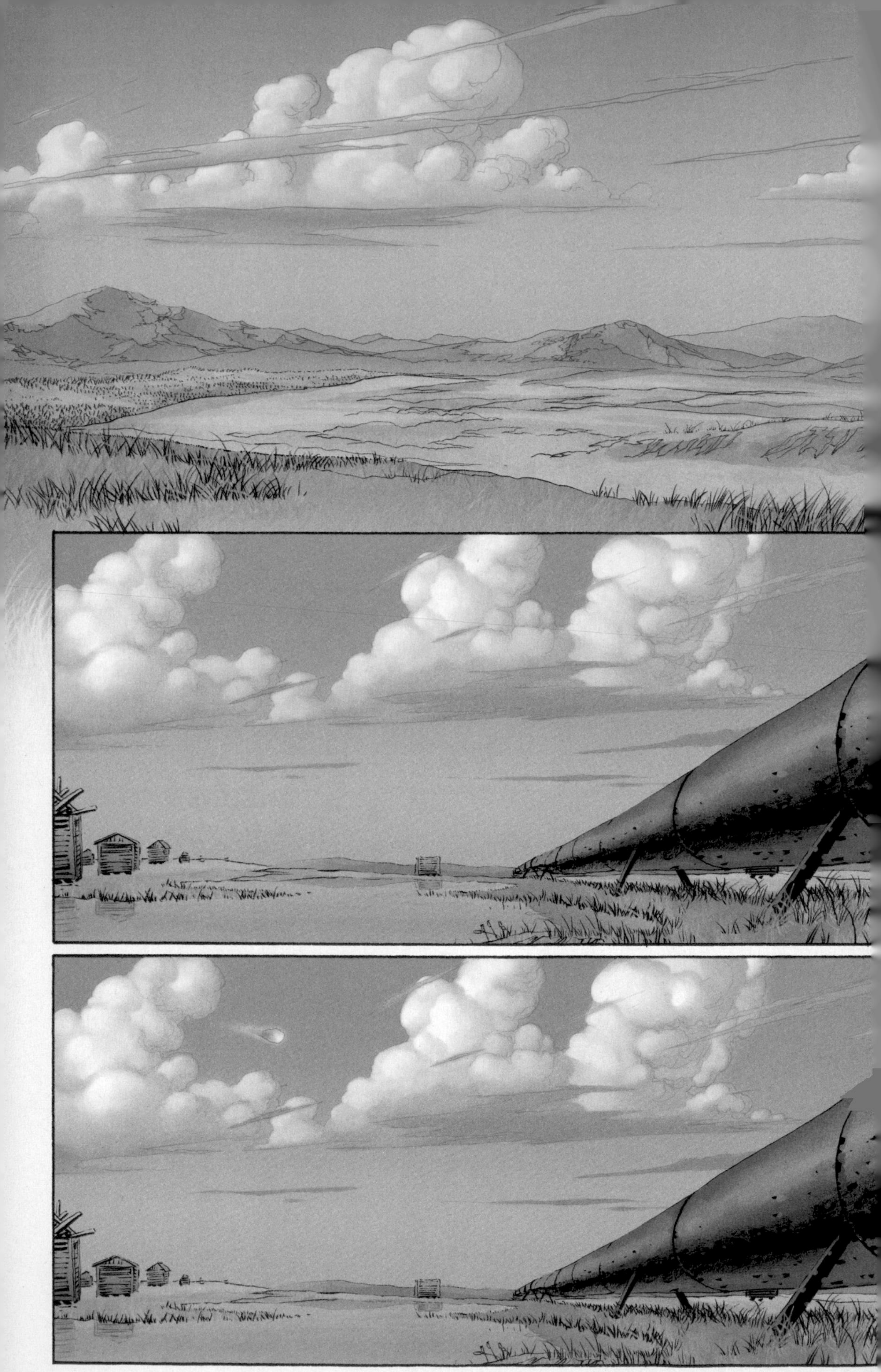

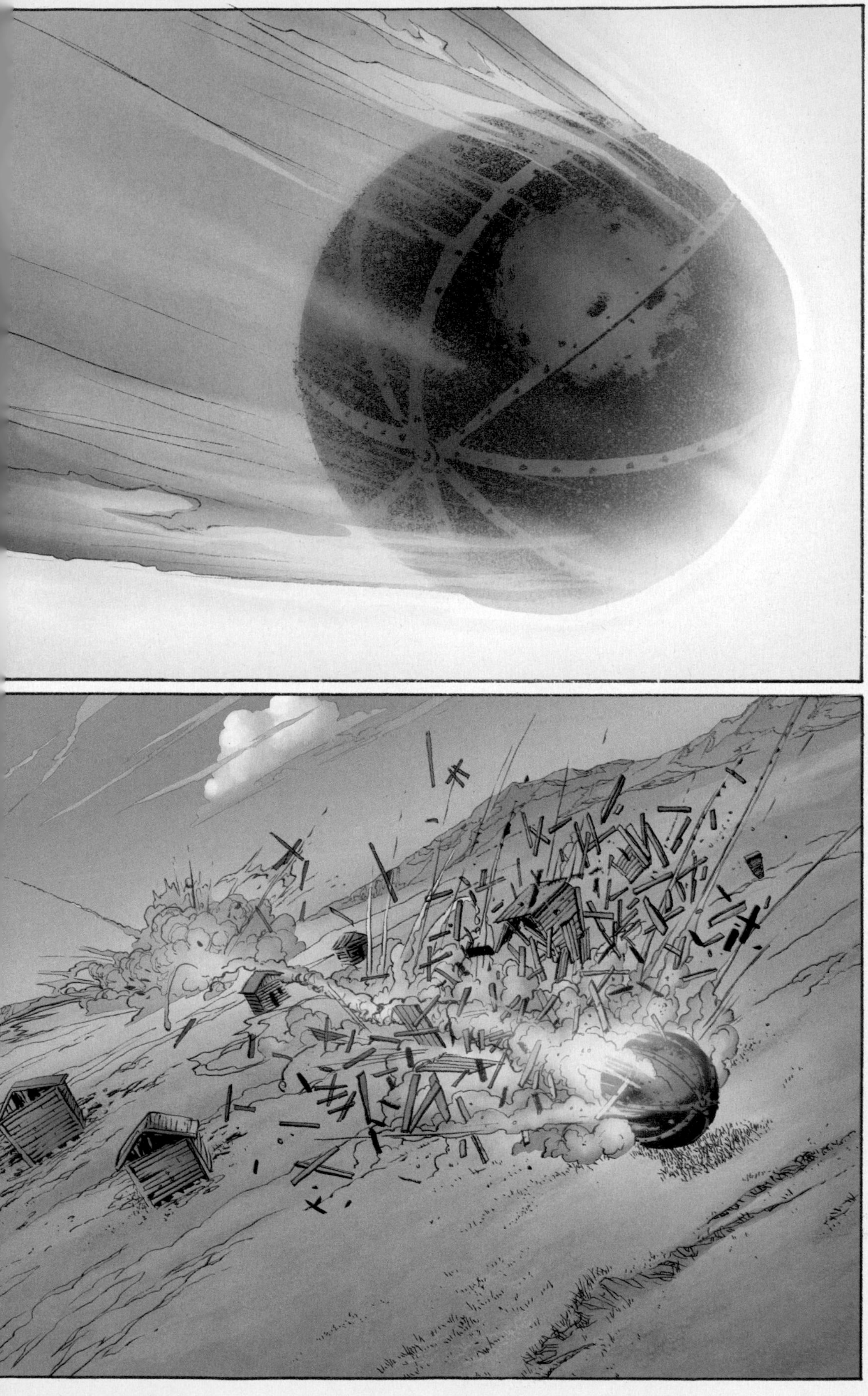

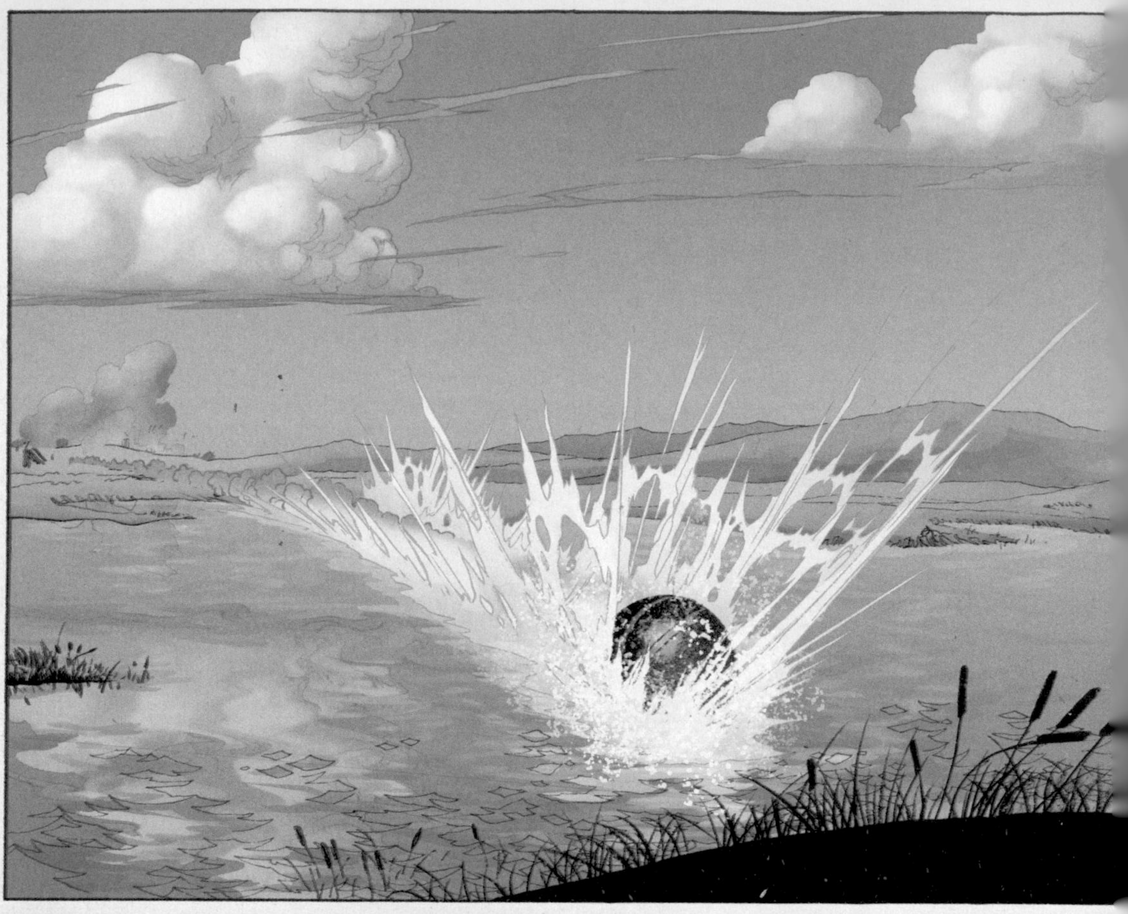

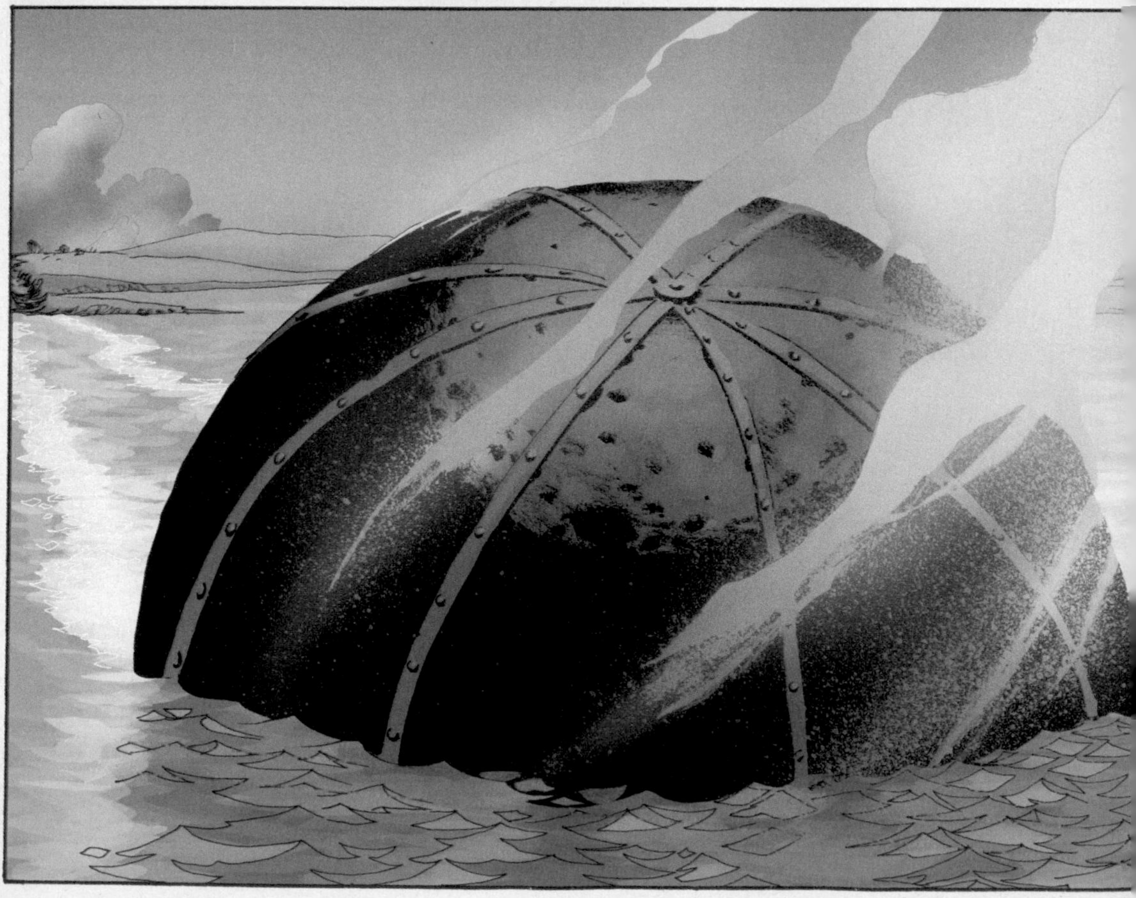

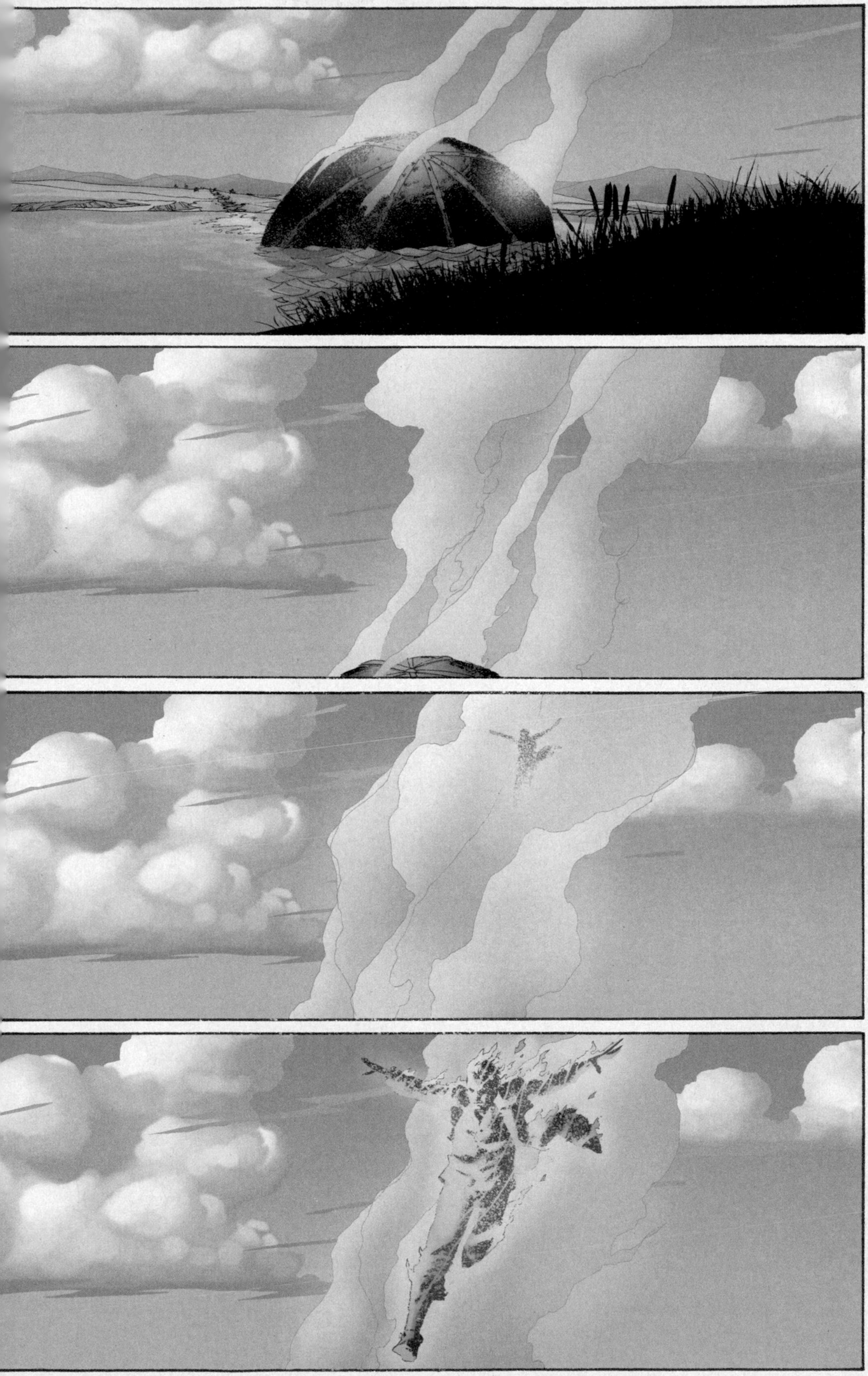

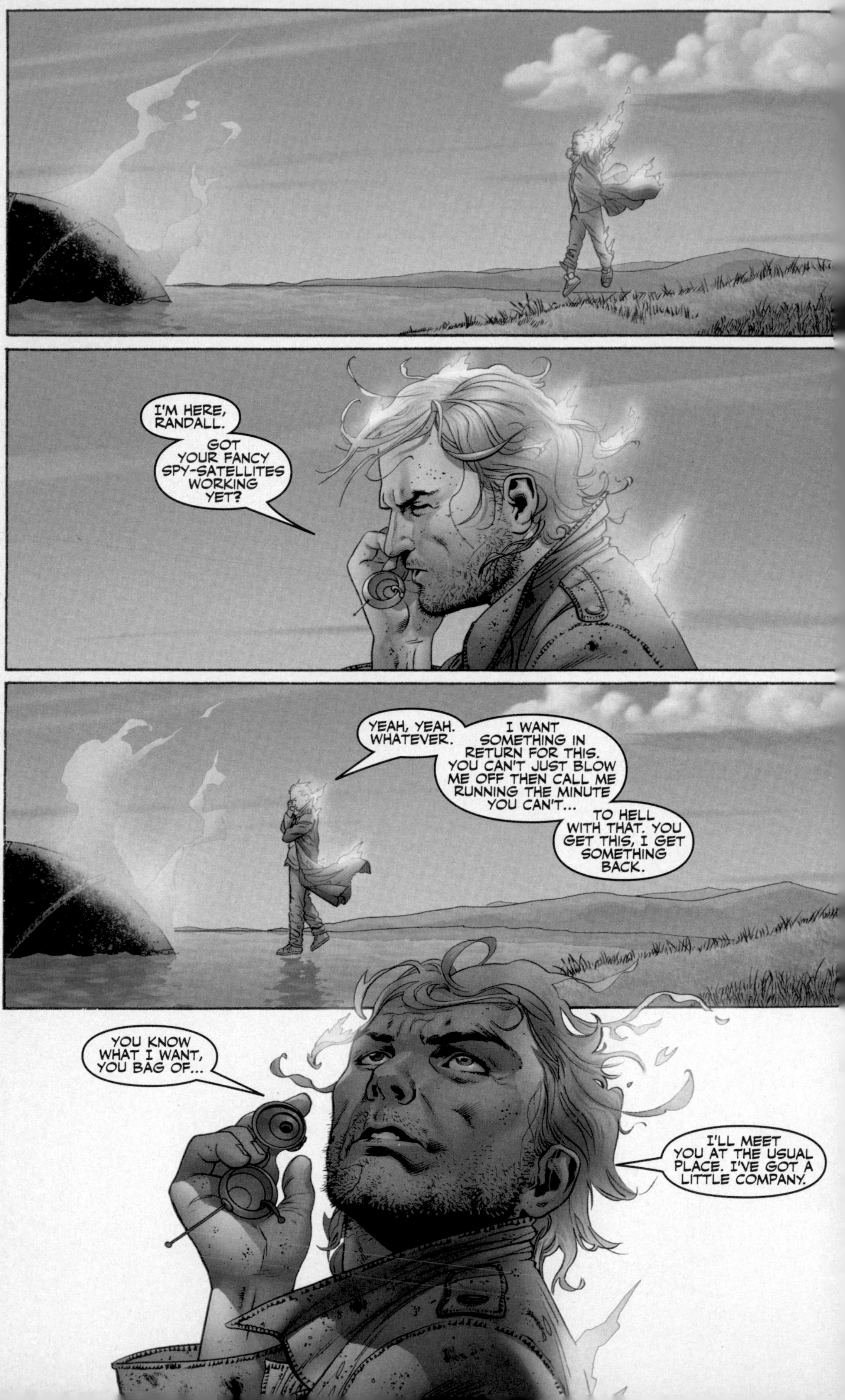
I'M HERE, RANDALL.
GOT YOUR FANCY SPY-SATELLITES WORKING YET?
YEAH, YEAH. WHATEVER.
I WANT SOMETHING IN RETURN FOR THIS. YOU CAN'T JUST BLOW ME OFF THEN CALL ME RUNNING THE MINUTE YOU CAN'T...
TO HELL WITH THAT. YOU GET THIS, I GET SOMETHING BACK.
YOU KNOW WHAT I WANT, YOU BAG OF...
I'LL MEET YOU AT THE USUAL PLACE. I'VE GOT A LITTLE COMPANY.

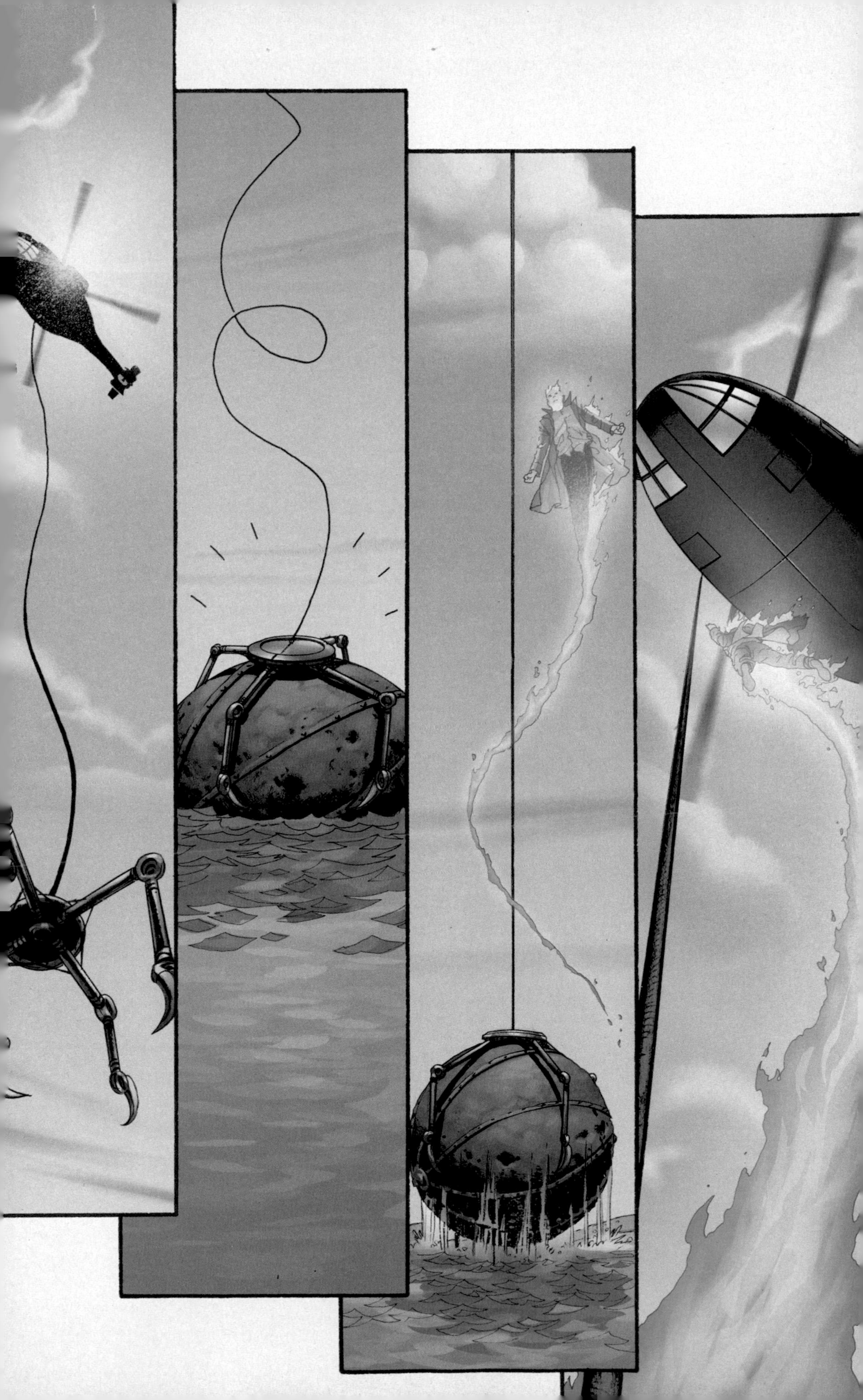

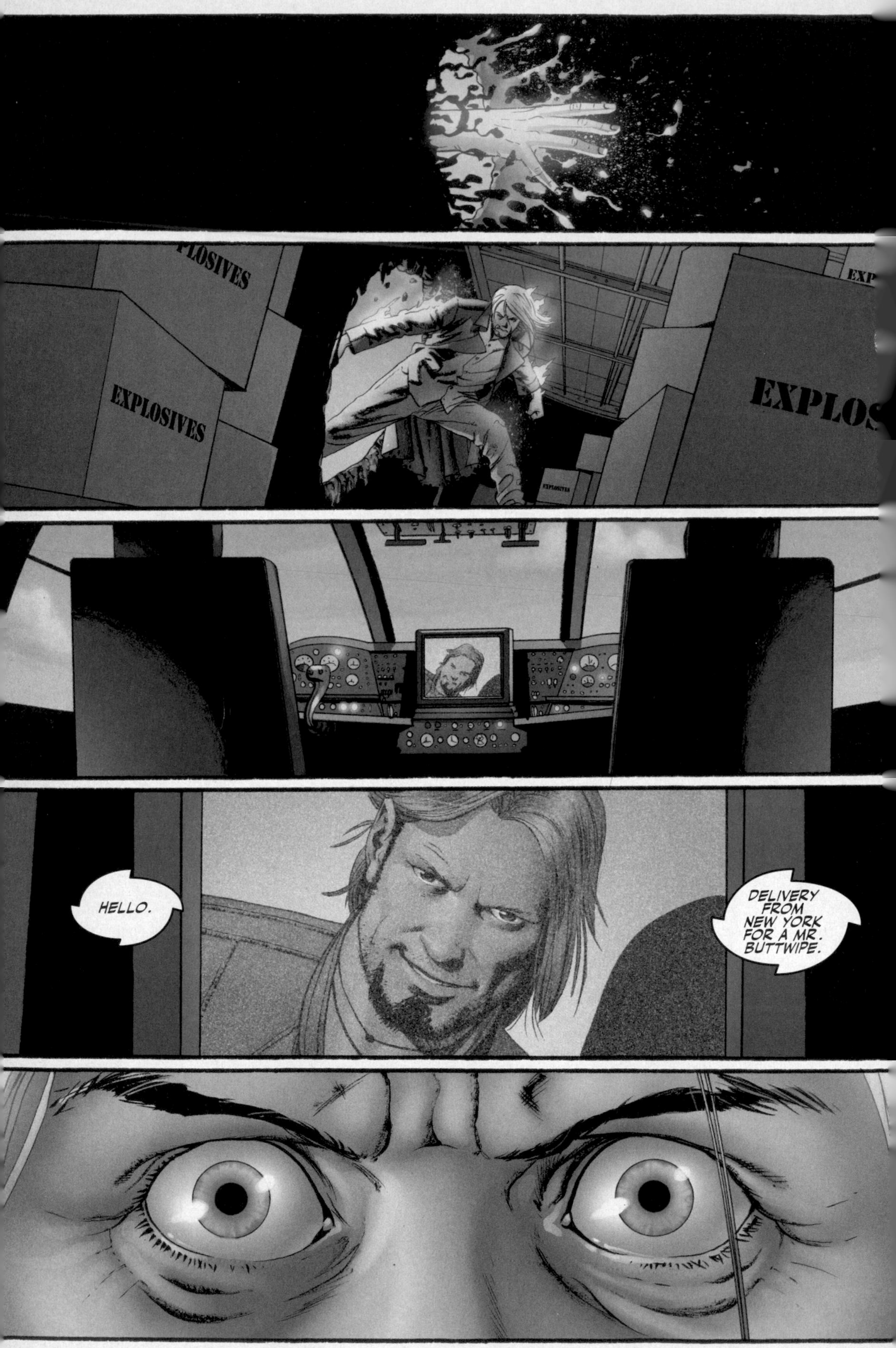
EXPLOSIVES
EXPLOSIVES
HELLO.
DELIVERY FROM NEW YORK FOR A MR. BUTTWIPE.

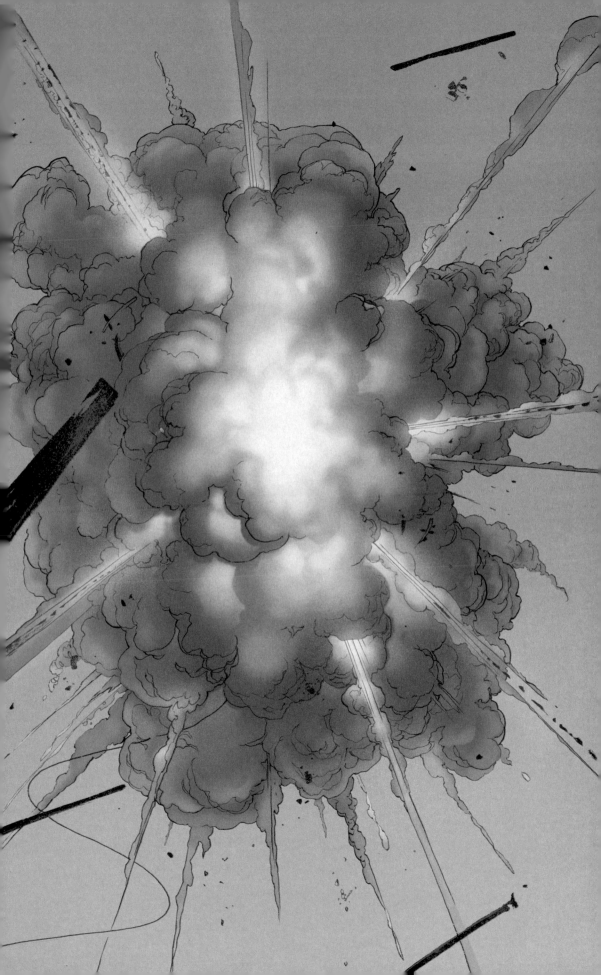

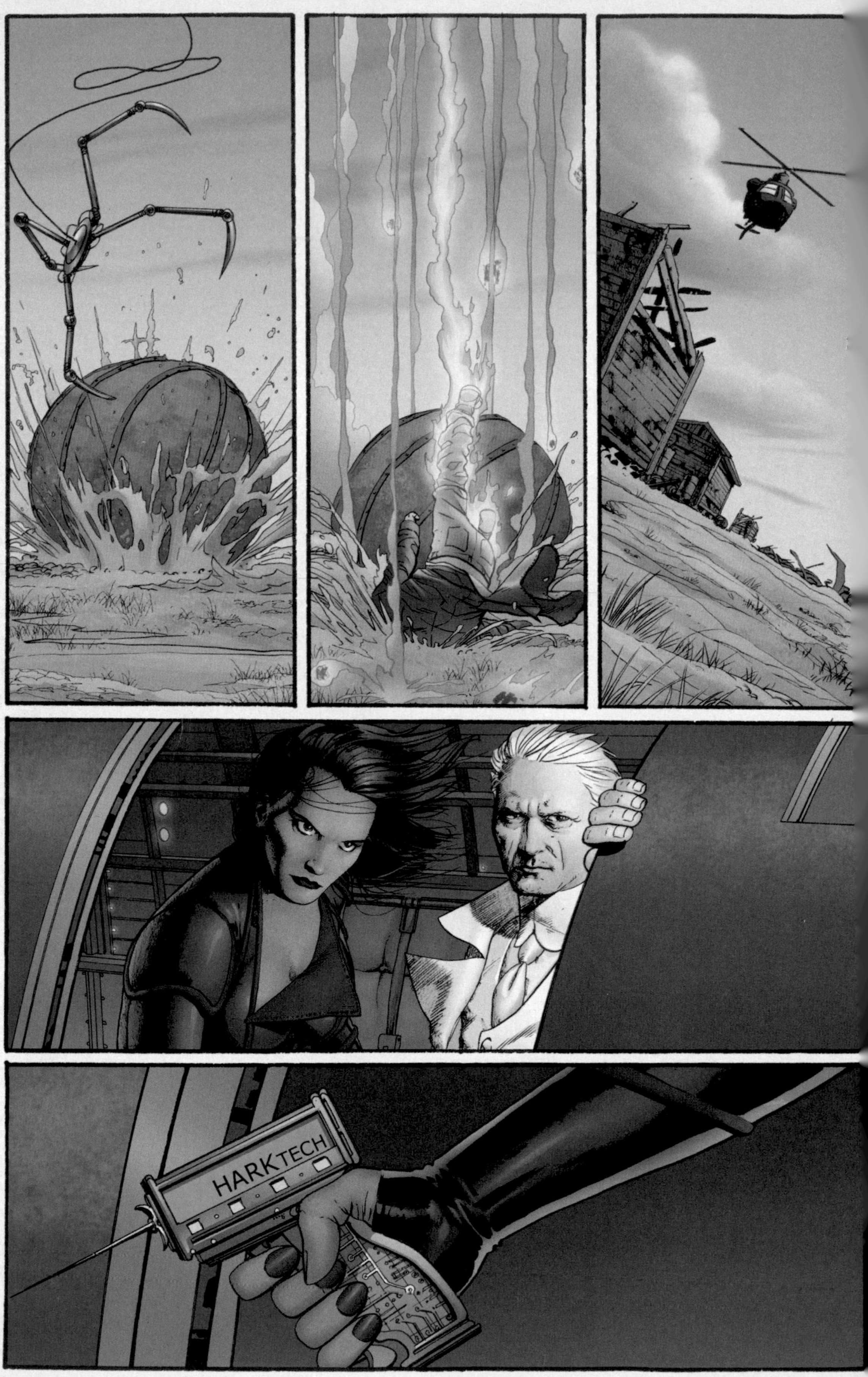
HARKTECH

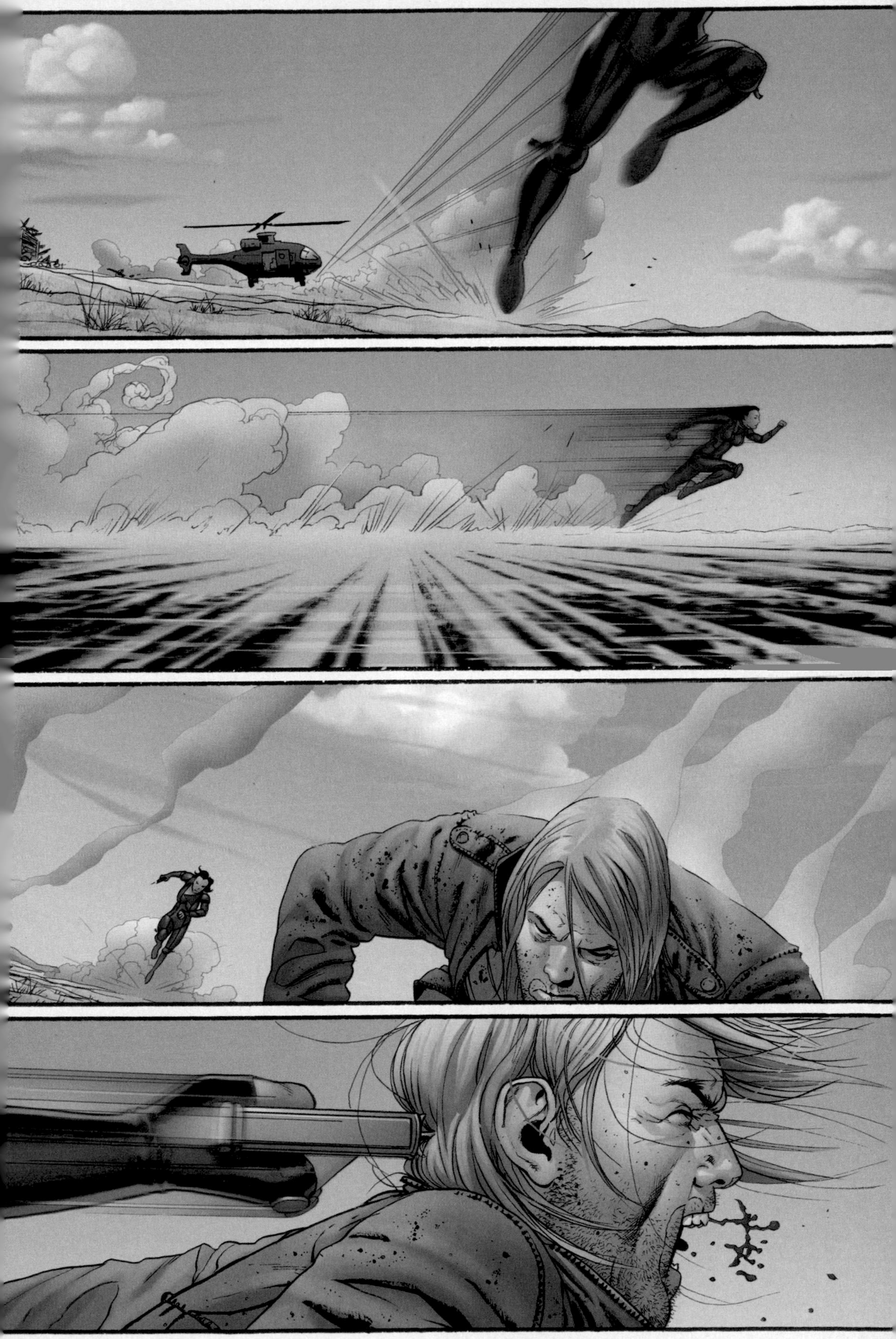

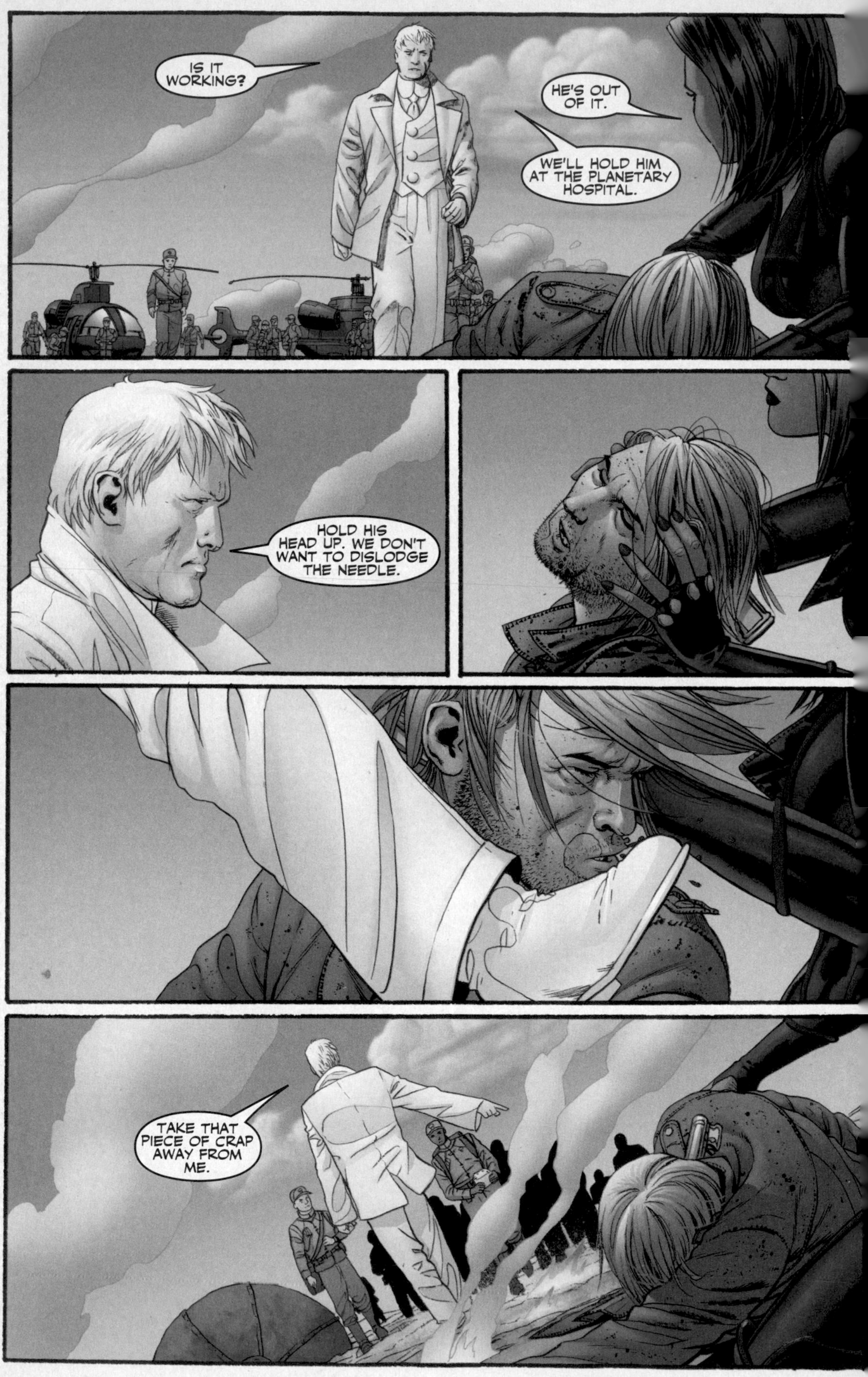
IS IT WORKING?
HE'S OUT OF IT.
WE'LL HOLD HIM AT THE PLANETARY HOSPITAL.
HOLD HIS HEAD UP. WE DON'T WANT TO DISLODGE THE NEEDLE.
TAKE THAT PIECE OF CRAP AWAY FROM ME.

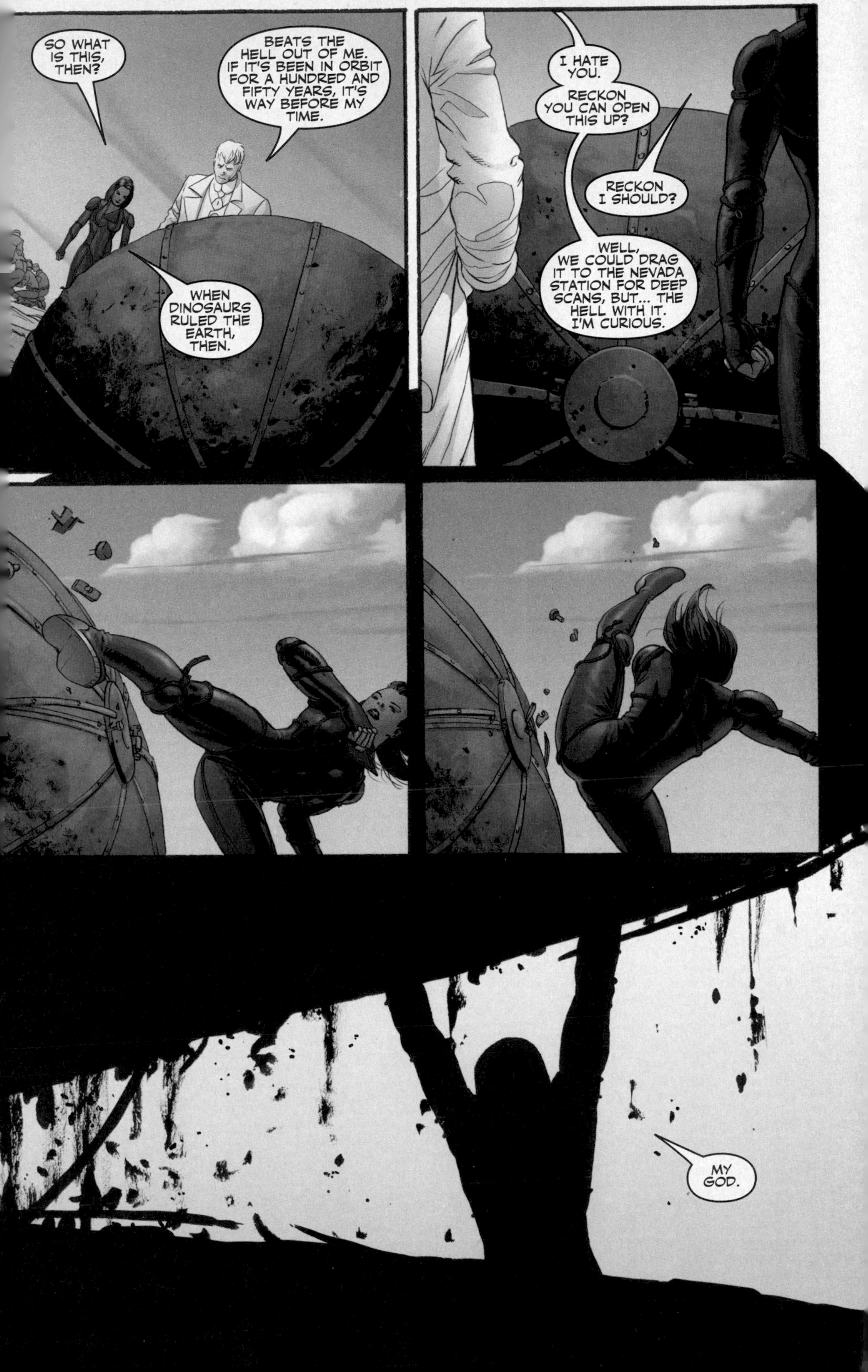
SO WHAT IS THIS, THEN?
BEATS THE HELL OUT OF ME. IF IT'S BEEN IN ORBIT FOR A HUNDRED AND FIFTY YEARS, IT'S WAY BEFORE MY TIME.
WHEN DINOSAURS RULED THE EARTH, THEN.
I HATE YOU.
RECKON YOU CAN OPEN THIS UP?
RECKON I SHOULD?
WELL, WE COULD DRAG IT TO THE NEVADA STATION FOR DEEP SCANS, BUT... THE HELL WITH IT. I'M CURIOUS.
MY GOD.

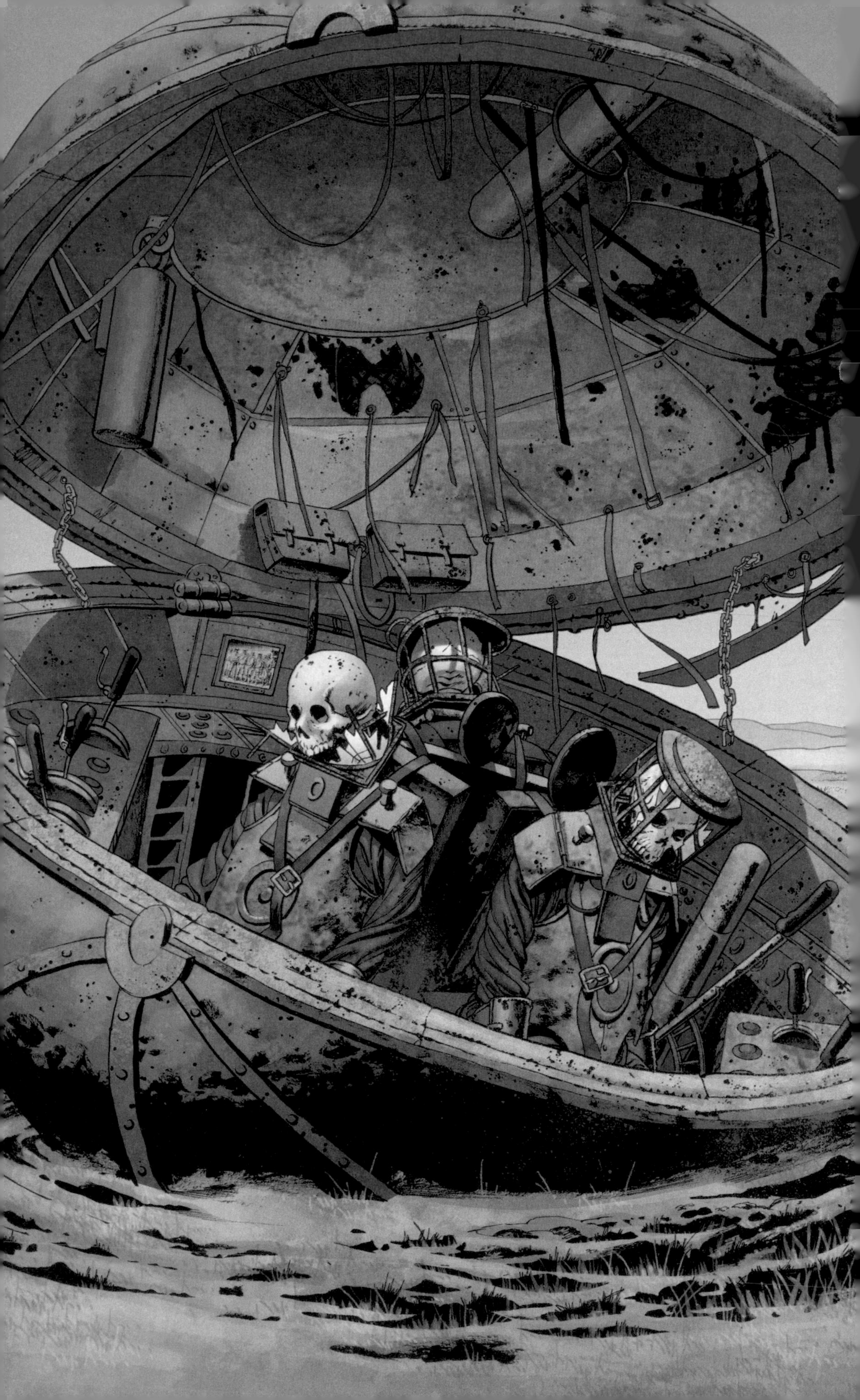

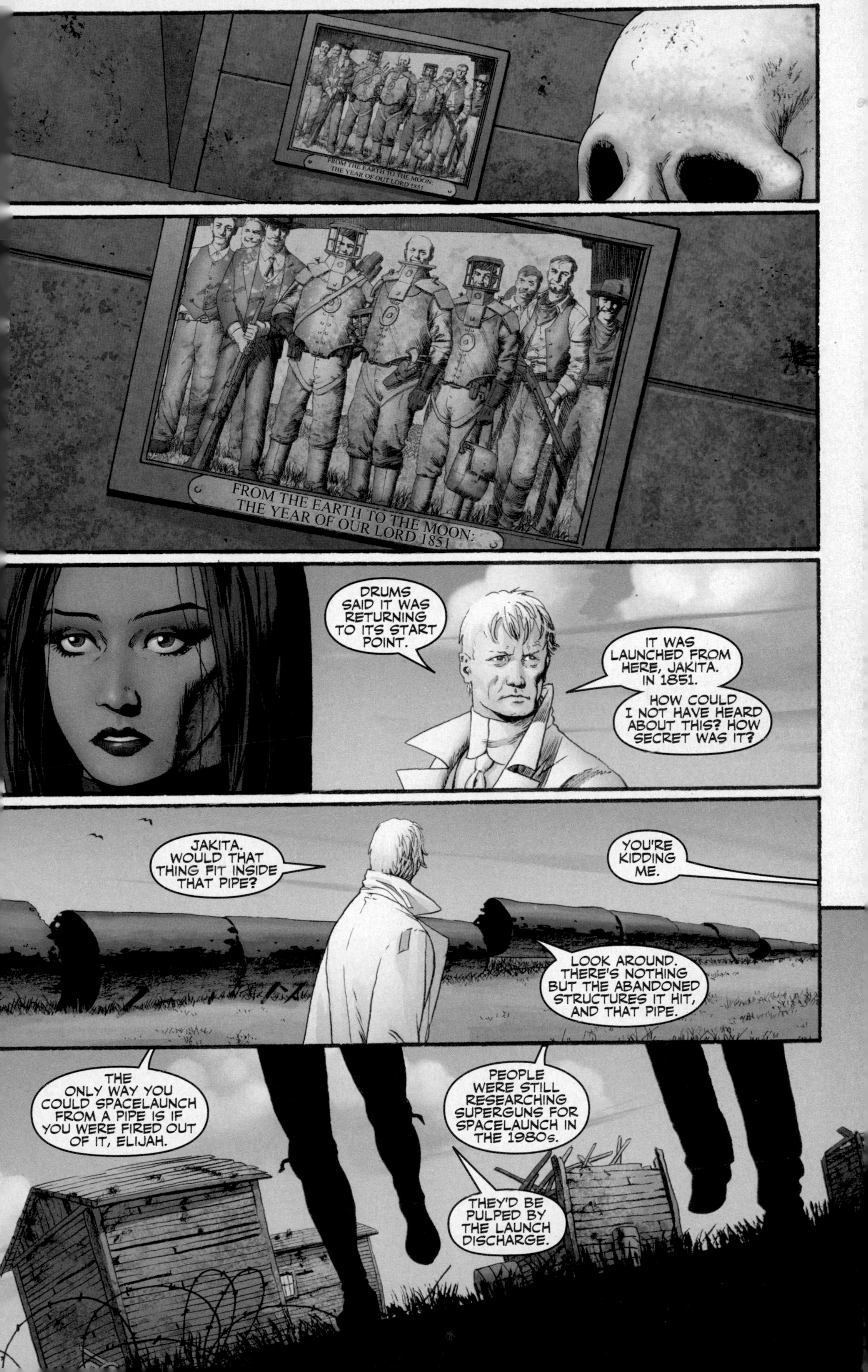
FROM THE EARTH TO THE MOON:
THE YEAR OF OUT LORD 1851
FROM THE EARTH TO THE MOON:
THE YEAR OF OUR LORD 1851
DRUMS SAID IT WAS RETURNING TO ITS START POINT.
IT WAS LAUNCHED FROM HERE, JAKITA. IN 1851.
HOW COULD I NOT HAVE HEARD ABOUT THIS? HOW SECRET WAS IT?
JAKITA. WOULD THAT THING FIT INSIDE THAT PIPE?
YOU'RE KIDDING ME.
LOOK AROUND. THERE'S NOTHING BUT THE ABANDONED STRUCTURES IT HIT, AND THAT PIPE.
THE ONLY WAY YOU COULD SPACELAUNCH FROM A PIPE IS IF YOU WERE FIRED OUT OF IT, ELIJAH.
PEOPLE WERE STILL RESEARCHING SUPERGUNS FOR SPACELAUNCH IN THE 1980s.
THEY'D BE PULPED BY THE LAUNCH DISCHARGE.

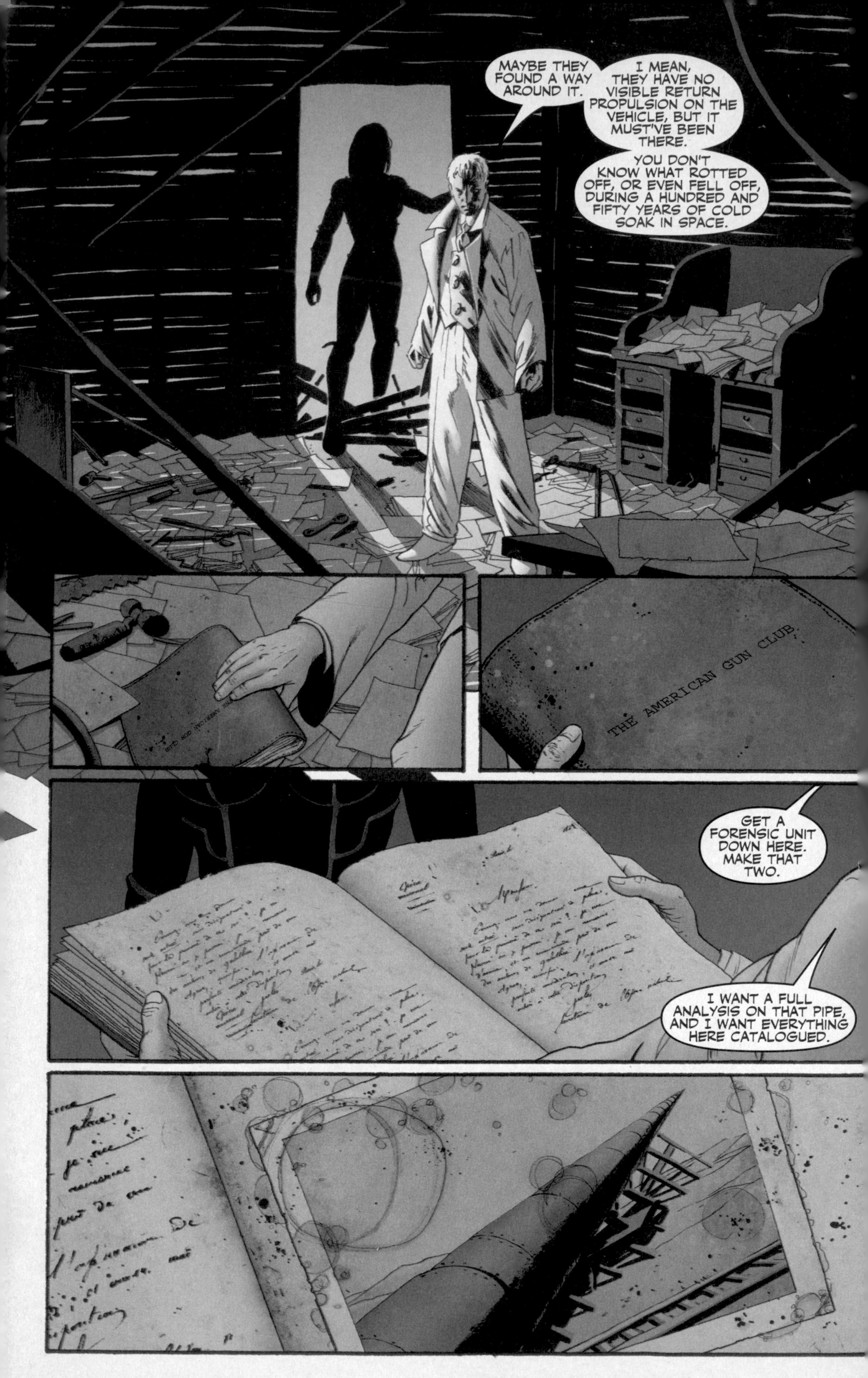
MAYBE THEY FOUND A WAY AROUND IT.
I MEAN, THEY HAVE NO VISIBLE RETURN PROPULSION ON THE VEHICLE, BUT IT MUST'VE BEEN THERE.
YOU DON'T KNOW WHAT ROTTED OFF, OR EVEN FELL OFF, DURING A HUNDRED AND FIFTY YEARS OF COLD SOAK IN SPACE.
THE AMERICAN GUN CLUB
GET A FORENSIC UNIT DOWN HERE. MAKE THAT TWO.
I WANT A FULL ANALYSIS ON THAT PIPE, AND I WANT EVERYTHING HERE CATALOGUED.

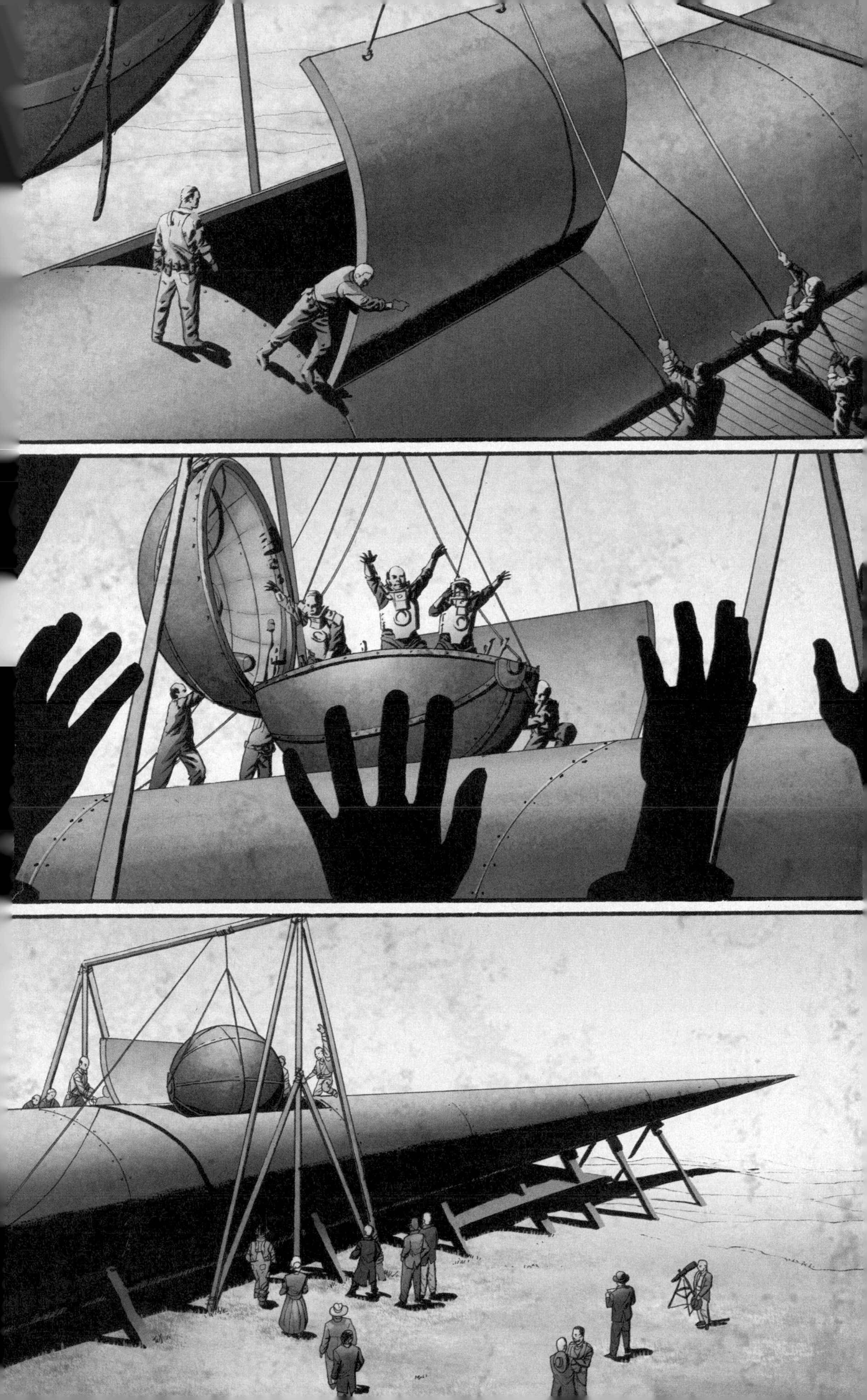

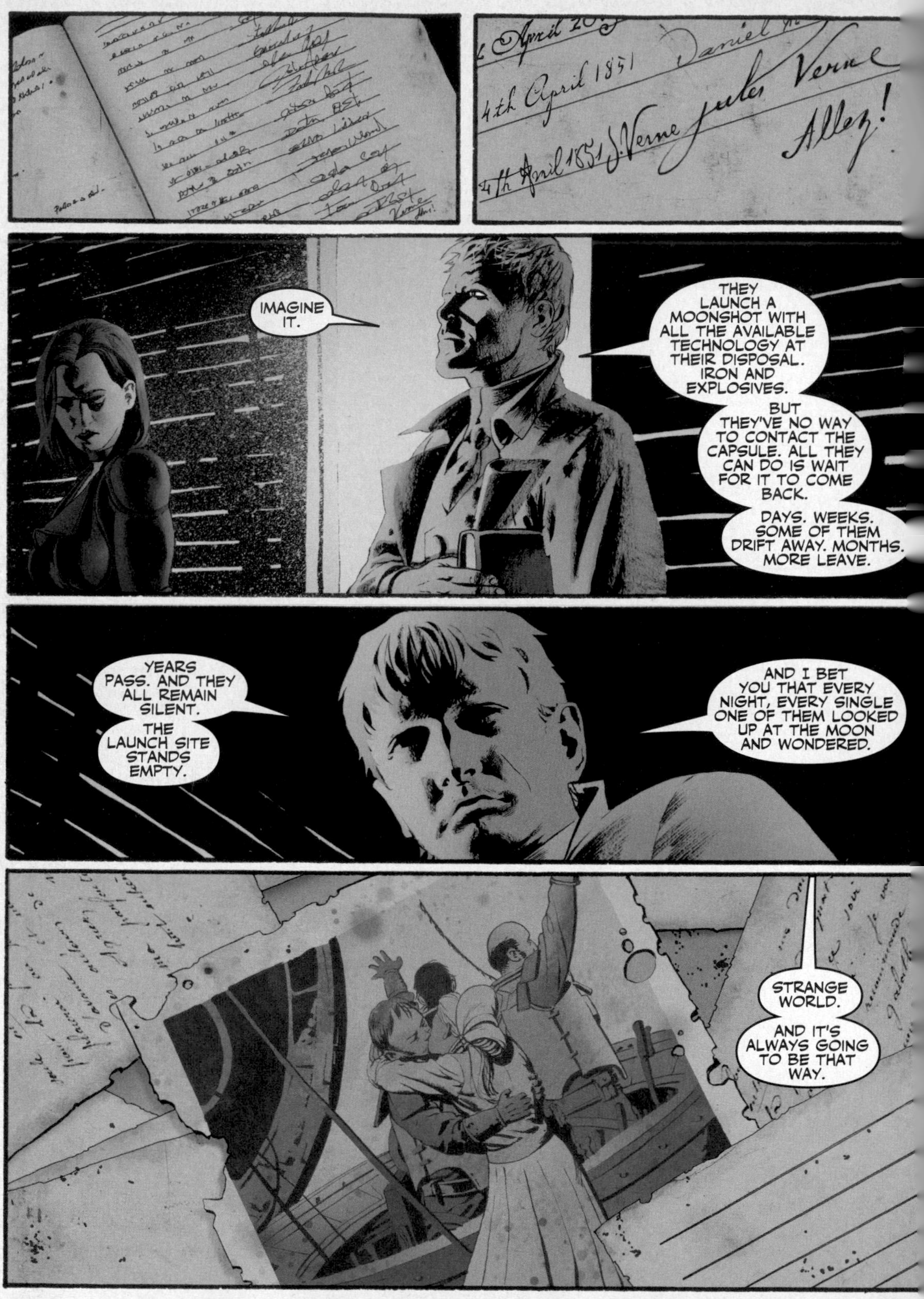
4th April 1851
4th April 1851 J. Verne Jules Verne
Allez!
IMAGINE IT.
THEY LAUNCH A MOONSHOT WITH ALL THE AVAILABLE TECHNOLOGY AT THEIR DISPOSAL. IRON AND EXPLOSIVES.
BUT THEY'VE NO WAY TO CONTACT THE CAPSULE. ALL THEY CAN DO IS WAIT FOR IT TO COME BACK.
DAYS. WEEKS. SOME OF THEM DRIFT AWAY. MONTHS. MORE LEAVE.
YEARS PASS. AND THEY ALL REMAIN SILENT.
THE LAUNCH SITE STANDS EMPTY.
AND I BET YOU THAT EVERY NIGHT, EVERY SINGLE ONE OF THEM LOOKED UP AT THE MOON AND WONDERED.
STRANGE WORLD.
AND IT'S ALWAYS GOING TO BE THAT WAY.

THE GUN CLUB

WRITTEN BY WARREN ELLIS ART BY JOHN CASSADAY
COLORING BY LAURA MARTIN LETTERING BY RICHARD STARKINGS
ASSISTANT EDITOR KRISTY QUINN EDITOR SCOTT DUNBIER

For Peter, Kelly Sue and Matt.

- Warren Ellis

Dedicated to the loving memory of Margaret "Mozell" Merrill.

- John Cassaday

To Randy, with my love.

- Laura Martin

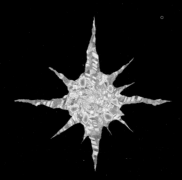

'arren Ellis *was born and raised in darkest England. He has been cited by merous critics as one of the finest creators currently working in the graphic rrative field. Among his many creations are* **THE AUTHORITY,** **ANSMETROPOLITAN,** *and* **GLOBAL FREQUENCY,** *the last of which has been tioned for an episodic television program. The innovative and much renowned ANETARY, done in collaboration with John Cassaday, is a work progress.*

hn Cassaday *was born in Texas, but New York City is his home. Highlights his career include Captain America and Astonishing X-Men. John's first major ork was for WildStorm, the much lauded western/horror series* **DESPERADOES.** *ortly thereafter he began his collaboration with Warren Ellis on the oundbreaking and highly acclaimed* **PLANETARY.***

aura DePuy Martin *has been employed by two comics' publishers and has eelanced for numerous others, winning awards for her work on* **PLANETARY, THE UTHORITY, JLA, Universe-X,** *and* **Ruse.** *She is currently working on* **PLANETARY,** *stonishing X-Men, I Am Legion,* *and* *The War, among other things. She lives Tampa with her husband Randy and her two animal kids, lina and Aku.*

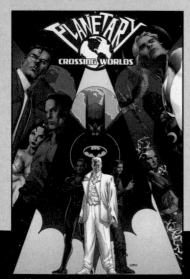

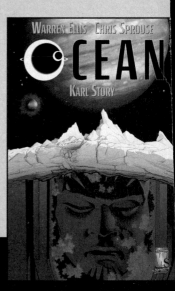